Sociology, Youth and Youth Work Practice

Working with Young People: Theoretical perspectives

Series Editors: Jean Spence and Sarah Banks

This critical series engages with the theoretical debates that most directly impact on work with young people.

The books offer perspectives from a range of disciplines, including sociology, psychology, education, social policy and criminology, with a view to drawing out the enduring ideas and debates that frame practice. Individually the books present accessible insights into the ever-changing purpose and functions of work with young people, while highlighting the settings and policy that structure current practice.

Together they offer a unique opportunity for readers to explore and challenge the ideas that inform their understanding of young people as a distinct yet diverse social group, and the implications of this for practice.

Published titles

Bradford: *Sociology, Youth and Youth Work Practice*

Forthcoming titles

Spence, Issitt and Banks: *Research Perspectives in Work with Young People*

Sociology, Youth and Youth Work Practice

Simon Bradford

palgrave
macmillan

First published 2012 by
PALGRAVE MACMILLAN

Palgrave Macmillan in the UK is an imprint of Macmillan Publishers Limited, registered in England, company number 785998, of Houndmills, Basingstoke, Hampshire RG21 6XS.

Palgrave Macmillan in the US is a division of St Martin's Press LLC, 175 Fifth Avenue, New York, NY 10010.

Palgrave Macmillan is the global academic imprint of the above companies and has companies and representatives throughout the world.

Palgrave® and Macmillan® are registered trademarks in the United States, the United Kingdom, Europe and other countries.

ISBN: 978–0–230–23798–8

This book is printed on paper suitable for recycling and made from fully managed and sustained forest sources. Logging, pulping and manufacturing processes are expected to conform to the environmental regulations of the country of origin.

A catalogue record for this book is available from the British Library.

A catalog record for this book is available from the Library of Congress.

10 9 8 7 6 5 4 3 2 1
21 20 19 18 17 16 15 14 13 12

Printed and bound in Great Britain by
CPI Antony Rowe, Chippenham and Eastbourne

Katalinnak, sok szeretettel.

Contents

List of Figures and Tables

Figures

Tables

Acknowledgements

I am grateful to the series editors Jean Spence and Sarah Banks for the invitation to write this book. They have been exemplary in keeping the book (and me) on track and in helping to see it through to completion with a degree of confidence that, frankly, has sometimes eluded me. Much of the inspiration for the book has come from courses that I have taught, with others, over a number of years at Brunel University. Writing is never an individual effort or achievement. It always entails the encouragement, support and help of others. Several people deserve particular acknowledgement. Mick Brent and Paul Allender both made substantial contributions to courses at Brunel and I have developed ideas taken from their work. Peter Seglow, Bob Gutfreund, Bernard Down, Val Hey and Fiona Cullen helped me develop my own sociological imagination over many years and I have borrowed from them. Colleagues in the Centre for Youth Work Studies at Brunel University have always been supportive and generous: Pam Alldred, Craig Johnston, Michael Whelan, Laura Hills and Laura Green in particular. Students on various undergraduate and master's courses have, often inadvertently, given invaluable criticism of my ideas and work over the years and they have helped to ground some of these. My doctoral students have been a source of inspiration and encouragement. I am grateful to the support of colleagues more widely at Brunel, past and present, and in the Schools of Health Sciences and Social Care, and Sport and Education in particular.

I am grateful to editorial staff at Palgrave Macmillan; Catherine Gray and Katie Rauwerda in particular deserve acknowledgement and Bryony Allen has been forensic in copyediting.

As ever, the most important debts are personal. To my friends and family, and in particular, Katalin, Tamás and Angela, thank you, and my sincere apologies for neglecting you at times when chapters needed completing.

Simon Bradford

Preface

This book explores sociology and the sociology of youth, and their significance for professionals working with young people. It is aimed at two constituencies. Principally, it addresses students on university courses preparing them for practitioner roles (youth workers, social workers, teachers, personal advisers, drugs workers and so on) and who are working to gain an understanding and capacity to theorize and explain young people's lives and experiences. The book will also appeal to established practitioners who want to reflect on their own work in order to better understand and explain the complexity and nuances of young people's lives by drawing on the sociology of youth. The book is intended to enhance an inquisitive and critical understanding of the concept of youth.

As a social category, youth as currently understood emerged as a consequence of rapid changes in the nineteenth century, associated particularly with shifts from so-called traditional societies to industrial, urban and capitalist modernity. Modern societies should not be seen as homogeneous. They are much more plural and ambiguous than some accounts suggest, with aspects of what is understood as 'modernity' and 'tradition' existing side by side. In such societies, young people became progressively positioned in a kind of structural 'no-person's land' leading to them frequently being understood and represented in deeply problematic and pathological terms. Youth (in the West, at least) has historically been situated on the boundary between constancy and change and in that sense is a *liminal* category, symbolically powerful and dangerous. Recent events in North Africa, the Middle East and Europe, including the UK (in nation states that include variously articulated aspects of tradition and modernity that exist sometimes in tension and at others in harmony), have demonstrated young people's capacity – their *agency* – to transgress some of the boundaries within which they have been locked. This makes the task of theorizing youth complex.

In some ways, generation relations in the West and elsewhere (as power relations) seem to have altered in certain respects in recent times. Youth's cultural and social capitals, increasingly embodied in digital technologies and practices, partially displace the cultural authority of an adult elite, contribute to apparently widening social distance and in some circumstances lead to declining trust between generations. This is expressed in some young people's visceral hatred of adults who symbolize illegitimate authority: politicians, police, teachers, social workers and others. Social policy has, too often, contributed to some young people's marginal status.

In sociology, the concept of youth has shifted to take account of the multiple experiences that constitute young people's lives against the backdrop of a world in which some aspects have changed radically while others have remained obstinately persistent. Some of these changes are associated with *global* processes that have become increasingly significant in reconfiguring how the social world is imagined and experienced (the growth of digital technology and social media, and increasing global flows of knowledge and people, for example). However, structures of opportunity invariably mirror, reproduce and exacerbate earlier patterns of inequality that are familiar across the modern world. In this broad context, sociologists have described and explained youth through accounts that focus on social relations (youth as occupying a special, often subordinate, position in relation to other social groups), social processes (youth as an emergent and transitional category and experience) and social difference (youth marked out through age, class, race, gender, sexuality and so on). These arguments reflect different underlying sociological perspectives and preoccupations. Inevitably, different approaches have been variously combined to generate novel theorizations of youth.

In the UK and in similar societies, various youth practices have developed over the last century or so (youth work or youth social work, for example). These have become professionalized and increasingly knowledge-based. This book reflects a conviction that sociology and, perhaps, sociologists have something important to say about the social world especially to those working professionally with young people. I am convinced that practitioners working with children and young people in a range of disciplines have much to learn from good sociology. Arguably, this is particularly so in circumstances where professional work with young people is contested and challenged, perhaps by recurrent disagreement about what it is for, what it seeks to achieve and why, inevitably, it is not always successful. Good sociological knowledge has the capacity to identify the, sometimes intractable, powers that shape the social world and that confront (or sometimes support) the interventions of practitioners. A critical and realistic appreciation of these factors can release practitioners from anxiety about their own capacity to intervene and change things by explaining how power 'works' in modern societies. In the context of 'deficit reduction' policies that disproportionately affect public professionals (and their clients), the organizations and services in which they work, these are vital understandings that this book seeks to cultivate.

The book considers these perspectives, positions and arguments and their relevance to youth practitioners.

The book is made up of eight chapters. Chapter 1 introduces sociology, considering its origins in the fundamental social changes that brought about European modernity, and it points to a distinctive imagination that captures a specifically *social* world. The chapter considers contemporary understandings of youth as a social category with its own characteristics, needs and problems in the context of shifts from traditional to industrial, urban and capitalist societies.

Chapter 2, although specific to the UK, explores young people's experiences of growing up since the Second World War. The chapter's analysis could be applied to similar countries although the social policy details referred to might vary. The broad argument is that public policy frameworks (in this instance beginning with the welfare state) shape young people's worlds through the particular structures of social and economic provision (and thus opportunity or disadvantage) that are provided. Representations of youth and how youth is understood as a social category intersect with the development of policy and practice interventions. This implies an implicit reflexive relationship between youth, on the one hand, and social policy and professional practices on the other.

Chapter 3 considers the concept of identity as constituted in relations of similarity and difference, and its relevance to understanding youth. Identity matters become significant when identity itself is brought into question. In other words, identity is a consequence of the changes that configure modernity and, especially, *late* modernity in which social difference such as class, gender or race became increasingly important. The chapter considers family, community, friendship and other personal relationships as sites of identity formation and construction.

Chapter 4 continues the exploration of the concept of identity particularly from the perspective of similarity and difference. Are the factors that make young people *similar* to one another as significant as those that make them *different*? The importance of generation is considered and the chapter identifies social class, gender and sexuality and race and ethnicity as specific examples of social difference that differentiate individuals' and groups' access to social power.

In Chapter 5, youth is considered as a focus of social anxiety, the concept of *moral panic* often mapping the social processes through which youth and young people come to be seen as problematic. Youth has become a sort of screen onto which broader anxieties about social change (specifically *adult* anxieties) have been projected and through which they are symbolized, often by the popular media.

Chapter 6 explores how space and place locate and constitute youth in the contemporary world. In the chapter, *space* is considered in social, material, and virtual dimensions. *Place*, it is suggested, is an aspect of space that is invested with specific cultural meaning by those for whom it assumes significance. Particular places (a shopping mall, a youth club or a sports arena, for example) provide settings in which young people's individual and collective biographies are imagined, lived and experienced. Chapter 6 also suggests how patterns of opportunity and inequality are invariably spatialized and how growing up in particular geographic regions, for example, shapes the nature and experience of youth.

Chapter 7 discusses globalization and citizenship and their implications for social change and social constancy. Processes of globalization *universalize* youth through constructing potential shared interests and solidarities, and simultaneously *fragment* and differentiate youth by creating patterns of inequality in relation to economic and cultural assets. Citizenship appears to be predicated on the idea of the nation state and Chapter 7 discusses two constitutive aspects of citizenship: citizenship as *entitlement* (for example social or civil entitlement) and as *practice* (as 'good citizenship'). It is relatively easy to see how these might be enacted in the context of the nation state but matters become more complex in a globalized world.

Chapter 8 argues that sociology is important for professionals engaged in work with young people and communities. In particular, it considers the production of sociological knowledge, including that by *practitioner-sociologists*, and professionals (such as youth practitioners) for whose work sociological understanding can contribute an important critical dimension.

Each of the chapters includes activities and exercises that are designed to encourage readers to explore aspects of their own experience and work with young people from a sociological perspective. Some of these draw on popular cultural sources (novels and films, for example) to exemplify and illustrate questions that are raised in the text. These activities can be completed by individuals or, even better, collectively in reading groups or class groups, and they are intended to provide opportunities to reflect critically and imaginatively in a spirit of curiosity. Further reading is suggested at the end of each chapter.

1

Sociology Matters

Sociological Perspectives and Young People

Introduction

This book begins from the conviction that sociology has great potential in helping youth practitioners understand young people, the world they live in and the professional practices that aim to support them. Sociology involves a special and unique way of thinking about the world that the book will introduce.

Insofar as thinking leads to doing, the aim is to influence how readers approach their practice with young people and communities. Sociological thinking aims to provide resources for analysis and change and is therefore inevitably implicated in questions of politics and power. Sociological analysis points to difficult questions that are sometimes problematic for government and decision makers: questions of freedom and security, wealth and poverty, consensus and conflict, stability and change. These are matters that those in power may prefer to ignore but for practitioners with young people, they are fundamental to day-to-day practice. The intention of this book is to open such questions to the sociological imagination so that youth practitioners – as *practitioner-sociologists* – can better understand their implications.

Most introductions to sociology refer to the ways in which societies shape the beliefs, conduct and identities of their members. Society is constituted in the groups to which people belong (families, communities or classes, for example), the institutions through which the social world is organized (education, welfare systems, politics and the law, for example), and the shared cultures and practices which differentiate one society from another. Essentially, sociologists claim that there is something important and unique about *the social* that helps us to understand a range of important questions. Sociologists are interested in questions like, 'Why do people (as shoppers, football fans or young men, for example) behave as they do? Are people born or made? Are people social or individual beings or both?'

1

Such questions underpin sociological and broader philosophical debates that have, sometimes, run on for centuries. This book will engage with some of these questions and offer an understanding of them in the context of professional work with young people.

Chapter 1 outlines sociology and the unique perspectives that it offers. As a discipline, sociology seeks knowledge and understanding of the social world through rigorous research, reflection and theorization. Many of the areas that sociologists are interested in are ordinary and everyday and will be familiar to many youth practitioners. Examples might be: how can shoplifting be understood in societies obsessed with shopping; does celebrity culture shape young people's aspirations and ambitions; are young men's views of what it means to be a young man in contemporary Britain shaped by biological or social factors; how and why has football become so established in some national cultures and not others; how does popular music help young people to express their sense of identity; and how are young people's emotions shaped by social processes and institutions?

A Brief History

Sociology as a Modern 'Science'

Before looking at the broad issues that sociological thinking can illuminate, this chapter briefly explores sociology's beginnings. The historical context can help us to define and understand some of the questions that sociologists are interested in looking at and the broad positions that they occupy. Sociological approaches draw on rational analytical thought. This involves identifying a problem, seeking, evaluating and interpreting evidence, and drawing conclusions. This approach underlies all scientific endeavours and derives from the philosophies of the classical world, but sociology, as the science of society, is a product of the 'modern' industrial and scientific age. It is these 'modern' origins of sociological thought that are considered here.

As science and rational thought began to offer an alternative to the dominant religious world view in late eighteenth-century Europe and America, social philosophers and scientists began to apply the tools of reason (logic and scientific method in particular) to social life itself. The optimistic aim of these 'logical positivist' social philosophers was simple. By painstakingly gathering facts, creating theories and testing them, they believed that everything was ultimately knowable and the mysteries of the universe would eventually become accessible to the scientists' investigations.

The first use of the term *sociology* is usually credited to a French philosopher, Auguste Comte (1798–1857), who argued that his new science of sociology had the capacity to define what should count as human progress and flourishing (Comte, 2010: 802). This is quite a claim, particularly as friends, adversaries or neighbours might disagree about what progress would look like and how human flourishing should be defined.

However, for the early sociologists, the so-called *scientific method* offered the guarantee that its reflections would lead to truth. Comte held the firm conviction that society could be studied scientifically through the methods of observation, experimentation and comparison that had developed within the natural sciences such as chemistry and biology. He also identified the sociological problems of social change and social stability and was determined to discover what appeared to him to be specific laws governing social order, what he called 'social statics', and those governing social change, 'social dynamics'. For Comte, the purpose of his 'new science' of society – sociology – was to uncover underlying universal laws that determined the ebb and flow of social life. As such, he was interested in similar problems to many contemporary sociologists.

Over to you...

Critical reflection

The idea of progress is quite complex and looking at the world around us it is difficult to believe that any of the early sociologists' convictions have counted for much at all. What would count as progress and whose progress would it be? What ideas of progress do you think underlie current political party positions in your own country?

What about the question of 'human flourishing'? In your view, what would a 'flourishing human being' be like and what kinds of social conditions and arrangements would be in place to encourage that? Should practitioners with young people be concerned with human flourishing and, if so, how does your work contribute?

One of the important, continuous defining features of the sociological perspective has been its combination of scientific method and moral concern. Despite claims for the 'value free' and scientific status of sociology, its origins and development have always been implicitly or explicitly connected with notions of improving the human condition.

Sociology is not only a body of abstract ideas and thought. It has to be understood in its *material* setting as well. The development of sociology was intimately bound up with the tumultuous happenings in the French and American revolutions of the late eighteenth century. The earliest sociologists, including Montesquieu (1689–1755) and Saint-Simon (1760–1825) were part of the surge of *Enlightenment* ideas that were developing a powerful critique of Europe's *ancien regime* based on feudal tradition and structured by the articulated powers of the monarchy, the aristocracy and the Church. This culminated in the French Revolution and the War of American Independence; both defined as *progressive* causes informed by and furthering Enlightenment ideas. Sociology, in embryo form, thus contributed to the intellectual underpinnings of revolution and this can be understood as an early version of a critical and sometimes *utopian* tendency in sociology. It is not too much of an exaggeration to argue that this is sociology, as Comte and others saw it, in the service of *human emancipation*.

Many sociologists, either implicitly or openly, take the view that sociology makes a contribution to progressive social arrangements, sometimes construed as some kind of emancipation or liberation (Becker, 1967; Foucault, 1988). In one sense, sociology's historic position has been to subject the world to relentless critique, as a *science* of society; critical questioning of the social world is intrinsic to the discipline.

Traditional and Modern Societies

The segmentation of society into age groups in which young people came to be allocated a particular position in relation to work, family, education and leisure is as much a characteristic of the industrializing world of the modern age as is the focus on science. The emergence of youth as a social category is bound up in shifts from traditional to modern societies.

It is useful here to consider how sociology has made distinctions between pre-industrial, industrial and post-industrial societies and the significance of this for the position of young people. Pre-industrial societies have been categorized as 'pre-modern', while industrial and post-industrial societies have been understood as 'modern' in terms of their economic, institutional and social characteristics.

Pre-industrial societies are often understood as 'traditional' societies based on at least the following characteristics:

- common values and beliefs centred on religious world views
- primary face-to-face relations (people know each other), ascribed (predetermined) roles
- extended families as forces of socialization and as the basis of economic production
- strong gender order and little social or geographical mobility

- systems of agricultural production and the extraction of natural resources from the earth
- gradual social change.

In pre-industrial societies young people are relatively tightly integrated into the community and the transition from childhood to adulthood is characteristically short (Ben-Amos, 1994: 236–42). Social reproduction means that in such societies young people remain in the same social category as their parents and undertake similar work to that of their parents.

The characteristics of modernity, which can be seen as beginning roughly in the mid-eighteenth century at the beginning of industrial society (Bell, 1976; Hall and Gieben, 1992: 6), are listed below:

- the nation state as the key territorial unit in which secular forms of power and authority operate, developing new imagined communities of place and belonging
- modern societies are monetarized exchange economies, large-scale systems of marketized commodity production and consumption, long-term and sustained property ownership and capital accumulation
- declining traditional social order of fixed and articulated social hierarchies and their dynastic authority (aristocracy and Church, for example), a specialized and complex division of labour, industrial capitalism and social class formation
- declining religious world view and ascendancy of secular and materialist culture with an associated knowledge economy characterized by individualism, rationalism and instrumentalism.

Modernity is characterized by the growth of industrialization and mechanized technologies for making things and managing people. It involves urbanization in which people move from the countryside into expanding towns. Modernity is associated with the establishment of newly defined nation states; for example, Italy and Germany became unified nations during the nineteenth-century modernization of Europe. Governance in modern states involves a range of centralized practices and institutions including the increasing audit and surveillance of the population. Most modern societies are, above all, *capitalist* societies based on systems of marketized commodity production and consumption.

With the emergence of capitalism in late eighteenth-century Europe, traditional inherited social relations of feudal power and dependence declined. Emerging social relations were profoundly shaped by the inequality between those who owned the means of production – factories and mines, for example – and those who had to sell their labour in order to survive. The growth of modern industry is associated with the shift from a family-based economy and a greater mobility of labour in terms of shifting work roles and the geography of work. In the process of industrialization, old ties and social roles are no longer necessarily appropriate, and young men in particular become freed from the necessity of occupying the same roles as their fathers. Technical education becomes more important and the school becomes an important site of training, replacing some of the previous functions of the family, again, especially for boys.

Further changes occurred with the emergence of what has been termed 'post-industrial society' in the latter part of the twentieth century, which can be also understood as a *knowledge society* in which information and knowledge are the main commodities. According to Bell (1976), post-industrial society remains a modern society, sustaining similar social relations even as industrialism declines. The growth of *knowledge economies* has profound implications for young people, especially in relation to the significance of education. These economies depend much less on physical capacity (for example as in heavy industrial work) than on the sometimes high-level skills that underpin service and knowledge-based work. Those without such skills are likely to be very vulnerable in these labour markets, making transitions to independent adulthood potentially problematic. These economies are characterized by increasing inequality of wealth.

The shift from the pre-modern into modernity is essentially characterized by a fundamental shift in the nature of social relations.

Over to you...

Critical reflection

Sociologically speaking, it is very important to distinguish between the terms *social relations* and *social relationships*. Both terms are used in sociology but with important differences. When we refer to social relationships, we mean the particular associations that we have with others (my relationship with my partner, my second year students or my next-door neighbour). If we refer to social relations we mean the general patterns of association that develop over time and become almost 'external things' that seem to have a life of their own. So we might talk about the social relations that occur in the context of age, gender or ethnicity (the general ways in which men and women or different cultural groups characteristically relate to each other in a particular society: we could refer to these as gender relations or ethnic relations). In these examples, you would probably want to argue that these social relations are characterized by persistent inequalities, at least in the specific context of the UK. Can you identify any societies where different age, gender or ethnic relations prevail?

The Influence of Marx, Weber and Durkheim

The key sociological thinkers of the late nineteenth and early twentieth centuries were interested to understand the changes from pre-modernity to modernity. While Comte might be known as the founding father of sociology, it was Marx, Weber and Durkheim who set the terms of reference for understanding contemporary social change. Each of them was preoccupied with understanding the extreme, and disruptive social changes in European societies associated with the apparently declining influence of custom and tradition in the late eighteenth century and the emergence of the modern industrial world. All three thinkers had particular perspectives on this 'crisis', and different understandings of it and attitudes towards it.

Marx

The German social theorist Karl Marx (1818–1883) remains the most powerful voice making the morally and politically *critical* case in the context of capitalist industrialization. His critique of capitalism in the mid-nineteenth century formed the foundation not only of a school of social thought, but of an ideal alternative socialist or communist economic and political system (see Marx, 1906, 1973; Marx and Engels, 1970). Social systems derived from these ideas crumbled in Eastern Europe in the last decade of the twentieth century but still exist in different forms and to different degrees in China, Venezuela and Cuba. There are many different strands of Marxist thought but they share some key principles.

First, Marxism holds to a *materialist* premise. Materialism is the view that the primary human reality is the material world. The realms of ideas and culture derive from the material base of society. In this social analysis this translates into a view that the *economic* relations that stem from the pattern of ownership and control of the means of production (factories and firms, for example) are the underlying and ultimate reality from which all other features of society take their shape. Changing society therefore entails changing the relations of production.

Second, Marxist thought regards the division of labour (the relations of production) as based on the *exploitation* of one group of people by another. The 'proletariat' (or working classes who own no productive property) have only their labour power as a commodity that can be sold in return for wages and are exploited by the 'bourgeoisie' who own and control *capital* – wealth, factories and units of production. Profit for the bourgeoisie depends on paying as small a wage as possible to the proletariat. The workplace is a place of alienation for workers who have no control over what they produce and how they produce it. It is also a place of struggle and conflict, as workers must constantly resist efforts to keep their wages low.

One extrapolation from this is the idea that in any particular society the bourgeoisie also control the production of ideas and as such produce a *dominant culture*, an *ideology* that serves the needs of the capitalist class. This argument figures prominently in relatively recent Marxist accounts of the sociology of youth, as Chapter 4 shows. To illustrate this, one might argue, as have some sociologists, that the period known as 'Thatcherism' in the UK (the period of Conservative party government from the late 1970s until the early 1990s) represents a particularly stark example of this cultural and ideological dominance when individualism, aspiration and greed seemed to be established anew. Although these were always present in the UK and elsewhere, they were reasserted then to set the foundations of the subsequent periods of government whose power rested on the continuation of competitive capitalist relations of production.

These two positions are accompanied and complicated by a further argument, the *third* main Marxist premise, that the history of all human society is a history of *class struggle* between two opposing classes: those who own and control the crucial form of property of the era (land, capital or knowledge, for example) and those who do not. This struggle results in periodic revolutions, such as the French Revolution in 1789, when new forms of property, *capital*, emerged within and superseded a feudal, land-based system. Between revolutions long periods occur during which 'contradictions', or system faults, accumulate until the point where the new forms of property and relations of production are strong enough to overthrow the old forms. Marx predicted a final revolution when the property-less proletariat (the working classes) would overthrow the capitalist bourgeoisie (those who owned the means of production) to establish the socialist era.

Different traditions of Marxist thought combine these three basic premises (materialism, capitalist exploitation and class struggle) to draw divergent conclusions but central to all these positions are arguments about *power*. Some Marxists, like the members of the so-called 'Frankfurt School' (for example Theodore Adorno, Walter Benjamin, Herbert Marcuse) writing from the 1930s to the 1960s – first in Germany and then in the US after fleeing Hitler – stressed the power of a 'dominant ideology'. This ideology maintains a cultural monopoly serving the interests of the capitalist class. Contradictions – system faults – may exist, but the subordinate classes are *bound* to fail in making inroads into the cultural monopoly of the capitalist class, at least until the final moment of revolution when they become fully conscious of the reality of class relations and their own alienation and exploitation. The tendency in this kind of analysis is to present the capitalist system as a 'cultural closed circuit' in which anything new or challenging created by subordinate groups from, say, jazz to punk rock to rap and hip-hop music, is instantly appropriated, that is, taken over and used by the dominant class to serve its own ends. It might be worth thinking, for example, about how capitalism has managed to 'commodify' (translate into a commodity from which profit can be extracted) popular music (see Longhurst, 2007). The sociology of youth culture in Britain from the 1970s onwards was much influenced by this view.

The Marxist tradition in sociology has nurtured a continuing concern with questions of social class, inequality, structures of power and the existence of chronic conflict in society and has fostered an agenda of social criticism. Indeed, much sociology from the mid-nineteenth century onwards developed as an ongoing debate with Marx and various Marxisms.

Weber

The German sociologist Max Weber (1864–1920) understood the transition to modernity firstly as a shift from societies stratified in terms of ascribed *status* (where people were born into a social position through family origin, or ethnicity, for example) to those stratified by *class* (in which social position was determined by economic interests and wealth), and secondly from social formations characterized by the mutual obligations of *community* to those characterized by the economic and often politically temporary relations of *association* or *society*. For Weber, modernity was characterized by systematic *rationality*, embodying the purposeful calculation of efficiency in the pursuit of specific and often economic goals, which superseded *traditional* characteristics in which relatively fixed beliefs and morality were transmitted from one generation to another (see Gerth and Wright Mills, 1967).

Weber's account of rational modernity marks out several features that can easily be recognized in day-to-day life:

- **new forms of social institution:** political, religious, social and economic institutions that have an apparently independent and autonomous existence
- **the emergence of large organizations:** organizational forms established to respond to a range of human needs and in which large sections of the population are employed (examples here would be political parties, churches, the education services and banks)
- **specialized division of labour:** a range of specialized occupations (the website Monsterjobs or local business directories give a sense of this)
- **the significance of clock time:** rather than time being measured by the seasons, clock time determines the detail of activity (most people's employment contracts specify their responsibilities in very specific time terms; social arrangements are invariably time specific)

- **self-discipline as a form of governance:** individuals required to manage their lives in accordance with notions of responsibility, achievement and efficiency (the skills that students are expected to develop at school or university, the so-called 'transferable skills' of being 'self-starters' or 'independent learners')

- **anonymity:** modernity can be seen as anonymous and impersonal with serious consequences for the emergence of a particular kind of 'self' and its life in emotional and personal domains.

It is worth reflecting for a moment on the consequence of such rationality. Weber pointed out that the dehumanizing properties of contemporary organizations and the obsession with clock time led to alienation and *disenchantment*.

Over to you...

Critical reflection

Reflect on this idea of disenchantment. Think about the experiences of young people you know or with whom you work. A good example here might be the way in which large secondary schools – academies, for example – operate for young people who arrive from much smaller-scale feeder primary schools. Are young people's experiences of the routines and impersonality that are so evident in some large schools alienating or dispiriting? Consider your own experiences with welfare agencies, government departments, banks or internet service providers where it seems so easy to get lost in systems and procedures and where you do not seem to be a person at all, simply a customer making certain kinds of demands that are dealt with according to pre-specified routines, often by automated responses. What are the consequences of such experiences for how we think about ourselves and for how we relate to people in those and other organizations?

Such experiences led Weber (and others) to think about modernity as a 'disenchantment of the world', driven by the forces of capitalism. Thus, the culture of modernity was characterized through the displacement of myth, magic and God (the 'enchanted' world shaped by mystery, metaphysics and spirituality) by science and logic. Of course, science's capacity to explain and emancipate (from the natural world) is in considerable tension with its coterminous capacity for disenchantment. Interestingly, a contrast can be drawn here between Marx's materialist position and Weber's emphasis on *non-material* variables as independent causal factors in social and economic change. Weber's most famous argument, for instance, holds that the *Protestant Ethic* (a commitment to hard work and the virtue of labour) was a prerequisite of capitalist development in the West. Weber argued that ideas and beliefs about the importance of being conscientious and hard working, associated with Protestant Christianity, were crucial in establishing European capitalism.

There is a powerful humanistic perspective in Weber's sociology that insists on the methodological importance of the human capacity for *empathy*, the ability to imagine oneself in the situation of someone else in a different time, place and set of circumstances. This capacity for *verstehen* (understanding) lies at the heart of Weber's approach: no analysis of any social phenomenon can be satisfactory if it fails to account for the motives of the individual actors. Weber, therefore, emphasizes the need to *connect* the analysis at the macro level (society in general and particular historical societies) with analysis at the micro level (individual actors). He argues that before our sociology can be adequate, it is vital to understand how people's lives make sense and have meaning *for them*. Weber, and the so-called 'phenomenologists', bring into sociology the idea that *individual human agency* is something that must be taken into account in explaining the social world.

The work of *symbolic interactionists*, deriving from George Herbert Mead (1863–1931) and Herbert Blumer (1900–1987), and expressed in the later work of sociologists like Howard Becker (b.1928), used phenomenological insights to elaborate the nature of small-scale interactions and the negotiation of meaning between individuals. Blumer identified the underlying principles of symbolic interactionism that form the basis of social order (see Mead, 1934; and Blumer, 1969).

● People act towards things and other people on the basis of the meanings they give them.

● Meaning arises from social experiences.

● Meanings are further interpreted and mediated through additional social experiences.

This broadly Weberian-derived approach (and its preoccupation with meaning and the experience of active agents) can be compared with that of Marx if class, gender or race are taken as examples. Marx's analysis would be to understand these as aspects of structured *social division* or *social difference*. These inequalities would be seen as inevitable consequences of the social relations (and *power* relations) of capitalist production, almost built in to the system of social relations that makes up capitalist exploitation. In contrast, the phenomenological perspectives deriving from Weber would analyse class, gender and race as social objects whose specific meanings and significance emerge and change over time through the processes and practices of social life and social interaction, albeit in the context of power relations.

Durkheim

Emile Durkheim (1858–1917), Weber's French contemporary and the third major sociologist of the late nineteenth and early twentieth century, focused on the shift from traditional societies to modernity (see Durkheim, 1970, 1976, 1984). He is often wrongly and unfairly understood as a conservative *functionalist*, unable to explain conflict, or careless of explaining the experience of individuals; none of these characterizations are accurate.

For Durkheim, the change in social relations to modernity caused by the development of industrial society was expressed primarily in the changing nature of *solidarity*. Durkheim understood solidarity as the *social cement* binding people together and forming a context in which they thought about themselves and their relations with others.

Modernity involved a change from *mechanical* to *organic* solidarity that reflects the shift from a traditional and communal society to one characterized by a complex division of labour (see Table 1.1). Durkheim's account of social life – *the social* – is seminal. Mechanical and organic solidarity are invariably understood as describing different forms of association: different types of actual society and different forms of social life. As Jenks indicates, however, they can also be used as metaphors for ways of thinking about the social (2005: 26). For example, mechanical solidarity characterizes a society based on similarity and resemblance between its members; organic solidarity suggests the interdependence of difference and diversity. Although occasioned by Durkheim's experience of and sensibility towards the shift from traditional to modern, the mechanical and organic metaphors retain explanatory power in the related change from modern to late modern in the contemporary world where both forms coexist.

Although, for Durkheim, the two versions of solidarity relate directly to two different types of society, what is most important here is his preoccupation with explaining the significance of the social. In a beautifully written passage from his *Rules of Sociological Method*, Durkheim sums this up:

> When I undertake my duties as a brother, husband, or citizen and fulfil the commitments that I have entered into, I perform obligations which are defined outside myself and my actions, in law and custom. Even when they conform to my own sentiments and I experience their reality subjectively, that reality does not cease to be objective; for it is not I who created these duties; I received them through education. ... Similarly, the believer, from the day he is born, encounters the beliefs and practices of his religion ready-made; if they existed before him it is because they exist outside him. The system of signs I use to express my thought,

the system of currency I employ to pay my debts, the instruments of credit I utilise in business relationships, the practices that I follow in my profession, etc. function independently of the use I make of them ... these are ways of acting, thinking and feeling which possess the remarkable property that they exist outside individual consciousness. (Durkheim, 1982: 50–1)

Table 1.1 Durkheim's distinction between mechanical and organic solidarity

Mechanical solidarity	*Organic solidarity*
Characterized by likeness and resemblance between members	Characterized by difference between members
Social bond based on shared morality (moralistic)	Social bond based on specialization and interdependency (utilitarian)
Strong collective consciousness; collective ideas stronger than the individual	Collective consciousness dispersed through complex division of labour; individual ideas strong
Proximate social horizon	Unlimited social horizon
Repressive law because deviance disrupts moral sentiments of group; punishment as ritually imposed to uphold collective morality	Restitutive law as deviance disrupts social order; purpose is restoration of order
Young people incorporated and absorbed into communal life with youth having a distinctive role and purpose in achieving social continuity and coherence	Young people alienated in a fragmented and dispersed division of labour and ambiguously positioned between the statuses of child and adult

The Durkheim quote above encapsulates an imagination that sees the word as irrevocably social and elaborated through an economy of symbol and meaning. For Durkheim, this means considering how everyday life is socially structured in three crucial ways.

1. The social is both *external* to the individual and *internalized* to become part of the person: it pre-exists the individual and becomes lived experience.
2. The social is *constraining:* it shapes the choices people make in life through tradition, law, education, and so on.

3. The social is *generalized:* it influences through the existence of shared or collective representations embodied in various symbols (objects like the Union Jack or the Crescent Moon, or ideas like democracy or time). It is these shared representations that create social solidarity and cohesion.

Common Themes in Marx, Weber and Durkheim

From Marx, Weber and Durkheim, three key components of 'the social' can be identified. First, and particularly in the work of Marx and Weber, the idea of *social difference* or social division prevails. This refers to how capitalist societies, but not exclusively those societies, are made up of groups (based on class, gender, age or ethnicity, for example) located in different positions of social power. Second, the idea of *social relations* is fundamental. Social relations are those associations that become persistent over time, as patterned entities and that appear to have autonomy beyond the individual. So in societies like those in Western Europe, North America or Australia characterized by gender inequalities, it is possible to talk about *gendered* social relations in which men and women are positioned and constrained in specific ways. Third, this work points to the importance of *social processes,* the activities that are regularized, routinized and lasting and that reproduce societies over time. For example, education is a very important social process. It enables children and young people to become participants in society through the acquisition of the 'right' kinds of knowledge, dispositions and skills. Economic processes are important in terms of the production and distribution of material goods that are necessary to keep societies running smoothly.

These three component elements are what, over time, form the basis of society as an experienced external reality. As Durkheim suggested, society becomes an object of study, a 'social fact', a 'thing in itself' or 'sui generis'. These components are crucial in *reproducing* society over time and giving it a kind of permanency and predictability. In relation to social difference, for example, inequality is worked out socially in clear and patterned ways. There is nothing random about how class, gender, race, disability and so on are socially organized, and this organization gives society a structural quality that is reproduced for new generations. Aspects of structure should not be overemphasized if that denies the possibility of human *agency*, that is, the capacity of women and men to make choices that impact upon and, potentially, change their worlds. However, to paraphrase Marx (Marx and Engels, 1968: 96), people make their own history (that is, make their own choices and decisions about their lives) but not necessarily in the circumstances that they would choose for themselves (that is, there are always external circumstances and constraints that curtail the capacity for choice). This problem of so-called *structure and agency* is well known and important (Archer, 2000: 17). One way of thinking about it is to see the conjunction of structure and agency as constituting the *freedom* in which people engage in everyday life. Freedom can only exist by virtue of participation and membership of social groups, rather than through any negative absence of constraint (Bauman, 2001: 18; Berlin, 1969). People are always caught in tension, a kind of dialectic, between being free and accommodating the demands which membership of society imposes. Indeed, freedom is both enabling and constraining: it could not be otherwise. That has important implications for educationalists: freedom is constituted in the processes of learning *how* to participate in society, acting with reference to one's group as well as in following individual desires. In this sense, freedom can be considered as a social *practice* (that is, how people 'do' freedom) rather than a *state of being*.

Modernity, discussed in this part of Chapter 1, is significant especially because it is the period in which the social category of youth also emerges and young people become understood as members of such a social category. The classical sociologists alert us to aspects of young people's class position (Marx), the status of youth itself (Weber) and the position of youth as a component in solidarity and social order (Durkheim).

Becoming (and Remaining) Part of the Social

Having looked at the emergence of sociology and some underlying ideas, this section briefly considers how people become members of societies – the ways in which they take on specifically 'social' identities – and the ways in which societies secure social order. So, the discussion considers what it means to be social. Are we born social or do we have to *become* social?

Socialization is the term generally used by sociologists to refer to the practices that exist in all societies to form their members as social beings. The processes that constitute socialization are also important because they help to answer the question, 'How is social order possible?'

Socialization is usually understood (often by politicians!) as a parental responsibility, or the responsibility of other carers, especially in a child's early years. Beyond that, various institutions undertake some of the functions through which children and young people become socialized: playgroups, schools, colleges, universities and perhaps youth services. Beyond this, churches and religious organizations, media and the labour market are among the institutions in which sociality is acquired and practised. The more complex a society, the more specialized skills are necessary to be 'socially competent' and the more varied become the institutions necessary to impart cultural skills and knowledge. It is through their material and social surroundings (construed as social relations, processes and differences) that individuals acquire the social knowledge, skills, attitudes and values that enable them to conduct themselves more or less competently in society. Social competence is learned through immersion in social institutions and the relations and processes that this entails. This, of course, is never-ending. Nick Lee's work (2001, 2005) on childhood is worth looking at here. Lee is critical of the distinction sometimes made between adult 'human beings' and child 'human becomings'. Lee's argument can be extended to youth. He suggests that human life is a process characterized by change, dependency, and interdependency and a constant state of 'becoming' for everyone. Perhaps this perspective, which concentrates on the idea of the process and dynamic nature of the life course, challenges some taken-for-granted ideas about socialization. That is certainly so if socialization is understood as a zero-sum process, a once and for all event that occurs in the early parts of human lives.

It would be a mistake to view societies' socialization processes as monolithic, 100% effective 'production lines' for the creation of perfectly adjusted and socialized individuals ready to take their place in their pre-planned niche in the social world. Some sociologists, particularly the so-called structural functionalists, seem to take this rather monolithic view of socialization and consider the behaviour of human beings as very much *determined* by society. However, other sociologists reject this as symptomatic of what Dennis Wrong (1961) famously referred to as the 'over socialized' concept of man, in which the uniqueness and individuality that symbolize our humanity have little place. Moreover, it does not account for social change.

Reflexivity

Sometimes, sociological thinking has assumed that people just 'get socialized' in the mechanical way that Wrong criticized half a century ago. Sociologists now tend to think about people as having the capacity to be more or less *reflexive*, a practice that Margaret Archer refers to as having an internal conversation with oneself: 'the regular exercise of the mental ability, shared by all normal people, to consider themselves in relation to their (social) contexts and vice versa' (Archer, 2007: 4). Archer argues that reflexivity is central to a person's sense of being a continuous self in the world. Without the internal conversation in which people pose questions to themselves, weigh up possibilities, speculate about themselves and their relation to aspects of their environments, people would simply not be aware that *social norms* (expectations or responsibilities, for example) have any meaningful application to anyone unless they know that they apply to themselves. In that sense, the social world presupposes individual reflexivity (Archer, 2007: 25–7). That means that the processes of socialization, particularly understood in terms of constructing *identity,* are active processes in which individuals are engaged and involved. Their involvement is shaped by patterns of social difference and social relations in which they are located.

Sociologists argue that the requirement to be reflexive has intensified as a consequence of changes associated with contemporary social life, and particularly because of the apparently increasing range of risks and opportunities that characterize Western societies and often associated with the consequences of economic and cultural globalization (Giddens, 1991: 10–34). Contemporary society is sometimes labelled as *late modern* or even *postmodern.*

The question of socialization highlights that there is something abstract about how some sociology represents the individuals through whom the social works. They often seem to be hollow and lacking in human substance and sometimes a little difficult to identify with. However it is possible, using the idea of reflexivity, to look at the relationship between the individual and social processes differently as an example from my own research with Val Hey illustrates (Bradford and Hey, 2007).

The following quotation is from a series of interviews with young people exploring their understandings of what it meant to them to be successful. The young people interviewed were very clear that their world was shaped by demands (from parents, teachers and, interestingly, from *themselves*) to 'make something of yourself', principally by taking advantage of educational opportunities that would lead to higher education, a career and personal satisfaction. They were also acutely aware of the difficulties this posed: acting in a highly competitive world, the distinct and real possibility of failure, the need to make *wise* choices and the prospect of making bad ones. Their school's response, and that of the young people, was to 'get focused' and to reflexively work on oneself in order to mobilize capacity and talent. One of the interviewees, Gandeep, who was part of a well-supported high achieving community (in school and outside), talked about the importance of 'focus'.

> 'I suppose if you know what you want and lots of things distract you ... Say girls and drugs and things like can get in your way and putting you off but if you are focused you get to the point ... I'd have to set my goals now and go for the career I want ... like if I achieved those goals in 10–15 years time I'd be quite happy.' (Bradford and Hey, 2007: 602–3)

This quotation shows how this young man engages in the processes of becoming successful (a key idea in socialization in Western societies). It entails careful and reflexive work by him on the self, designed to shield him from the temptations of the world in his attempted construction of a successful career. Clearly, there are several important processes going on here, almost in the background. The school operated to instil in these young people the importance of success and the means of achieving it, the young people's families were encouraging and invested time and money in supporting their children, friends and peers created a setting in which it was considered 'cool' to work and achieve and, finally, the young people themselves exercised a constant reflexive monitoring of their lives and achievements, making the necessary adjustments and accommodations. Gandeep's situation can be understood as embodying the relations, process, and divisions of socialization. Had other young people's experiences been researched, very different approaches and outcomes might have been discovered.

Sociology seems often to be concerned (rightly in some ways) with the impact of ideas, ideologies and, broadly, with things that go on inside people's heads. Socialization is sometimes presented as a problem of getting people to think the 'right' thoughts and know the 'right' kinds of knowledge.

Embodiment

Bryan Turner (1992: 83–100) offers an engaging way of understanding the problem of socialization more broadly. He suggests that all societies must attain 'bodily order' by resolving the problem of the physical body, thus reminding us of the specifically *embodied* nature of human agency and the significance of *embodiment* in becoming social. Turner points out that human beings are bodies! This is particularly important in relation to young people. Youth, and perhaps more specifically *adolescence*, is nothing if not an embodied experience for young people. Think here about natural bodily changes, social practices such as piercing and body decoration or seeking bodily pleasures through sex, alcohol or drugs, for example. Although these are not specific to young people, they assume great significance in youth. Importantly, by acknowledging the significance of the body the importance of social difference and social relations arises. Human bodies are organized in terms of age relations. They are gendered: the body appears that of a man or a woman. They have racial and ethnic features: the body is marked by certain characteristics that are given meaning and understood as expressing race or ethnicity. Bodies are classed: although the ubiquitous jeans and trainers have partially masked class, the ways in which the body is dressed – formally or informally in particular circumstances – can be decoded in terms of class.

Young people's bodies are also the sites upon which they engage in *consumption* of different kinds: music, fashion, dance, substances and so on, in the context of wants and desires created by a ubiquitous consumer capitalism. Consider, for example, the extent to which young people – perhaps young women especially – invest in their bodies in order to achieve an identity shaped by prevailing notions of *beauty*. Different young people are likely to acquire different capacities for this kind of *body work*, not least in terms of their economic resources. It is not difficult to see how the body has become the vehicle for the reflexive construction of a visual identity in contemporary societies and the extent to which capitalism has specifically created and sustained youth-oriented markets focused on the body. Importantly, the normative requirement to have a beautiful, fit or appropriately clothed or pierced body (the *performativity* of bodily identity) inevitably leads to disappointment. This can result in psychological damage and dislocation for many young women (Frost, 2001, 2005). Other writers have shown the extent to which the *imagined* bodies of gay young men can become a source of stigma and homophobic rejection (Barron and Bradford, 2007: 240). Many youth, social and health workers will be very clear about the high levels of eating disorders and other embodied mental health problems among young people in Western societies at the present time.

Turner uses the term *body* in two ways in his analysis. He refers to *individual* bodies and the *social* body or population, and suggests that achieving social order (in both senses: an ordered population as well as ordered physical and individual bodies) has four dimensions that exist in time and space, and in relation to internal and external aspects of the body. He suggests that societies devise means of achieving these four aspects of socialization and order: in a sense, the processes of becoming and sustaining sociality. The following categories are drawn from Turner's work.

1. **Reproduction:** social continuity through time; literally ensuring that bodies are reproduced through the work of health services and the provision made for parents and their children.
2. **Restraint:** concerned with the 'internal' control of desire and passion; self-discipline is important here and part of the function of the institutions of socialization.
3. **Regulation:** control and surveillance of population in social space: consider the ways in which young people are subject to all sorts of surveillance while they are in public space particularly (such as curfews).
4. **Representation:** establishing or communicating personality and identity in the social domain; particularly significant for young people in their construction of social identities through the processes and practices of consumption.

The importance of Turner's analysis is that it moves beyond an abstract notion of socialization, and identifies the material processes that act upon particular bodies at specific historical points. Turner's work points to the concept of *social control* that, although often poorly defined in sociology, refers to all the processes that are intended to reinforce conformity in any society.

Over to you...

Critical reflection

Using Turner's four categories as a framework (reproduction, restraint, regulation and representation), identify how your personal interaction or professional work contributes to any or all of these. You might draw out a table indicating aspects of your interaction or work that can be located in each. This will demonstrate something of how you, or your employing organization, contribute to young people becoming and remaining 'social'.

Most importantly, we need to remember that bodies are not all the same but are inscribed by social difference and division. Thus, bodies are racialized, gendered, or placed on a register of ability and disability, for example. Different bodies are regulated in different ways and come to convey different social meanings in the context of particular relations of power.

In reading Turner, one realizes that the concept of social control is related to questions of order and how societies organize and regulate collective lives. Often, social control is intimately linked to questions of *power* and how power relations operate in societies. Two important theorists whose work opens up very important questions of social processes, social control and power are referred to here. Basil Bernstein's research from the 1950s onwards into the sociology of language has been enormously generative in showing how language constructs, positions and regulates identities. That is to say, language has real social power; it is 'one of the most important means of initiating, synthesizing and *reinforcing* ways of thinking, feeling and behaviour which are functionally related to the social group' (Bernstein, 1971: 43). In research on family and socialization, Bernstein identified two speech codes (ways of talking) that he characterized as having roots in different family and class cultures and experiences. In one type of setting (associated with but not exclusive to some working-class cultures), Bernstein argued that a *condensed* and *positional* speech code operated that situated speakers in very clear ways. When children ask, 'Why do I have to do this?' the child is told, 'Because I say so' (a response based on hierarchy), 'Because that's what boys do' (a response based on gender role) or 'Because children should do as their elders tell them' (a response based on age relations). Such positioning forms of speech, Bernstein argues, lead to a grid of identities and categories in which individuals are situated and come to understand themselves.

This condensed form of speech contrasts with what Bernstein refers to as the *elaborated* and *personal* speech code that is characterized by a pattern that celebrates the autonomy and uniqueness of the individual rather than an identity or categorization based on position. When the child asks, 'Why can't I do that?' the response might be, 'Because mum is worried about what might happen', 'Because I have a headache' or, 'Because dad will be very disappointed', or 'How would you like it if you were a cat?' Mary Douglas argues that in this setting the child is free from the rigid grid categories and positions of the condensed speech code but 'is made a prisoner of a system of feelings and abstract principles' (1996: 29). Bernstein's work is not so much concerned with the content of these speech codes (the words used or the slang in which something is expressed). Rather, the codes operate as representations of particular social relations within which group (class) members understand themselves, and their social function is to police these understandings. Bernstein controversially pointed out that schools are invariably organized on the basis of elaborated codes and therefore children whose socialization consisted in condensed forms of speech (that is, *positional* rather than *personal*) were, inevitably, disadvantaged (Bernstein, 1975).

In his account of social control, Michel Foucault (1977, 1979) makes related points about the crucial role of language in the form of *discourse*. For Foucault, discourse refers to the ways in which it is rational (normal and expected) to speak or write about a particular object or topic in a particular way. For example, he was interested in the multifarious ways in which modern societies came to think about matters like sexuality, madness or criminality and how dominant discourses shaped or even controlled political, social and cultural agendas. Discourse can be contrasted with the more specific term *ideology* that always deals with matters of politics and the social–cultural distribution of power.

Foucault argues that modern societies are characterized by a range of *disciplinary* apparatuses (schools, factories, prisons and so on) and techniques (examination, assessment or appraisal, for example) that operate through supervision and surveillance. Disciplinary power is based on the deployment of 'scientific' knowledge (produced, for example, by professionals and academics) that is used to analyse and categorize human beings in specific ways. Consider, for example, the ways in which 'psychological knowledge' is used to describe and categorize individuals in a range of settings and circumstances: industrial organizations, hospitals, clinics, counselling agencies, therapeutic communities and so on (see Henriques, et al., 1984). Think about the way in which knowledge derived (however indirectly) from the 'social sciences' is used to develop techniques to 'manage' or regulate young people in various ways. A possible recent example lies in the work of John Huskins (1996, 1998), which informed the development of a range of services for young people such as the Youth Achievement Awards adopted by UK Youth. Huskins was interested in identifying a universal framework for defining young people's involvement in youth work. By identifying this by means of a developmental stage model, Huskins claimed that youth work could be much more effectively planned, managed and evaluated. Normative practice models like this mark out a range of needs and experiences, which are claimed to offer universal principles for managing *at risk*, or *excluded* young people. The knowledge underpinning the models comes from a combination of psychology, sociology and professional practices of various kinds.

These examples contribute to what might be referred to as a *discourse of adolescence*, signifying all the ways in which specific meanings and understandings have become associated with the idea (the *discourse*) of adolescence. For example, adolescence is a 'naturally' problematic period, young people need special kinds of intervention or difficult adolescent experiences lead to difficult adulthood. The point for Foucault is that these discourses are made up of what he refers to as *power-knowledge*. By this he identifies how knowledge is deployed to shape particular social relations (of gender, age, or race, for example).

This underlying power-knowledge constructs young people as both 'subjects' and 'objects'. It forms specific kinds of human identities that, Foucault argues, are intended to internalize particular kinds of sociality and *normality*, similar to Bernstein's arguments. Individuals are shaped or produced by the 'discursive practices' (knowledge-based practices like education, therapy, management and so on) that come to colonize particular societies at particular times. It is argued that the 'technicians' of these practices, social workers or youth workers, for example, respond to their clients in terms of the frameworks of knowledge that are established and reproduced through their practices.

Practices and processes of socialization and social control are far from monolithic and, clearly, are only partially effective, and different institutions or practices of socialization may be in conflict (churches, homes or peer groups, for example). By acknowledging the various domains and levels of the social (the family, the school or the media, for example), a range of complex interactions is evident within whose conjunctions social identities are formed. Socialization could be seen as an example of practising freedom and is both active and lifelong. Becoming and remaining social – in other words, exercising freedom – is neither cultural nor social imprinting, but is complex and multilayered.

Youth, Sociology and Young People

Youth is an important (and symbolic) concept that has emerged historically in both sociology and public consciousness over the last hundred and fifty years or so. That is not to suggest that there were no young people – *youth* – before, say, 1850. However, the way in which youth is understood as distinctive and having special characteristics, as an 'in-between' or *liminal* social category, as inherently troublesome and as requiring services designed to meet its specific needs is typical of *modern* societies in the global North.

Several writers have pointed to the long historical development of cultural views of youth (see Griffiths, 1996; Ben-Amos, 1994) which came about through the displacement of young people from the controlled environment of rural communities and the domestic economy to newly developed urban spaces of living and employment as societies moved from their traditional to modern forms. In traditional society young people had been subject to the social control of peer and elder guidance in their transition from the (legitimate) irresponsibility of childhood, and admittance to adulthood was often marked by ritual or celebration.

Some key processes are responsible for growing attention being given to young people in the nineteenth century and for the associated emergence of a social category: youth. These underlie contemporary anxieties about young people and have meant that age is retained as an important aspect of social difference.

● The separation of childhood and youth as specific social categories as a consequence of legislation protecting children and young people; the curtailment of employment hours, for example, created leisure as a distinct temporal space.

● The extension of schooling.

● The growth of scientific knowledge – particularly psychology – about young people.

● The proliferation of social, moral, legal and other discourses in which young people emerge as particular subjects positioned in particular ways.

Clearly, it is impossible to regard youth or young people as an entirely universal category. Social difference, in the form of class, gender and race, for example, has shaped young people's differing experiences of being young. One only has to compare the lives of, say, early twentieth-century English working-class young women whose schooling was completed by the age of thirteen with those of young men of the same era born into aristocratic or professional families who were sent to public school and then to university. Their experiences and the meaning of youth for them (and those around them) were quite different.

Social difference and division of similar kinds continue to mark out the opportunities and challenges faced by young people. However, despite the vast academic, policy and media interest in the category *youth*, commentators have noted that youth remains a slippery and ambiguous category (Griffin, 1993, 2004; Valentine, 2003; Jones, 2009). As a concept, youth has mirrored the development of sociology in the twentieth century with different theoretical positions shaping the sorts of questions sociologists have asked about youth.

Some sociologists have come to see the present time (say from the mid-twentieth century onwards) as having particular characteristics and being a kind of 'sub-period' of modernity itself. For Bauman (2007), the current period can best be understood by using the metaphor of *liquidity,* drawing from and extending Marx's dictum that in capitalist modernity, 'All that is solid melts into air' (Marx and Engels, 1968: 38). According to Bauman (2007), *liquid modernity* embodies distinct social processes that compound social anxiety and uncertainty, all having implications for young people. It is possible to identify at least five particular elements of this modernity, all of which have implications for youth and young people:

- Social institutions and social forms that embody the routines and patterns of a predictable daily existence no longer have fixed shape or identity; for example, work experiences are no longer fixed or solid points in people's lives from where they might navigate their life course. As a case in point, for young people in the UK, where one million young people are unemployed in 2012, it is hard to see a future in the labour market and beyond. Recurring redundancy, retraining, and reinvention of self become the norm (see Sennett, 1998, for an account of the personal consequences of 'liquid labour').

- Domestic politicians have diminishing capacity to mediate local conditions as power shifts into uncontrollable global spaces (finance and media, for example, are now moved across boundaries at the click of a mouse). The global recession shows just how entangled national economies have become, encouraging national states to curtail their previous functions (to provide services or protection to the vulnerable members of their societies) which become left to the market and private initiatives.

- Collective responses to individual vulnerability (undertaken hitherto by the welfare state) decline as do attendant social solidarity and community. Collective identities are degraded and competition heightened. Society becomes understood as no more than a matrix of network connections rather than something solid and structured. For young people and others, this enhances tendencies towards instrumentalism and away from collaboration.

- Late modern liquid societies lose the capacity to think and plan long term because stable and permanent organizations and institutions capable of this are dismantled. Life (at societal and individual level) becomes a 'short-term' series of 'projects and episodes' rather than a narrative that holds a promise of development or progression. For young people, identity and transition to adult status (and any economic independence that this confers) becomes an experience of stops and starts, with little sense of sequence, rhythm or advance in the absence of 'future'.

- The responsibility for resolving the difficulties entailed in this late modern life are devolved to individuals who are encouraged to exercise responsible choices in the life project. Rather than *conformity* to rules being at a premium, the emphasis becomes placed on individuals' *flexibility*, that is, changing direction, abandoning commitments and old loyalties for fresh ones and pursuing opportunities on the basis of availability rather than preference. For young people, this means the constant injunction to be 'up for whatever comes', to be increasingly reflexive and to reinvent self according to external demands.

This liquid or *late* modernity is expressed and embodied in various aspects of youth transitions in the post-recessionary world that underline the sense of uncertainty and unpredictability many young people currently experience. Social difference impacts on young people's capacity for resilience and their ability to withstand the challenges faced. The nature and meaning of youth as a social category is thus shaped by the social conditions in which it is produced.

Over to you...

Critical reflection

Thinking through the kind of society that Bauman maps out (some people find his work very pessimistic), can you identify examples of the five elements identified above and ways in which your personal interaction or professional work with young people seeks to compensate for these or alleviate their effects? For example, the shifting nature of institutions (the institution of work or the institutions that make up specific service provisions might be examples) seems to underlie much of this. Where specifically do your interventions impact on that?

Despite so many radical changes, the idea of youth retains considerable symbolic power in Western societies. As a common-sense category, the term *youth* has become encrusted with layers of social meaning over time, reflecting a range of social, moral and political preoccupations and anxieties. As John Davis (1990) has argued, youth has become a kind of screen onto which the social anxieties and hopes of adult generations have been periodically projected. In some ways, late modernity could be seen as a period in which fascination and fear of young people are increasingly widely expressed. *Fascination* is reflected in the enormous social energy expended in writing about youth, making films and television programmes about youth and, generally, offering a continuous cultural commentary on the affairs of youth and the condition of young people. Interestingly, many adults (with the complicity of expanding health and fashion markets) seek to extend their own youth for as long as possible. *Youthfulness* has become a valued cultural commodity despite the simultaneous *fear* that many adults commonly express about youth themselves. The proliferation of social policy that focuses on young people signals that youth, like childhood, has become one of the most governed sectors of human existence in Western societies (Rose, 1999). Readers who are youth practitioners might like to consider the extent to which, and *how*, their work contributes to that.

Summary and Conclusions

Chapter 1 offers a broad introduction to sociology, covering its origins in the fundamental social changes that brought about modernity in Europe. Sociology's distinctive imagination and an understanding of the specifically *social* world were also identified as important features of sociology.

Most importantly, Chapter 1 showed how contemporary understandings of youth as a distinct social category with its own needs, characteristics and problems are a consequence of changes that occurred from the eighteenth century onwards, especially in ostensible shifts from traditional to modern societies. The processes of industrialization and urbanization associated with capitalism were especially significant in the emergence of youth as a modern social category. This is not to say that young people didn't exist prior to modern times; rather that the meaning and position of youth alters according to broad historical and social changes.

Sociology emerged as a consequence of a modern and critical reflexivity that developed in the midst of immense changes in Europe in the nineteenth century. Sociology responded to, and offered an account of the meaning and significance of these shifts. It was based on the attempt to rigorously research and theorize *scientifically* – that is, on the basis of scientific method and reason – what the changes might mean for those caught up in them. This was powerful, radical and, for those in traditional positions of authority (in the church, for example), profoundly threatening as sociology articulated an agenda based on broad Enlightenment principles. Sociology's historically progressive position has been largely maintained since the nineteenth century. More recently, this progressive agenda has reflected discourses of social justice and fairness that have characterized much sociology of youth.

As Chapter 1 has shown, for Durkheim and the classical sociologists of the nineteenth and early twentieth centuries, all life is encompassed by the social and nothing should be considered beyond a specifically *social* explanation. Sociology should be thought of in terms of both knowing *and* doing, and the continuing endeavours of sociologists to analyse social affairs *and* contribute to changing the world remain very significant. For youth practitioners, these twin aspects of knowing and doing are vital. Without good, rigorously researched and critically theorized knowledge of young people and the influences and circumstances that shape their lives, policymakers and practitioners are unlikely to be able to make good decisions about either policy or practice matters. Youth practitioners' use of their *sociological imagination* as is an essential part of this.

Further Reading

- Jones, G. (2009) *Youth*, Cambridge: Polity Press.

  A comprehensive overview of the main approaches to the sociology of youth.

- Plummer, K. (2010) *Sociology, the Basics*, London: Routledge.

  Plummer's book is packed with ideas and illustrations of key sociological theory.

- Oakley, A. (2007) *Fracture. Adventures of a Broken Body*, Bristol: Policy Press.

  Oakley offers a fascinating sociological account of the social context and processes of embodiment as she narrates her experiences of breaking an arm while in the United States.

2

Growing Up in the Present

From 1945 to the 2000s

Introduction

Chapter 2 argues that to understand the position of youth and young people in current times one should *first*, know something of the social policy and economic contexts in which post-war youth emerged as a social category and, *second*, understand the specific cultural contexts in which youth is constructed and to which it contributes. For example, what is now understood as *youth culture* in the UK emerged against the background of the development of the welfare state in the 1950s. Perhaps because of a demographic 'bulge' in the post-war youth population, youth became highly visible in the post-war period, generating broad and often exaggerated social anxiety. The development of what came to be named as a 'generation gap', in which the young appeared to have different values and interests from their parents' generation as the 1950s progressed, came to fruition in the youth cultures of the 1960s as the 'bulge' generation reached the age of majority. Chapter 2 considers youth in the UK as a paradigm example to explore how discourses of youth emerge and are reproduced in the context of policy, political economy and culture.

Much of the sociological literature suggests that in the West, youth is a cultural phenomenon of the 1950s and 1960s. However, David Fowler's (2008) excellent history of youth culture from 1920 onwards, suggests something of a 'cult of youth' after the First World War (Fowler, 2008) and there is evidence of distinctive youth groups and movements at the start of the century (for example Gillis, 1974; Davies, 2008). Historians have contested whether youth culture as such existed prior to this (Ben-Amos, 1994; Griffiths, 1996). What is important about the second half of the twentieth century in the UK and other modern societies is the extensive social preoccupation with youth as a distinctive and apparently universal social category, considered problematic both for society and for young people themselves, and which raises questions about the position of young people as 'citizens' or 'citizens-to-be'. This has implications for contemporary young people who are inheriting a world in which, arguably, technological change is rapidly deconstructing the social categories and certainties of the past, including the idea of a universally understood concept of 'youth'.

While all historical periods are times of change, the second half of the twentieth century demonstrates a number of very significant social trans-formations that provide a background to understanding contemporary young people and the phenomenon of youth. However, it is important not to concentrate *exclusively* on change. Sociology has the capacity to identify the relationship between change *and* continuity. For example, sociology can help to explain poverty and inequality as continuing general social questions, and in terms of the ways in which the features and experiences of poverty and inequality change over place and time such that in the UK they are different today from the immediate post-war period, and different in the UK from other parts of the world. Such understanding can then be linked in turn to other social relations and categories. Thus sociology can analyse how poverty has affected working-class youth with reference to changing youth–class relations and subcultural practices. The work of the sociologists in the Birmingham Centre for Contemporary Cultural Studies in the 1970s and 1980s focused its attention particularly on such matters. Sociology can also explain changes and continuities in terms of wider social categories involving political economy and institutional power. Since the 1990s the Teesside sociologists of youth (see, for example, Shil-drick and MacDonald, 2006, 2007) have been particularly focused on these matters. These different interests tell us something about the changing importance of the condition of young people and questions relating to youth in UK society.

In sociological terms, the era from the Second World War in the UK can be understood in three broad historical periods. Sociologists *model* historical periods in terms of their distinctive economic, cultural and social character-istics. It is important to remember that these models are approximations, a kind of 'shorthand' devised to represent and explain the main trends in any given period of historical time. Each of the three periods can be understood in terms of a *zeitgeist*, or spirit of the age, which expressed dominant polit-ical visions and an imagined 'good society'. Importantly, each period must be viewed in the context of changing global conditions and events: the demise of the Soviet Union, the expanding European project or the rapid modernization of China and India, for example. These historical periods contained ideas of what it meant to be a 'responsible citizen', thus having particular relevance for youth and the institutions (education and youth services, for example) that shaped their lives. The three periods are dealt with here as 'political consensus' (late 1940s to 1970s); the 'challenge to consensus' (1970s to late 1990s) and 'between the market and the state' (late 1990s to 2010).

The Post-War Period and 'Political Consensus'

This period, and its implications for youth in the UK can be characterized in the following way.

Table 2.1 Political consensus

Post-war political consensus	Late 1940s–1970s
Dominant political rationality	Post-war demands for social change and residual perceptions of wartime consensus lead to post-war 'Keynes-Beveridge' settlement and 'political consensus'; social and institutional reform aimed at diminishing inequality; 'social citizenship' and individual rights to welfare balanced by collective obligations; rational social planning through the deployment of *neutral* expertise; belief that the state could underwrite social progress
Characteristics of public policy	Relatively comprehensive, collective and *centrally managed* system of social insurance, education, health, employment and welfare benefits
Significance for young people	Expanding services for young people, especially after the 1944 Education Act and the Albemarle Report (Ministry of Education, 1944, 1960). The significance of this for young people lay in the emergence of specific services (the Youth Service is an example) that aimed to support them in particular ways and according to specific definitions of youth and youth need. Tacit acceptance that education was a means of inclusion and opportunity. Youth seen as a broadly universal or essential category

Two principal domestic components characterize the post-war period in the UK: the emergence under the Labour government of 1945–1951 of the welfare state based on the work of Sir William Beveridge and a Keynesian approach to managing the UK economy based on the work of the economist John Maynard Keynes. Keynesianism proposes the active involvement of government, central banks and the public sector in stimulating economic demand and reducing unemployment to stimulate economic growth. Under this system of political and economic management, working-class young people were beneficiaries of generally improved social services and in particular they were able to access employment opportunities and education which had been hitherto unknown. Full employment led to new levels of affluence among young people, which impacted upon the development of a specific youth-oriented retail market and the development of distinctive youth styles and culture. The main social concern about young people during this period was their perceived difference from the parent generation, a so-called 'generation gap' that raised concerns about social continuity and the ability of the new generation to become disciplined workers and citizens.

The post-war political position of both the Labour and Conservative parties (effectively until the early 1980s) was marked by a duality of providing a welfare state while also becoming integrated into an increasingly global (and eventually neoliberal) capitalism. This period has been described as a time of agreement or *settlement* between the main power brokers. It was, in fact, characterized by a number of settlements understood to have embodied *consensus* in the relationship between the state, the economy, civil society and the public sphere, and referred to by Esping-Andersen as the 'golden age' of welfare (1990). This arrangement – an assumed political and social consensus – is sometimes also referred to as the 'political settlement', although not all commentators accept the idea of consensus. For an excellent challenge to the so-called 'myth of consensus' see Butler (1993).

It is worth noting that this period is characterized by a growth in academic sociology in the UK, with university sociology departments being established and expanding. Research-based (empirical) sociology was very much part of the underlying post-war commitment to progress, and it was in this period that the beginnings of a distinctive sociology of youth began to emerge. This sociology understood youth as a preparatory phase for adulthood in which young people would become appropriately socialized. The concern here lay with aspects of social reproduction and generational continuity, and the function of youth in this process (Parsons, 1942; Eisenstadt, 1956).

This period of consensus was supported by seven key ideological and organizational elements:

1. 'Reason' and 'progress'
2. Social and political consensus (real or imagined)
3. Universal citizenship discourse
4. Rhetoric of citizenship

5. Mixed economy of welfare
6. An organizational settlement
7. Commitment to full employment

as outlined below.

'Reason' and 'progress'

Ideas of 'reason' and 'progress' underpinned much of the thinking about welfare and the state at this time. For Beveridge, progress would be achieved through the state and civil society cooperating in the calculated and systematic alleviation of the five 'giant evils' ('want', 'disease', 'ignorance', 'squalor' and 'idleness'). This view assumed that the rising generation, benefiting from welfare state provision, would reproduce its conditions and beliefs in the future.

Social and political consensus (real or imagined)

Assumptions about the nature of British society, its citizens and the most effective ways of responding to their 'needs' underlined the importance of social and political consensus. The provision of state welfare, including health services, education and housing, was a means of securing citizenship and consolidating a sense of national identity; welfare was an integrating force ensuring that individuals or groups did not become marginalized as a consequence of poverty and of ensuring that class conflict did not create social instability and crisis. Though it addressed class distinctions to some degree, it is important to acknowledge that other social inequalities, including gender and age were institutionalized by the terms of welfare. It was in this context that specifically class-related, and male-dominated youth subcultures emerged as young people were situated as relatively secure 'adults-to-be'. Young men in particular had earning power but few family responsibilities. They had leisure time to define in their own terms and with reference to their expectations of the future.

Universal citizenship discourse

The idea of *universal citizenship* was important to consensus; in Marshall's words, citizenship status was given to members of the national community (1963) and constituted in individual rights and responsibilities concretely established through a range of state and civil institutions. In this view education – including youth work – would be important in the formation and socialization of good citizens. Social change could be managed in a progressive and orderly way, with welfare mitigating social conflict. Such an understanding contributed to the idea that problematic youth in general, and young people as individuals 'with problems', could be 'managed' through institutional intervention including the provision of general services such as youth clubs, night classes and sports facilities, while problematic individual young people could be managed through the intervention of social workers and rehabilitative 'treatment' within the framework of juvenile justice.

Rhetoric of citizenship

In creating a sense of British identity (and thus consensus through 'solidarity'), the language of citizenship is important in obscuring differences due to class and income. Citizenship discourse is one way in which vocabularies of difference (race or class, for example) can become absorbed into rhetoric of common identity. This points towards the symbolic and instrumental value of citizenship embodied in the post-war consensus and which continues to be important. However, citizenship is an elastic status that can be 'extended, given, restricted and withheld' (Coffey, 2004: 43). This was crucial in relation to increased migration from the Commonwealth in response to calls for labour to help rebuild the post-war UK economy, and in relation to contemporary debates in Europe about *who* exactly counts as a citizen.

Mixed economy of welfare

The idea of a 'mixed economy of welfare' meant that the state guaranteed minimum universal benefits while simultaneously leaving individuals with the freedom to extend and build on this through their own actions. Beveridge expressed this view in the metaphor of the 'extension ladder', establishing a framework of welfare, incorporating state, private and voluntary initiatives (Standing, 2009: 36). For young people, a meritocratic ideology of achievement encouraged aspiration for some while supporting those who 'failed' educationally or could not climb the career ladder out of the working class. In some ways these class-based identities shaped distinctions between youth cultures (for example between the mods and rockers) and exacerbated class divisions that would later materialize under Thatcherism in the 1980s.

An organizational settlement

The post-war consensus also incorporated what Clarke and Newman (1997) refer to as the 'organizational settlement' through which the welfare state could be managed and its practices administered. The organizational settlement entailed two specific elements: 'bureaucratic organization', stressing efficiency and impartiality, and 'professionalism' emphasizing the importance of expertise in resolving complex human problems. It is in this context that the Albemarle Report (Ministry of Education, 1960) set the terms for the professionalizing of youth work through a statutory youth service. The expansion of state professionals provided careers for some young people from working-class backgrounds in nursing, teaching and youth work, for example, arguably shifting established class identities and incorporating the most educated working-class young people into a consensus view of citizenship.

Commitment to full employment

The post-war commitment to full employment (Standing, 2009: 37–40) incorporated the idea that participation in society really meant participation in paid work by all those who were capable. The concept of *social inclusion*, used frequently in the late twentieth and early twenty-first century in Europe and the UK, has its precedent in the immediate post-war years. In the UK, being included in society meant having a paid job while *exclusion* signified being outside of the labour market. Thus education, training and socialization for young people were directly linked to their expected futures in the labour market. The grammar school system was designed to encourage social mobility and to deploy individual talents to those areas of the labour market that needed specific skills, thus enabling the most able from the working classes and lower middle classes to escape their class backgrounds. However, also built into the educational system was an assumption that social classes would generally reproduce themselves in the next generation, and the secondary modern schools and private schools retained very clear and distinctive functions of social reproduction. Meanwhile, education for young men and young women was related directly to a highly gendered labour market that disadvantaged young women.

It is worth reflecting here how social consensus, and associated ideas about citizenship penetrated 'official' youth service and youth work discourse during this period and, despite social change, their continuity beyond the immediate post-war period. The idea of citizenship formation in a very broad sense (and sometimes not using the term *citizenship*) has always been significant in the purposes of youth work, in whatever guise. Its rhetorical use, as suggested earlier, seems particularly marked in UK reports about youth work, including the Albemarle Report (Ministry of Education, 1960), the Hunt Report (Department of Education and Science, 1967), the Milson-Fairbairn Report (Department of Education and Science, 1969) and the Thompson Report (Secretary of State for Education and Science, 1982), all of which rely on motifs of citizenship in one form or another. More recently, citizenship education has become a formal part of the school curriculum and the new National Citizen Service being developed by the UK coalition government is also predicated on the discourse of citizenship.

In their different ways, these youth service documents are characteristic of the state's approach to youth. All identify how young people can or *should* be helped to understand the process of 'growing up' in terms of the responsibilities of 'mature' citizenship at a variety of levels, but in a context where citizenship rights have been simultaneously withheld from them through franchise law, social policy and benefit reforms. The documents are based on a view of society that privileges consensus: integration, adjustment and the flattening of any difference arising as a consequence of social relations. They do not address the differences between young people, the tensions between youth and other social groups, or the potential of dissent or conflict between citizens about the nature of citizenship.

It is important to remember the ideological significance of ideas like citizenship, and to be aware of the ways in which they can be deployed in the attempt to paper over all sorts of 'cracks' in the social structure that indicate the presence of difference and inequality. Critical sociologists have had much to say about all of this, pointing to the structures of disadvantage and inequality that have increasingly characterized young people's lives in the UK and other societies (MacDonald, 1997; Henderson et al., 2007; Thomson, 2009; Roberts, 2009). Perhaps the key debate here has been the extent to which young people's transitions into responsible adulthood are shaped by the social circumstances that position them, partially delineated by policy, and the resources that are available to them for making 'good decisions' about their lives and futures. By virtue of their membership of groups or communities – based on class, ethnicity, friendship or faith, for example – young people are able differentially to draw on support, encouragement and help in decision-making about aspects of their lives (Bradford and Hey, 2010).

The expansion of youth work following the Albemarle Report (Ministry of Education, 1960) signalled a general move towards the regulation of youth work expertise through professionalism and bureaucratic organization (the 'youth service') in the post-war period, reflecting consensus assumptions about welfare. Professionalization reminds us of Weber's position on power and status, especially the argument that powerful groups seek to effect *closure*, and prevent others from encroaching on their position. Youth workers have argued consistently that 'social education' (as the dominant rationale for youth work from the 1960s onwards), and more recently 'informal education', is a complex set of practices which demands *professional judgement* based on accredited knowledge and skill, achieved through an extended period of training. This fitted well with the managerialist assumptions of welfare state ideology. Youth workers, like related occupations in education, health and welfare, have pursued professionalization as an occupational strategy calculated to achieve status and authority in the occupational domain. Beginning with the Albemarle Report, they have had some success. From 2010, in the UK, it became necessary for a *qualified* youth worker to be educated to at least degree level.

It was the articulation of the 'political–economic' (full employment and labour security), the 'social' (welfare services and provision) and the 'organizational' (bureaucratic professionalism) settlements which formed the basis to post-war consensus, and which underpinned the development of the British welfare state. These framed the institutional parameters of youth and constructed the professional expertise that would address the condition of youth.

Challenges to the Settlements: Emerging Neoliberalism

Table 2.2 offers a summary of this second period.

Consensus economics (from Keynes), and its welfare superstructure (from Beveridge) continued to develop throughout the 1950s and 1960s. However, the 1970s introduced fundamental challenges to the settlements and to notions of consensus.

Four principal reasons can be identified for the disruption of the political and economic assumptions that underpinned these in the UK: failure of 1960s modernization programmes led to a disillusioned electorate, economic difficulties in the 1970s, rising unemployment and increased public expenditure; world recession in the 1970s; a volatile and fragmented UK electorate reflecting specific interests, identities, movements and nationalities necessitating the main parties raising their political profiles in order to present a populist image to electors; and the increased and unashamedly ideological character of British politics.

The rise of a 'new right' and a 'new left' facilitated the demise of the consensus through political and ideological conflict. Several authors have suggested that these factors are part of a wider international crisis in state authority in the context of globalized economics and capital accumulation through corporate *multinational* business (globalization is considered in Chapter 7). In practical terms, a global 'politics of the budget' has, since the 1970s, taken centre stage in controlling public spending. Recessionary influences besetting the global economy since 2008 make this even more critical in countries where social expenditure is *the* prime target for government cutbacks. The conditions facing contemporary young people (in many countries in Europe and beyond) have their roots in the emergence of neoliberalism in the mid-1970s and its subsequent political dominance since the 1980s.

Table 2.2   The challenge to consensus

The challenge to consensus: Neoliberalism	*1970s–late 1990s*
Dominant political rationality	The politicization of welfare; 'New Right' reaction to 'welfare dependency'; politics of the budget; rejection of the idea of the state as key actor in welfare; attack on collectivized provision and an emphasis on individual prudence and responsibility; stress on *obligations* rather than rights
Characteristics of public policy	Demand for accountability and 'value for money' from public services; injection of 'market discipline'; fragmentation and flexibilization of welfare through 'internal market', 'contracts', 'mixed economy of care' and 'partnerships'; management shifted from 'the centre to the periphery' and increased role of managerialism; the emergence of the 'quango state' (quasi-autonomous non-governmental organizations: 'arms-length' organizations funded by government) and blurring the boundaries between 'public/private' and 'state/voluntary' provision, including services for young people
Significance for young people	Collapse of youth labour market; increased sense of vulnerability and uncertainty for some young people (shaped by class, gender, place and race, for example) and their futures: 'risk'; extended and fragmented transitions for many young people, damaging opportunities for independence and for achieving the status of 'adulthood'

Over to you...

Critical reflection on reading or watching a film

It was suggested earlier in this chapter that the post-war consensus might have contained the 'seeds of its own destruction'. Reflecting on the settlements that constitute the consensus, the 'political–economic' (full employment and labour security), the 'social' (welfare services and provision) and the 'organizational' (bureaucratic professionalism), can you identify reasons why underlying post-war discourses of family, employment and professionalism may no longer have provided a basis for consensus by the 1970s and from then onwards? For example, how have discourses of family or identity shifted from those of the early post-war period?

One way of thinking about this is to consider how these ideas were (and are) constructed in popular culture. For example, to get a sense of ideas of the *British* working-class family in the 1950s and 1960s, consider some of the so-called 'kitchen sink realism' dramas of the period, often created by young people who had working-class backgrounds and had benefited from a meritocratic educational system. Films like *Saturday Night and Sunday Morning* (1960) and *A Taste of Honey* (1961), and television productions like *Cathy Come Home* (1966) are good places to start. The arrival of *Coronation Street* in 1960 was an example of how working-class British life was represented at the time. Novels and plays by Allan Sillitoe (for example *The Loneliness of the Long Distance Runner*) or Nell Dunn (for example *Poor Cow*) also offer important representations of post-war working-class life. In looking at or reading these, you will gain a very clear view of the British family and identity. If you watch *A Taste of Honey* you will be able to detect real tensions about these matters.

From the 1970s onwards (and specifically as a consequence of Thatcherism in the UK and Reaganism in the US) a constant challenge to the welfare state was advanced. Both political Left and Right were critical of the consensus welfare state through the 1980s and 1990s. The Left cited the welfare state's failure to alter the position of disadvantaged sectors of society. The political right (the so-called New Right) was critical of welfare state bureaucracy, its inefficiency and its tendency to create dependency on benefits (Clarke and Newman, 1997).

The term 'New Right' (Barry, 1987) was a convenient way of grouping a number of related ideas and themes, although there was divergence between some of them. The apparent synthesis of these ideas in a political programme led to forceful critique of consensus politics and welfare provision advanced by Margaret Thatcher in the UK, Ronald Reagan in the US, and their successors. The New Right position in 1970s and 1980s Britain, and reflected in other parts of the world, focused on a number of key areas that symbolized the erosion of moral authority and social order, mobilizing public opinion and concern around a number of key concerns. These can be understood as the ideological out-workings of struggles about imagined societies, often conducted in terms of arguments polarized between fairness, equality and social justice *and* tradition, hierarchy and authority. There are three key arguments here.

1. The welfare state had been instrumental in undermining traditional institutions (particularly the family) that had been the guarantors of moral and social order.

2. In extending individual rights, 'progressive' social legislation had facilitated the growth of radical social movements (particularly the trade unions and the women's movement) that, it was claimed, had also eroded the authority of traditional institutions. The predominance of 'rights' rather than (or at the expense of) 'obligations' was understood to have had a similarly destructive effect.

3. Encouraged by 'child-centred' teaching methods, poor parenting or diverse lifestyles, for example, 'permissiveness' was alleged to have swept across the UK, again threatening 'traditional' morality and established authority.

Perhaps the important issue here is the extent to which these ideas, regarded in the 1980s and early 1990s as the province of politicians on the right, have now become almost mainstream politics and social thinking in the UK, the US, Australia and many European countries. One particular argument, enthusiastically pursued by politicians of all the main parties during the past few years, is how welfare provision has created a 'culture of dependency' (an idea fervently promoted by sections of the media) allegedly undermining personal responsibility and individual initiative. This is a view that is not peculiar to politicians of any single party, and most politicians want to be seen to encourage 'enterprise' rather than reliance on 'state support' of various kinds. This discourse of enterprise and personal responsibility holds considerable power across political (and indeed popular) positions. It has had real implications for young people.

Charles Murray, for example, was a highly influential political commentator in the early 1980s. He singled out young people in the debate about a so-called *underclass*, allegedly a sector of society that can be distinguished from the *respectable* working class (IEA Health and Welfare Unit, 1996). For Murray, three factors lead to membership of the underclass: illegitimacy, violent crime and dropout from the labour market. The dependency that he asserted is constituted in the receipt of welfare benefits he considered largely responsible for the growth of this group. Murray argued that some young men have grown up with no strong role models, leading to a lack of family discipline and an absent sense of responsibility. Without regular employment, Murray suggested, these young people become involved in crime and drug use. Murray's solution lay in the withdrawal of benefits from single parent families (essentially young parents) who would then give up their children for adoption and would have to take whatever employment was available rather than relying on state benefits to support a new generation of underclass children.

Sociologists have been enormously critical of Murray's arguments pointing out that they are invariably racist, they stigmatize young women, that there is no evidence that any group holds markedly different values in relation to work than those of the majority of the population and that the vocabulary of underclass tends to exclude and pathologize specific groups of young people. Nevertheless, Murray's ideas have been influential and much of the broad social policy agenda of the past 20 years has, in the UK and elsewhere, been shaped by Murray's position. Benefits, in particular, have been progressively withdrawn from young people, who have had to rely on their families for social and economic support, thus increasing their dependency at a time when there is an expectation of increasing individual *independence* and responsibility, regardless of age (Jones, 2009: 140).

Over to you...

Critical reflection

New Right arguments rest on particular views of 'human nature', that is, what people are really like underneath. What is your view of human nature? To what extent do you think that social arrangements (the way in which a particular society is structured or organized) shape human nature, or are social arrangements themselves a product of human nature? What underlying view of human nature can you identify in your own service or organization? What are the implications of this for your professional approach to young people?

What was understood as New Right ideology is a fusion of two other political perspectives. Its roots lie first in orthodox conservatism, which embodies a particular view of human nature, and entails specific social arrangements. Its underlying principles can be summarized in three ways (the reference to 'conservative' signifies an *ideological* conservatism rather than, necessarily, a political party). *First*, if left to their own devices, people are fundamentally weak, selfish, irrational and aggressive. *Second*, because human nature is as it is, authoritarian government is necessary to secure order and to regulate people's conduct, thus managing the fear of impending disorder. *Third*, social inequality is natural. Conservative ideology holds that some people are innately superior to others. As Edmund Burke, an early conservative theorist put it, society operates 'a fixed compact sanctioned by the inviolable oath which holds all physical and all moral natures, each in their appointed place' (Burke, 1790: 144).

The logical consequence of New Right perspectives (ironically, almost an 'anti-social' stance) is to encourage the view that there can only really be *individual* solutions to *individual* problems: universal or collective responses have no place in this view of the world. This general position has obvious implications for the provision of public services and public welfare. The analysis offered seems blind to the extent to which individual circumstances may be the consequence of particular social relations or structural inequalities.

From the late 1970s, rapid restructuring of the economy occurred under the stimulus of policies of 'free market' privatization and deregulation: neoliberalism. Five important aspects of change are identified here, all of which had major implications for young people and in which youth came to be understood as a social problem:

- the new service and knowledge economy
- feminizing the labour force
- flexible labour markets
- the social geography of the labour market
- youth labour markets and the transition from school to work.

Although these changes are especially marked in the period from the late 1970s, there is considerable historical continuity into the present time.

The New Service and Knowledge Economy

There has been significant structural change in the world economy since the early 1970s. In the UK in 1978, 6.9 million employee jobs (29%) were in the manufacturing industries. This had fallen to 3.0 million (11%) by 2007. In contrast, for example, financial and business services accounted for about 2.5 million jobs in 1978 but by 2007 this had grown to nearly 6 million (about 20% of jobs). Add to this a further 6.5 million jobs in distribution, hotels and restaurants (from 4.5 million in 1978), just over 7 million in public administration, education and health (from 5 million in 1978) and the shifts that occurred in the UK labour market are plain to see. This has had implications for young people in terms of the kinds of skills and dispositions required for employment, with a higher demand for 'soft skills' and 'interpersonal skills'. Work in the service sector has often become non-unionized, poorly paid and insecure (the 'Mc Jobs' phenomenon), and may offer little to young people seeking to achieve some status and independence through their labour market participation.

Throughout the post-war period a gradual transformation occurred as a 'new stage' of capitalism emerged. This was called by some (for example Daniel Bell in America and Alain Touraine in France) the 'post-industrial' stage, because of the prominence of services and information and the decline of manufacture and the old 'smokestack' and extractive industries (steel, coal and other manufacturing). As suggested in Chapter 1, this can be understood as a form of late modernity. The new growth sectors became the service industries: finance, administration, retailing, catering, tourism, health and welfare, personal services (from beauticians and masseurs to therapists), myriad consultancies and so on. The computer revolution and the rise of the 'knowledge industries' transformed service activities perhaps even more dramatically than manufacturing. As Daniel Bell argued (1996), knowledge, particularly theoretical knowledge, became *the* crucial factor of production in the 'post-industrial' economies of the Western world. One effect of this has been to render a range of traditional skills rapidly obsolete and to require a new set of (usually computer based) practical skills and of person-to-person 'interactive' skills from the workforce.

Feminizing the Labour Force

The skills most spectacularly made redundant over the past 30 years in the UK and elsewhere are the craft skills of manual work and the unskilled labour at the 'bottom of the pile' in building and construction, manufacture and extractive industry. These were predominantly jobs held by men. Since 1979 roughly 80% of all the jobs lost in restructuring processes have been jobs taken by men: while roughly 70% of all the new jobs created were *understood as* women's jobs (that is, they were predominantly in retail or the service sector and, as such, generally lower paid). Between 1992 and 2007, the number of people economically active in Britain rose by 2.3 million to 30.7 million. The majority of these were women, of whom there was an increase from 12.4 to 14.1 million.

The reasons for the increased involvement of women in paid employment are complex but generally, much service sector work (person-to-person) in retailing and personal services requires skills culturally understood to be *natural* to women and had historically been undertaken by women. Such work uses interpersonal skills that have been seen as essentially feminine, and in a context of gender inequality and assumptions about women's primary role in the family, such skills attracted a lower wage rate than male work. Insofar as the service sector has expanded, the labour market has become increasingly *feminized* and, combined with the loss of power of trade unions, this has resulted in a relative loss of earning power for workers. There are thus implications for this in terms of class and other inequalities structured into the global labour market.

Hochschild (1983) referred to feminized work as requiring 'emotional labour', characterized by face-to-face or voice contact with members of the public in the work setting, a requirement that the worker exercise a degree of control over their own emotions in the work setting and the requirement to produce an emotional response from another person as part of the work performance. Examples would be working in a restaurant, care work or working in a shop (in all of these the worker is expected to smile at the right time and gain the confidence of the customer or client through being friendly and helpful). In this sense, the emotional repertoire of the individual worker becomes a key component of the worker's capacity (Bolton, 2005). In communities where gender norms are rigorously defined, these capacities continue to be identified as feminine with implications for personal and social identities that are reproduced within education and the family as well as in the labour market. These inevitably impact upon young people and their attitudes and expectations.

At least as important as feminization is the fact that the 'flexibilization' of the labour market has involved the widespread replacement of full-time by part-time, temporary and casual jobs. For example, some British retail chains have withdrawn full-time contracts from their employees and offered in return only part-time contracts. Some women may be more inclined than men to accept part-time work both because it fits their domestic responsibilities (which are still not gender-neutral) and because part-time work is typically paid less well than full-time ('breadwinner') jobs that are understood as 'men's' jobs. In areas where there are high rates of male unemployment (such as ex-mining and shipbuilding areas) men are finding it necessary to accept these jobs, or remain unemployed and possibly accept their partner as the major breadwinner. These changes disturb traditional patterns of socialization and have significant implications for the formation of gender identities and adult role expectations among the young people affected.

Flexible Labour Markets

In analysing developments in the labour market, the contrast that many sociologists draw is between a 'Fordist' system (modern and industrialized) – that is, mass factory work organized around the principle of the assembly line – and the post-Fordist 'flexible firm', typically organized around smaller units and coordinated and controlled via information technology and characterized as late modern and post-industrial (Sennett, 1998: 46–63; Standing, 2009: 139–40). The labour market of the flexible firm is one in which only a minority of workers have careers or jobs with lifetime contracts, company pension schemes and guaranteed employment rights.

Some sociologists and economists have argued that the contemporary labour market can be understood in terms of primary and secondary sectors (Standing, 2009: 38). The *primary labour market* comprises occupations that are considered white-collar, professional and high management in which workers enjoy substantial benefits that contribute to personal satisfaction and challenge, high income, job security and career advancement. The *secondary labour market* comprises jobs that offer little of the benefits received by those in the primary labour market (incomes are lower, hours longer or part-time, job security less and they offer little in terms of personal or career development). Typically, these are low-skill, routine and blue-collar jobs increasingly found in the lower reaches of the service sector (cleaning, retail, or security, for example) and in routine assembly line work. Many young people, women and members of black and (other) minority ethnic groups are located in these parts of the labour market. Trends towards casualization of parts of the skilled sector (for example the use of short-term consultants in professional and managerial settings) mean that some professionals are also located in the secondary labour market.

The new *'core'* workers in the primary labour market (in manufacturing, such as car plants, or services, such as banks or retailing) must learn to be adaptable problem solvers and team workers at ease with the new information systems through which they monitor and control the flow of work in their enterprises. Many of them will be managers, technicians or professionals of various kinds.

Many workers are found in the *'peripheral'* labour force – the secondary labour market – as part-time, temporary or subcontracted (self-employed) workers. These groups do not have the guaranteed employment rights, pension schemes and perks of the 'core' workers and are therefore cheaper to employ and easier to discard. It is worth noting that professional and managerial workers (lawyers, accountants, business analysts, designers and so on) are increasingly likely to find themselves in this casualized peripheral sector.

The deregulation of wage and salary structures that has accompanied the development of the new flexible labour market in the past 30 years has depressed wages at the lower end of the income range and created a large mass of insecure, poorly paid part-time and temporary workers, especially at the base of the service sector: in catering, cleaning and retail services most of all. Women, ethnic minorities and young people are especially likely to find themselves in this sector of the labour market.

The Social Geography of the Labour Market

The structural changes of the past three decades have resulted in a skewed geography of employment and unemployment in the UK (Dorling et al., 2007). The new, knowledge-based service industries are clustered disproportionately in the South East of England while de-industrialization has blighted the old industrial areas of Wales, Scotland and the North and

Midlands of England. Cities such as Liverpool, Newcastle, Stoke and Glasgow contain large 'pockets' of de-industrialization. High rates of persistent 'structural' unemployment characterize those areas, especially among male manual workers. While the country as a whole has had unemployment rates of between 7% and 10% since the early 1980s, the areas of the most acute de-industrialization such as Liverpool or Tyneside have had rates more than double the average and not infrequently as high as 50% among unskilled young males.

A further factor that worsens the problem in areas of de-industrialization is the fact that professional and managerial workers operate in national (and increasingly in *international*) labour markets, but unskilled and semi-skilled people are trapped in local labour markets. This renders the structural, long-term unemployed immobile and unable to escape the effects of de-industrialization in their home areas. Young people are particularly vulnerable here.

Youth Labour Markets and the Transition from School to Work

The early 1980s recession (beginning in 1980–81) caused a sudden and catastrophic collapse of the youth labour market in the old industrial economies such as the UK, from which it has never really fully recovered (Brooks, 2009: 1). The transition from school to work (and therefore the transition from economic dependence to *relative* independence and subsequent recognition as a 'citizen') has thereby been lengthened in a dramatic way. It has been accompanied by polarization in the positions of young people in terms of qualifications, occupation and earning power. The most disadvantaged, and least qualified school leavers face low paid, poor quality and insecure employment as well as periods of unemployment (Kemp, 2005: 153). This is an inversion of the situation that benefited the post-war generation of young men and has, since then, systematically destabilized working-class gender identities and expectations. Neoliberal ideology has emphasized individual responsibility for failure while systematically removing the welfare benefits which had previously offered some level of security for the displaced and excluded. Indeed, so-called 'welfare to work' policies (including the New Deal for Young People developed in the UK) were based largely on a deficit model emphasizing young people's lack of employability, and in effect blaming them for their worklessness. However, it is important to acknowledge the complexity of these policies and to see them as not *only* coercive. Some young people are able to take advantage of the support that they provide in terms of improving skills and knowledge (ibid.). Structural factors in the economy, geographical location especially, shape labour market opportunities and are thus decisive factors in determining young people's futures. In the UK, the progressive removal of entitlement to housing benefit and income support from 16 to 18 year olds, begun in the 1980s and continued thereafter, has rendered them dependent on their families who, in the areas of severest de-industrialization, are often themselves living on state benefits. Despite government claims to guarantee a training place for all 16 year olds, it is estimated that there has been a consistent 9% of the cohort who are 'NEET' (not in education, training or employment) (Department for Children, Schools and Families, 2009).

In the UK in 1993 over 10% of those officially registered as unemployed were young people aged 19 and under. By 1997, 13.6% of young people aged 16–25 years were unemployed. In 2009, this had risen to 19.1% of the age group. Throughout this period, government policy designed to cope with the problem has included compulsory youth training schemes of various kinds that have removed 16–18 year olds from the official labour market, and, recently there have been attempts to make it easier for young people to return to education even after having left full-time schooling at the minimum school leaving age.

These changes in youth transitions into the labour market focus on the link between social inclusion (as citizenship) and labour market participation. The crisis precipitated by youth unemployment raises questions about the ability of (some) young people to become 'satisfactory' citizens. In these circumstances, the main policy thinking has focused on facilitating access to the labour market, including special programmes such as those established in the UK, for example by the Manpower Services Commission in the early 1980s, and the range of schemes for improving the vocational qualifications of the workforce, which have continued in various forms since the early 1980s. Research on the problem of the transition from school to work in the period beginning in the 1980s (Mizen, 2004) emphasizes that one response of young people themselves has been to stay on in full-time education after reaching the minimum school leaving age in order to avoid unemployment and/or the government training schemes. As Brooks points out, it is necessary to recognize that educational transitions should now take account of sites other than schools, especially further and higher education, and the implications that these have for young people negotiating interdependent and competitive knowledge economies (2009: 220–1).

Since the 1980s, sociologists have taken *transition* as an organizing concept in the sociology of youth. As Jones (2009) suggests, the focus on transition questions whether young people are best understood in terms of social relations (that is, the relation between the state and particular age groups which create dependencies) or as merely engaged in (temporary) transitional processes that result in the achievement of adulthood. The literature on youth transitions opens up a key debate in the sociology of

youth, namely that about the relative significance of the factors that constitute youth as a *homogeneous* category and those that emphasize its *heterogeneity*. By focusing on labour market transitions, it is plain that young people
from disadvantaged backgrounds on slow-track transitions experience
extended dependency while the possibility remains for other young people
to fast-track into adulthood. Clearly, any linear model of transition is
entirely inadequate for understanding the circumstances of young people
and sociology has emphasized the growing complexity and inequality of
transitions since the 1980s. This has meant that youth must be understood
as an increasingly heterogeneous social category. The concepts of structure
and agency mark out the category of youth by encouraging us to ask: *which*
young people are able to make autonomous choices about their lives and to
what extent are different groups constrained by social institutions and
mediated by social difference (class, gender, tradition and so on)? Clearly,
some young people are able to make *relatively* more autonomous choices
than others as they reflexively negotiate the effects of power, shaped by
their access to economic, social and cultural capital and mapping their transitions. Young people's lives are, of course, not only shaped by labour market
transitions. Such a parsimonious view of young people as little more than
human capital is confirmed in social policy that frames 'social exclusion' in
terms of labour market participation.

The nature of youth transitions has shaped the interventions made by
youth services. In the UK since the 1980s, youth practitioners have been
involved in a range of interventions supporting young people in their
labour market transitions: developing so-called life skills, encouraging
young people to be enterprising and providing information and counselling where necessary. Youth policy priorities have, inevitably, been shaped
by the broader political and policy environment that is mapped out here.

Between the Market and the State: Third Way Politics

This period can be summarized as shown in Table 2.3.

In the UK, the New Labour government of the last three years of the
twentieth and first decade of the twenty-first century incorporated but also
recast some of the ideas that emerged in the 1980s and 1990s, mobilizing a
particular brand of conservatism within its own political perspective. The
virtual collapse of the post-war settlements that constituted the welfare state
had irrevocably altered the landscape of education that New Labour inherited in 1997. New Labour social policy evolved through a commitment to
the developing narrative of the so-called 'Third Way', influential in several
late modern societies. This was a response to perceived 'globalization(s)', the

Table 2.3 The 'Third Way'

Third Way policy	1997–2010
Dominant political rationality	Acknowledgement that both state and market have vital roles in public service provision in a complex, globalized knowledge economy; personal responsibility *and* individual freedom; equality of opportunity
Characteristics of public policy	Mixed economy of service provision incorporating competition, marketization, privatization, joined-up policy, service integration; preventive, early intervention, rights agenda covering all aspects of integrated services for children and young people; policy initiatives reshaping services for young people
Significance for young people	A deficit discourse of youth; young people increasingly experience vulnerability and risk; surveillance (through e.g. Anti-Social Behaviour Orders (ASBOs), control orders, dispersal orders), 'responsibilization' through welfare to work policies; fragmentation of youth as they are targeted by state professionalism and bureaucracy

rapid emergence of 'knowledge economies' (Kenway et al., 2006) and the development of a so-called 'reflexive modernity' (Giddens, 1998, 2000).

Third Way politics circumscribed a new ethics stressing an accommodation between individual freedom *and* personal responsibility that its proponents believed to be appropriate to a radically altered (global) world and also offered a normative framework in which to situate welfare policy including education and services for young people. The choice for the welfare state in the global economy was indicated by New Labour early in its period of government, as between a 'privatised future, with the welfare state becoming a residualised safety net for the poorest and most marginalised; the status quo ... or the Government's third way – promoting opportunity instead of dependence, with a welfare state providing for the mass of the people, but in new ways to fit the modern world' (Department of Social Security, 1998: 19).

The Third Way retained a central corpus of New Right ideas that shaped policy in education and services for children and young people. It has been understood as a kind of 'hybrid'; an attempt to reconcile different political positions (essentially those understood as 'left' and 'right') through the synthesis of elements of both. While embodying elements of the neoliberal agenda discussed above, it also departs from that agenda by affording the state a substantive, but flexible, role in the provision of education and services for young people. It contains a critique of the unregulated market, yet acknowledges the place of the market in service provision and development. Many critics have indicated that the Third Way was deeply ideological in that it was an attempt above all to win consent and support for a political programme defined as an attempt to *modernize* existing services (this is a different use of the term *modern* than that introduced in Chapter 1 and refers essentially to 'updating'). The term *modernize* is, of course, equally ideological and used to win political support and legitimacy. Who could possibly oppose modernization?

The principal elements of Third Way ideology borrowed from earlier neoliberalism as applied to public service provision (including services for young people) could be seen as the following:

- **marketization:** for example the importance of *competition* in the commissioning and provision of services
- **privatization:** for example the involvement of the *private sector* in the provision of services
- **managerialism:** a discourse characterized by ideas of rationality and calculation that provides legitimation to changes in service organization and delivery
- **promotion of education and training for the labour market:** for example the crucial public services preparing young people (and others) for the labour market
- **central policy and budgetary control** with decision-making devolved to the periphery.

To some extent, UK New Labour's ostensibly tough response to young people (embodied most clearly in the rhetoric of 'tough on crime and tough on the causes of crime') was countered by an increased range of initiatives designed to develop services and provision for work with specific groups of young people. This was symbolized in the work of the Social Exclusion Unit (SEU) established to 'cross-cut' government departments and to report directly to the prime minister. Note the continuity with the consensus commitment to an 'inclusive' society as against the divisiveness of the neoliberal agenda that emerged in the 1970s and 1980s: the Thatcher period. The SEU conducted research and consultation on a range of topics that had ascended the New Labour agenda, influenced as the 1980s Conservatives had been by the Charles Murray-inspired underclass thesis: teenage pregnancy, truancy, and young runaways. These representations of *particular* young people (with, arguably, very specific needs) in terms of social and individual problems linked with an overall assumption that youth transitions to adult citizenship were *structurally* risky for society and for young people themselves. Yet they were often *generalized* to construct a discourse of youth in which *all* young people were characterized in problematic and pathological ways. This, of course, has provided 'ideal copy' for the media and led to young people's lives being often unfairly caricaturized and misunderstood through stereotypes and labelling (Davis, 1990; Osgerby, 2004).

A series of key ideas emerged through the SEU and became powerful motifs in policy and practice with children, young people and families, further fragmenting the concept of youth to render it a series of sub-populations, to the point that it is sometimes difficult to speak meaningfully of a universal social category of 'youth'. *Social inclusion* (generally defined through the prism of labour market participation), *social cohesion* (expressing the discursive power of 'community') and *equality of opportunity* (rather than equality) were the key elements in a constellation of concepts shaping education and social policy and professional practice through the decade. There was a marked distinction between these ideas and traditional Labour party 'redistributionist' ideology designed to increase equality (largely rejected by New Labour as it was predicated on what was seen as an outmoded socialist and class analysis). As the early New Labour white paper on lifelong learning, *Learning to Succeed,* put it, the vision 'is to build a new culture of learning which will underpin national competitiveness and personal prosperity, encourage creativity and innovation and help to build a cohesive society' (Department for Education and Employment, 1999:13).

This was an attempt to reconcile ideologies of competitiveness with discourses of personal fulfilment and social order. Education and learning (including informal work with young people) became the means of achieving a range of governmental objectives by aligning outcomes for the nation in a global economy ('national competitiveness') and goals for the domains of local neighbourhoods and communities ('social cohesion') with the desires and aspirations of individuals ('creativity' and 'personal prosperity', for example).

A distinct policy framework evolved quickly in the New Labour era that shaped diverse aspects of young people's lives and created a much more fragmented discourse of youth. This framework also signalled 'intensification of state influence over the lives of the young' (Mizen, 2004: 176). The drivers for this were complex but included the outcomes of the Laming inquiry into the death of the child Victoria Climbié at the hands of her carers, a political commitment to wider participation and co-construction of services, public mistrust of professionals that relate to questions of power within the state, demands for modernization and new forms of service organization. The framework was characterized by prevention and early intervention with *at risk* groups, safeguarding *vulnerable* groups, fostering a rights and entitlements agenda by promoting 'the voice of the child' and integrating professional services.

Some very positive aspects of this framework and its contribution to improving services for children should be acknowledged (for example Sure Start, Children's Centres, free nursery places for three and four year olds, substantial numbers of children no longer living in poverty, child trust funds). For young people, increased academic performance at secondary level and participation in higher education were undoubted achievements. However, New Labour, arguably, also contributed to the problematization, pathologization and, to some extent, criminalization of youth during its period in office.

A great swathe of social legislation relating to youth offending and social exclusion, from the Anti Social Behaviour Act to the implementation of Youth Inclusion Projects (YIP) and so-called 'Respect Agenda', were implemented under New Labour. A number of these initiatives concentrated on young people in *public space.* Anti-Social Behaviour Orders (ASBOs), for example, undoubtedly contributed to criminalizing young people's use of outside space as they were inclusive of an increasing range of conduct and behaviour defined as 'anti-social' – an elastic term that is difficult to define in any clear way. The use of curfews and exclusion areas forbids a section of society, *young people*, from congregating in public space at set times (see, for example, Goldsmith, 2008). Griffin's (1993) observation that young people are seen as simultaneously 'risky and at risk' can be borne out in the wave of Third Way social policy. Within much of the anti-social behaviour legislation of this period is a seemingly explicit wish for the erasure of young people from public space. The deployment of ASBOs, youth curfews, increased surveillance and the use of community wardens and police serve to highlight that groups of young people are often an unwanted and unwelcome presence in public space: streets, parks and playgrounds (Squires, 2008). Many young people, unable to exercise power as consumers, have become the 'collateral casualties' of contemporary consumerism (Bauman, 2007: 117) largely as a consequence of their position in the labour market. This offers a contrast to the 1950s and 1960s when, although characterized in partially problematic terms, young people were also the focus of proliferating markets for leisure and consumable goods: they had acquired some limited market power (Bennett, 2001: 9).

Over to you...

Critical reflection and reading

Do you agree that New Labour policy initiatives had the effect of 'pathologizing' young people? Can you identify any benefits of New Labour youth policy and for whom? What evidence would you draw to support your arguments here?

ASBOs, curfews and surveillance were predicated on early preventive intervention with *at risk groups*. The idea was to intervene before young people's conduct escalated to become a problem. The idea of *at risk* was a key underlying concept that continues to be used to justify, in policymaking and practice discourse, particular types of intervention into young people's lives. Perhaps one of the most important contributors to the literature in this area is David Farrington (1996). Farrington amassed an impressive array of quantitative and qualitative analysis, from which he and colleagues developed a range of recommendations on the attempt to reduce and prevent youth crime.

Farrington's work is of current interest particularly in the context of so-called 'evidence-based' policy and practice that has emerged. Farrington's main argument rests on the power of 'risk analysis' that seeks to identify a range of variables that are believed to predict the emergence of crime among specific groups and *protective* factors that militate against the emergence of crime and the development of criminal identities. The concept of *risk* is central to Farrington's work and provides the dominant discourse in explanations of crime in contemporary Britain. Farrington's work also denotes a view that crime is reproduced through family and neighbourhood structures. More widely, for example, there seems to be some consensus that the following are among the precipitative factors (*risk factors*): family violence and conflict, poor parenting styles, drug and substance misuse, truancy, delinquent peer groups, and lack of social cohesion.

Farringdon's work exemplifies an empirical tradition in sociology, promoting a 'gold standard' of quantitative, positivist, experimental research designs. These contrast markedly with more critically oriented traditions that seek to identify the significance and meaning of particular life experiences. It is possible to critique Farrington's approach. For example, it is unclear how these risk factors may be contingently connected and which are more important at which times in relation to which groups and individuals. While a correlative relationship between crime and the factors themselves may exist, that is not to say that the relationship is necessarily anything more than tenuous. As argued elsewhere, intervention in young people's lives is invariably justified by the argument that young people are somehow vulnerable and the idea of vulnerability underlies their at risk status for society. By identifying that status (for example in the terms described by Farrington), 'early *diversionary* or *preventative* intervention is thought possible. Rather than privileging characteristics which are thought to reside *in* individuals, the concept of "risk" concentrates attention on abstract factors which constitute an individual as being "at risk"' (Bradford, 2004: 250). The point here, of course, is that virtually anything can be included as a risk factor! Given the power of prevailing negative discourses of youth that emerged under New Labour, many aspects of young people's conduct could be construed as placing them at risk and, thus, open to targeted intervention and, potentially, to criminalization.

Summary and Conclusions

Chapter 2 has explored the contexts in which young people have grown up in the UK since the Second World War. While specific to the UK, the analysis made in the chapter could be applied to other similar countries although the details of the arguments might vary. The broad argument is that public policy frameworks (in this instance beginning with the welfare state) shape young people's worlds through the particular structures of social and economic provision (and thus opportunity or disadvantage) that are provided. It has also been suggested that representations of young people and how youth is understood as a social category coincide with the development of policy and practice interventions. There is an implicit reflexive relationship, therefore, between youth, on the one hand, and policy or practice on the other.

In Chapter 2 it has been argued that the post Second World War period in the UK can be understood in three broad historical periods, all of which have important sociological implications for youth and young people. Again, these periods and their underlying elements are mirrored in similar late modern societies. The first period, roughly from the late 1940s to the 1970s, was characterized as a period of relative *consensus* in which broad political agreement existed on the provision of a comprehensive system of public welfare including education, health, housing and social insurance. Youth was understood then as a universal category preparing young people for achieving adult status typified by secure employment and family formation. Public services supported these transitions that were further secured by a labour market characterized by full employment. This is the period in which youth culture emerged through proliferating consumer markets (fashion, films and music, for example) fed by young people's relative affluence, and encouraging the idea of a possible generation gap.

The second historical phase ran from the early 1970s to the late 1990s (with continuities beyond this) and was characterized as a period of neoliberalism that challenged the post-war consensus. During this period the so-called New Right sought accountability and value for money in public services. Economic recession in the early 1980s led to the collapse of the youth labour market. This resulted in an increased sense of vulnerability and uncertainty for many young people in which social difference (class, gender, race and place, for example) powerfully influenced structures of opportunity. Youth transitions became protracted, complex and risky, undermining young people's opportunities for independence and for achieving the status of 'adulthood'. Youth was increasingly understood as a *problematic* category in itself rather than in terms of generational difference or conflict.

The so-called Third Way was the third period identified in Chapter 2. This moderated but retained aspects of neoliberalism. In particular, problematic and deficit discourses of youth prevailed through this period and young people experienced increased vulnerability and risk in their transitions to adulthood. In order to manage the 'problem of youth', policy became more authoritarian and various strategies of surveillance (through ASBOs, control orders, dispersal orders, and so on) were deployed to contain youth populations. Policy further sought to increase young people's capacity for responsible conduct (the process of *responsibilization*) through welfare to work policies. State professionals and bureaucracy targeted specific youth populations (young single parents and so-called NEETs, for example), which further fragmented youth as an essential or universal social category.

As Chapter 2 has suggested, in each of these historical periods government can be understood as attempting to realize an imagined society in which youth has a particular status and which has been understood as requiring particular interventions by the state. Each period has distinct characteristics but the underlying policy perspective is that youth has been understood in increasingly problematic and pathological terms, often supported by the politically Right dominated media.

Further Reading

- Coffey, A. (2004) *Reconceptualizing Social Policy. Sociological perspectives on contemporary social policy*, Buckingham: Open University Press.

  Coffey offers a specifically sociological account of UK social policy, drawing on concepts like citizenship, identity and the body to explore policy developments in what she refers to as *postmodern times*.

- Davis, J. (1990) *Youth and the Condition of Britain. Images of adolescent conflict*, London: The Athlone Press.

  Davis's account of youth as symbolic of wider social change alerts the reader to youth's cultural significance in the post-war period.

- Barry, M. (2005) *Youth Policy and Social Inclusion. Critical debates with young people*, London: Routledge.

  Barry's collection gives a broad account of the main policy initiatives and developments that have shaped young people's lives in the first decade of the twenty-first century.

3

Growing Up in Public and Private

Youth, Transition and Identity-Making

Introduction

A central question in sociology concerns the nature of social order and cohesion and its maintenance and reproduction. Since the 1990s, sociologists have tended to concentrate on factors that signify *difference* rather than looking at aspects of the social world that might be understood as shared and collective in forming social bonds. Identity enables individuals to define the contours of their own selves in relation to others. Identity is constituted through practices of classification, boundary definition and the making of meaning that these practices entail. Thus, to fully understand identity, the interplay of similarity with difference must be understood. If difference is given too much focus, collective aspects that also render the world *social* are missed. Indeed, one point that will be stressed throughout Chapters 3 and 4 is the fundamentally *social* nature of identity.

Over to you...

Critical reflection

Select someone who is currently in the news. This could be a sports person, a politician or even a historical figure. First, what can you say about them that describes and maps their individual character, their personality and uniqueness? (You might say something about what they do, their contribution to a particular field, their friends and family, what they are like – as far as we know.) Overall, what kind of person is this? Second, what can

---

you say about this person's location in a specifically social setting: what might you say about their class position, their gender, sexuality or their ethnic or racial origins? What might it be about these aspects of social structure that made them who they are?

The point here is that identity can be thought of as both individual and social. However, Marx argued that it is not 'the consciousness of men that determines their existence, but their social existence that determines their consciousness' (1859, in Marx and Engels, 1968: 181). Marx's point is a basic and important sociological argument that the ways in which people think about themselves, their place in the world and their relations with others is shaped by the kind of society in which they live. So, celebrities undoubtedly have particular 'personal' characteristics but these can only really be fully understood in the context of their broader social positions. For young people, this means that their construction of identity is influenced by their social place and position. For those working with young people, it is crucial to have an understanding of the factors that shape the formation and experience of young people's sense of who they are, the way they understand themselves and are understood by others and the sorts of lives that they might live.

Identity, Youth and Transitions

The sociologist Zygmunt Bauman (2004) points out that it is only relatively recently that questions of identity have become of concern in sociology and to sociologists. He makes the intriguing suggestion that the interesting questions are not about identity per se; rather, why it might be that questions of identity are important *now*. People become aware of identity in circumstances where identity becomes questioned or vulnerable in some way. This is Bauman's point. It is in Western societies that there is, apparently, a sense in which one's place in the world is less certain, more risky or vulnerable than it may have been at other times. Some sociologists have presented evidence challenging this view, which is considered later in this chapter (Spencer and Pahl, 2006: 206).

Bauman argues that people are no longer born into their identity, for example in terms of social class origins, but are required to make or construct identity themselves. This is what Anthony Giddens refers to as the experience of contemporary life becoming a 'project of the self' (1991) and what Beck and Beck-Gernsheim refer to as 'the "elective biography", the "reflexive biography", the "do-it-yourself" biography' (Beck and Beck-Gernsheim,

2002: 3). In 'late modernity' according to Giddens, a sense of identity can be understood as a kind of story that one tells about oneself to self and to others. This is something upon which people work and reflect over time and is a continuing and social process. So identity becomes less a package of *received* personal characteristics (although these may still be one way of thinking about it) and understood more as a narrative or a story in which individuals are agents delineating their own identities, defining the relevance or meaning of where they have come from, who they are now and where they want to go.

Giddens' argument suggests that people are now expected to 'craft' a sense of who they are through the resources available. In some contemporary worlds, this often implies the construction of self through consuming certain kinds material objects: technology, fashion, music, sport and a range of other cultural artefacts. This is especially important for young people as they grow up. Adult identities no longer, necessarily, follow on *naturally* from childhood identity as it becomes possible for some young people to imagine futures different from those implied by received identities. Education may be particularly important here.

Youth as Transition

Youth has invariably been understood as a time of transition from childhood to adulthood, and the idea of transition has been foregrounded in recent sociological analysis of Western youth, as that period between childhood and adulthood has been extended and the future has become less clear in terms of the certainties of the past. The scope of analysis includes physical and bodily transition associated with sexual and biological maturity, transitions in cognitive and thinking capacities, transitions that entail the development of new skills and abilities that will support adult life, and a range of changes that involve transitions from one identity status (one kind of self and position) to another and that imply the acquisition of more or less independence or autonomy. Above all, the use of the term *transition* points to the dynamic process factors that shape the life course and its constituent pathways that can be understood in terms of both time and space. These become especially problematic in a period when, arguably, people are no longer born into clear or fixed collective identities: classed or placed identities, for example.

So, the interest here lies first, in the *temporal* quality of transition and its patterning across historical time in particular societies. For example, how is transition structured, what normative frameworks prevail and how do these change? In the UK, for example, youth transitions are structured by social difference (class and gender, for example) and reproduce extant patterns of inequality. Second, how transition is experienced in the micro-settings of everyday life is crucial (Holdsworth and Morgan, 2005: 25). Attention to these micro-settings (family or school, for example) points to individuals' lived experiences of time and exposes the detail and texture of transition. As well as transitions having temporal qualities, transitions are both *spatialized* and *emplaced*: transition has to occur 'somewhere'! Wyn and White (1997) have suggested that much of the literature has, implicitly, presented transition as a spatial metaphor. In this, young people are understood as being situated on a landscape that is mapped to identify the *pathways* or *trajectories* along which their transitions proceed. While helpful in terms of emphasizing the dynamic aspects of young people's lives and their construction of identity, the transition metaphor has some limitations (see Table 3.1).

Table 3.1   The metaphor of transition

Dimensions of transition	*Young people's lived experiences of growing up*
Transition as linear and one-way: e.g. education to employment	Transition is multi-directional: experience of moving forwards and return (e.g. unemployment, return-to-learn); shaped by social difference (e.g. class, gender and race)
Uni-dimensional	Multi-dimensional: labour market transition intersects with other aspects of life course transition (e.g. personal relationships, partnerships, setting up home) but these becoming less synchronized
Finality: point of arrival (e.g. a job, adulthood, maturity, independence)	Life course as a state of becoming (e.g. changing relationships, changing jobs, changing residence); adulthood a problematic and variously defined state; maturity socially constructed; independence never absolute and subject to a range of factors
Marked out by chronological/ biological age	Age socially and culturally constructed; shifting social meanings of age
Transition structured horizontally	Horizontal and vertical dimensions: age and generation, peers and others

Source: Adapted from Wyn and White (1997: 99)

Youth can be considered as a specifically *liminal* state as well as a transitional status. This implies an 'in-between' stage, a space that is socially and symbolically marked by ritual and located *outside of* mainstream space and time. The concept of liminality comes from the work of the anthropologist Victor Turner who, in turn, borrowed the idea from Arnold van Gennep. Van Gennep was interested in the rituals – *rites of passage* – that accompany the move from 'one cosmic or social world to another' (1961: 10). These moves might be changes of status (marriage or an engagement of some kind); changes of place (perhaps a new address); changes of position (a new job) or changes across time (New Year celebrations). As Hendry points out (2008: 77), these occasions are invariably ritualized: marked in particular ways that celebrate and protect the movement from one state to another. For example, dressing in special clothes, sending gifts and cards, eating special food or holding parties are all ways of marking these transitions (one might think here, for instance, of stag or hen nights in which people engage in ritualized behaviours to mark the status changes associated with marriage). Van Gennep identified a range of social and cultural status changes: birth, childhood, puberty, betrothal, marriage, pregnancy and so on (Van Gennep, 1961: 3). His analysis suggested great similarity in the forms of these ritual occasions, mirroring a universe 'governed by a periodicity which has repercussions on human life, with stages and transitions, movements forward, and periods of relative inactivity' (ibid.). This can be seen in relation to youth in Figure 3.1.

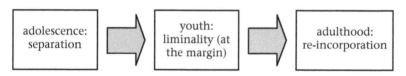

Figure 3.1 Young people and transition

Victor Turner argues that transitions, of which growing up is one, are marked out in three phases: separation, margin and re-incorporation. The middle phase – *margin* – can be seen as a threshold across which individuals pass in order to become re-incorporated in their new cultural and social status. The margin is regarded as 'signifying the great importance of real or symbolic thresholds at this middle period ... though *cunincular*, "being in a tunnel", would better describe the quality of this phase in many cases, its hidden nature, its sometimes mysterious darkness' (Turner, 1975: 232). Turner identifies the individual in transition as a traveller whose status is marked by ambiguity and uncertainty; it is a boundary state, inside yet also outside of conventional social categories, space and time. The *liminar* exists on the borderlands of the shared symbolic and cultural order and young people – youth – are 'neither one thing nor the other'. Like other liminars, the traveller's betwixt-and-between state is often associated with danger and pollution: the *stranger* is perhaps the iconic identity here. In short, outsider-hood leads to an anomalous and, as in the example of young people, often feared position.

The liminality of youth transition is on the threshold, in a 'no-person's land' between what have, historically, been understood as the relatively clear social identities of childhood and adulthood (the latter especially being an increasingly uncertain category and thus undermining any sense of a clear 'end point' to transition) and, as such, is characteristically a space in which social taboos are broken 'most of which will again be tabooed once the stage of liminality is over. But for a brief time liminality encompasses every possibility and potentiality. It is society's natural crucible for social experimentation' (Martin, 1983: 50). As Victor Turner suggests, liminality contrasts markedly with the hierarchy, differentiation and organization of 'normal' society; it is what he refers to as 'communitas'. Communitas is always sacred, pure and ecstatic (Turner, 2012). As Martin asks in relation to modern Western societies, where else would one expect to find 'the primary expression of ... communitas than ... among the young, poised between the protected but dominated structures of childhood and the responsibilities of adult (and elite) roles?' (1983: 51).

Over to you...

Watch a film and critically reflect

There are many novels and films that identify youth's liminality. The film *Human Traffic* tells the story of a group of Welsh young people on a weekend of clubbing, drug use, hedonism and pleasure. The film touches on a range of topics (youth culture and subculture, drug use, alienation from work, for example) but is interesting in the sense that the weekend's experiences of ecstasy (literally and metaphorically) seem to create the kind of 'communitas' to which Turner refers.

In Andrea Arnold's film *Fishtank*, 15-year-old Mia wanders alone through the post-industrial wastelands and marshes of metropolitan Essex (liminal landscapes, par excellence!). Mia is 'betwixt and between' in more ways than one. Although, superficially, there appears little ecstasy in her life, the sense of being a traveller in a difficult landscape is palpable in this film. Mia's identity is ambiguous and sometimes confusing for the viewer and, indeed, to those around her. Eventually, she appears to be drawn back from the margins and re-admitted to some kind of mainstream. Try to watch these films and see if you agree.

These ideas about transition help us to see how young people in Western cultures are invariably seen as anomalous and threatening: they don't fit the mainstream cultural categories of 'child' or 'adult' and are somehow 'betwixt and between', neither one thing nor the other. Young people threaten social coherence, with real implications for their capacity to make their identities. Their liminal status can mean occupation of uncertain and ambiguous social and cultural space somewhere between 'child' and 'adult', between 'dependency' and 'independence', and between being understood as 'responsible' or 'irresponsible'. It is important, of course, to acknowledge that those categories are no less problematic than the liminal status of youth: when does adulthood start, what cultural meanings attach to childhood and what counts as responsible in any given setting? One should also not assume that liminality is experienced in a negative way: as *Human Traffic* suggests, there is the potential for much pleasure in liminal space. However, one should be cautious about the extent to which liminal space is necessarily open to creative appropriation. Young people's capacity and resources for empowerment, and thus for successful negotiation of transition, remain differentially distributed according to social difference and division (Song, 2005: 72). Some young people's experience of liminality (for example those who are poor or disabled) may disadvantage them further.

Liminality is a complex state that points up articulations between structural factors and young people's lived experiences (Holdsworth and Morgan, 2005: 23). As Mary Douglas points out (2002), anomalous and liminal categories attract different kinds of responses. Youth, considered in abstract and as a universal category could be seen in such terms. Douglas argues that all cultures must take account of and deal with the anomalies that are inevitably produced as a consequence of their classificatory norms and practices.

Sociology and Youth Transition

The growth of sociological interest in youth transitions (Wyn and Whyte, 1997; Shildrick and MacDonald, 2007; Roberts, 2009) reflects the conditions of late modernity in which traditional routes into adulthood have become increasingly fragmented, protracted and non-linear (Jones, 2002). For many young people the ritual markers of independence or adulthood (a job, a place to live and a new family, for example) have all but disappeared and the liminality of youth becomes extended.

Valentine (2003) argues that youth transitions are socially constructed around a 'normative framework' (a linear movement from dependence to independence) intersected by issues such as gender, class and sexuality. However, various individualization theories (for example Ulrich Beck, 1992) suggest a tendency away from such structurally determined transitions towards individualized and apparently proliferating choice in late modernity. Beck (1992) refers to three elements of this movement towards individualization.

1. **Disembedding:** through which individuals are 'liberated' from their customary ties of family, locality and tradition (this means that for some young people the sense of boundary between youth and adulthood is no longer clear, and young people engage in conduct previously identified as adult).
2. **Loss of security:** where religion and traditional belief systems fail to offer appropriate guidance. Beck sees this as a process of 'disenchantment' (young people may access adult interests and responsibilities earlier or later).
3. **Re-embedding:** in which new forms of social relationships and commitments are formed and which provide a sense of 're-integration' through which young people construct a sense of identity: for example friendships, partnerships or interest groups.

Within this apparently expanded landscape of choice, young people's transitions have become difficult to navigate and, if transitions appear to be protracted or incomplete, then there is a growing possibility that individual young people are blamed for their own marginal status. However, this focus on individuals (often exaggerated in terms of its explanatory power) should not be taken to mean that 'the social' (in the form of class or gender, for example) is no longer important in shaping young people's views of education and their futures. The work of Bradford and Hey (2007) shows how it is possible to misunderstand the effect of individualization as a process in which the social somehow becomes expelled from everyday life.

Private and Public Worlds

Families, Communities and Friendships

Insofar as identity is mediated through family, community and friendships of different kinds, identity itself is constructed in social (and material) space: it is never free floating. These social spaces are especially significant to and for young people. Family, community and friendship are important material and symbolic sites on which they construct and maintain a sense of who they are.

The family can be understood as an economic institution that traditionally reproduces the existing relations of social power, particularly through the domestic (gendered and age-related) division of labour. It is also an educational and cultural institution, the main setting in which, both literally and metaphorically, aspects of the social become reproduced through the socialization of the next generation and the patterning of internal social relationships and social difference.

As well as considering family as an institution, it is possible to think about it in terms of its 'interior life': those practices and lived experiences that constitute family life itself and that are formative of the identities of young people. Carol Smart (2007) points to the importance of what she calls a 'family imaginary' in shaping identities. By this, she refers to the way in which families and their influences are as much the outcomes of our imaginations, memories and capacities for making representations (images) as any specific institutional properties that they might also have. Family memory and memories, especially, have real power in creating the settings in which people define who they are and where they come from. Consider, for example, the enormous cultural energy that is currently invested in tracing family roots through genealogy and family records, images and material objects of different kinds. This popular genealogy is a prime example of the significance of 'identity work'.

Over to you...

Research and reading

In thinking about family, try to get hold of some photo albums that tell a story (or stories) about your family. How far back can you trace your family? Who are the key players and what do you know about them? Are you aware of 'family stories' (the kinds of stories that get told and retold, perhaps at special family occasions) or perhaps 'family secrets'? Can you identify any special family objects: ornaments or bits of furniture, for example? What place do they have in 'representing' aspects of your family and how do you feel about these? What do they tell you about your own family and how you 'think and do' family, and how do they contribute to making you who you are?

Ideas about UK family life have tended to assume (to *imagine*) the existence of a 'conjugal nuclear' family unit having at least some of the following broad characteristics:

- primary relationships between husband, wife and children rather than extended family of more than these two generations and living in close proximity
- a man and woman: separate household in which responsibilities are towards one another and not to other kin
- based on monogamy and romantic love between a man and woman, understood as 'natural' rather than culturally specific
- marriage as an institution in which individuals seek security, intimacy and personal satisfaction.

This definition of family is quite exclusive of other kinds of partnerships and family forms, for example gay and lesbian partnerships or lone parent families, families with live-in nannies or au pairs, families where children are not with their parents (they may be looked after elsewhere or in a residential school) and 'arranged' rather than 'love marriages'. Moreover, such a model of family might only account for a relatively short period of people's lives, especially in societies with increased longevity. It also fails to recognize the influence of global families and how family means various things and is practised in different ways across different cultural settings (Morgan, 2011).

Over to you...

Critical reflection

One of the challenges in thinking about family is to identify clearly what we mean by the term. Before you go any further, reflect on your own family circumstances and try to answer the following: who do you consider to be 'family' to you and what is the significance of family for you? How might class or race shape views of family, for example?

When I thought through the two questions above, the following ideas occurred to me. For a start, family is probably defined by *kinship* (all societies have kinship systems as a basis, but there is great variation in family form historically and culturally) and therefore aspects of 'blood' and 'marriage' are important. But there are people in my family who are not 'blood relatives' nor married to a blood relative. Nonetheless, I consider them part of my family (a cohabiting partner of a relative might be an example here).

The second thing that comes to mind is that there are different types of relatives: 'close' relatives (my partner, mother or sister) and those more 'distant' relatives (for example cousins who I see very rarely). This gets more complicated when I think about my partner's side of the family. Although our marriage establishes relationships with many other people (made more complicated by the fact that none of them live in England) it is difficult to know where in my 'family map' I would place some of these people.

The third point that I identified was the importance of family 'being somewhere': while it is located in *social* space (in terms of relationships with others), family is also set in *material* space. Thus, for many, the household and the home has become an important aspect of family life. For some families (refugees or migrants, 'homeless' families or families in hostel accommodation, for example), this aspect of material location can be problematic. This signals a very important aspect of family life, namely that of privacy and intimacy where individuals relax and 'become themselves'. In other words, family home is a space where people create aspects of their identity. There are specific ways in which young people create their identities in this space, particularly in 'bedroom cultures' that have become significant to many young people through the growth of new technologies (Lincoln, 2004). Private and intimate forms of domesticity emerged in modernity, particularly as a consequence of industrialization, as craftwork and the production of goods moved out of the domestic sphere and into specialist factories and workshops. This designated an important separation between home and work and the change in family as an economic unit of production to become one of consumption. In some circumstances, paid work is beginning to move back into the home and this may have consequences for contemporary family relationships.

My fourth point concerned the extent to which reconstituted households and re-partnering (perhaps after divorce or death, for example) characterized parts of my overall family. No doubt there are similarities in many families. Finally, it struck me that some aspects of family may entail matters of choice (although this is clearly a cultural variable) whereas others do not.

What could be learned from this? First, there is a diversity of family arrangements in the UK at the present time: no single form of family. Class, race and ethnicity, in particular, shape family form. Migration to Britain and other European countries from South Asia and African-Caribbean countries has meant that different family practices, forms and structures have emerged and different young people develop different expectations and identities in the context of their families. Second, families seem to be constituted within shifting boundaries and the structures of families appear to be changing: who is in or out, and who leaves or joins (perhaps through divorce or marriage, for example). There are three fairly obvious shifts that may be very important in the lives of young people and that have significance for the extent to which young people construct meanings around identity and family: cohabiting families with non-married partners; families reconstituted through divorce and re-partnering, and families with same-sex partners.

The discussion so far suggests that it is difficult to give a precise definition to the term *family*. The meaning of family is shaped by beliefs and practices and is historically specific. Therefore the plural *families* is probably more appropriate than any singular notion of family. Dynamic aspects of the concept of family and the importance of self-definition should be recognized, meaning that family is sufficiently inclusive and fluid to accommodate definitions that family members themselves might apply to it. However, one should also ask when relationships become 'familial', how different kinds of relationships in this category can be distinguished, and how one might know the extent of such family forms. Why is it that some definitions of family prevail, especially in terms of assumptions made about 'normal families' in social policy and benefits regulations, for example?

Although family might be seen as a contested term, some family discourses have been particularly powerful in recent years. The term *family values*, for example, keeps emerging in politics although politicians themselves have recognized the dangers of invoking this idea in the public domain, as the media have been all-too quick to identify those who are thought to have transgressed in their family responsibilities. The questions here, of course, concern *which* values, *which* families, what is acceptable and what is not? As difficult as it is to identify in substantive terms these values, it is clear that family has powerful symbolic capacity. As suggested in Chapter 2, the post-war consensus assumed the stable, nuclear family constituted by a male worker with dependent wife and children. This continues to impact upon the social value accorded to particular families and to the prosperity, status and identities of those experiencing difference.

In asking about the significance of families, questions are really being asked about what families, as social institutions, are for. Three important changes can be identified in this.

First, patterns of marriage and divorce have changed in the UK (and elsewhere) with increasing cohabitation suggesting a shift in social values. The frequency of re-partnering and the significance of various *stepfamily* arrangements and the inevitable challenges these pose for many young people should be acknowledged. Those changes are connected partially with the broad liberalizing agenda that emerged through aspects of 1960s youth counterculture in Europe and elsewhere. This raises questions about the purpose of marriage in the 'project of the self' where individuals actively make identity through their own efforts and choices. High divorce rates in many Western nations seem to challenge the idea of romantic love as offering a sufficiently robust basis for a partnership and perhaps similarly emphasize that life and relationships are matters of personal choice; part of the reflexive elaboration of identity.

Second, the increase in the number of lone parent families has been significant. Potentially, children and young people growing up in these families are more likely than others to experience poverty and other forms of social exclusion. They may still be stigmatized where the normative model of the conjugal nuclear family retains its position as part of policy or in idealized media representations.

Third, there may be some evidence that shifting family dynamics have created new settings in which children and young people grow up. Some analysts suggest that family life has become increasingly democratized over recent years and that families have departed from a model in which men dominate. Arguably, cultural changes have altered views of children and their rights and a restructuring of dominant discourses of parenting now accommodate negotiation and consensus rather than the enforcement of conformity (Beck and Beck-Gernsheim, 1995; Beck-Gernsheim, 2002). Despite this, very high levels of male domestic violence continue in the UK and elsewhere (Harne and Radford, 2008).

These three factors have created very specific conditions and spaces in which young people engage in the practices of identity construction.

Over to you...

Critically reflect and research

Considering these aspects of family, what significance does family have for you? Who do you count as your family? Are those you identify 'blood relatives' or do you include others in your own sense of family? You might reflect on how you feel (good or less good) about your family, and the importance of your family in your own pathways to adulthood.

Considering young people with whom you work or know, what is the significance of family for them? Does this vary according to their social backgrounds? In particular, what is the role of family in the context of constructing a sense of self and identity?

Youth practitioners have invariably needed to take into consideration not only the family context of young people's lives, but also the extent to which young people are influenced by or identify with specific *communities*. Sometimes this has been formally acknowledged in policy as in the publication of *Youth and Community Work in the 70s* (HMSO, 1969) which had a significant impact on the organization of youth work in England and Wales during the 1970s. In Scotland the relevance of community education was established in the Alexander Report (HMSO, 1975) while in Northern

Ireland, the development of the youth service after the *Recreation and Youth Service (NI) Order* (1974) was directly connected to questions of the role of young men in community conflict there. Community was also recognized in New Labour's community cohesion agenda. Acknowledging and addressing questions of identity and identification with community is a necessary element of any constructive intervention with young people. The adoption of a community dimension enables youth practitioners to broaden their work to respond to a range of social factors that are important in shaping the contexts in which young people grow up.

A specific focus on community, evident in policy during the 1960s and 1970s, and then again during the New Labour period of 1997–2010 in the UK, can be understood as a response to fears that community is somehow threatened or dead and that the weakening of social ties embodied in the emergence of an increasingly globalized, late modern, mass culture is problematic for social stability (see, for example, Stacey, 1960; Wilmott and Young, 1960 or Frankenburg, 1966). As Bauman has argued, the desire for community can be understood as a quest for security and safety in a modernity characterized by risk and uncertainty (Bauman, 2001).

The earliest, and perhaps most well known sociological analysis of community came from Ferdinand Tönnies (1955; 1887) and was lodged in the transition from small-scale rural life to urban and industrial settings in the late nineteenth century. He proposed the two concepts of *Gemeinschaft* and *Gesellschaft*, roughly designating the distinction between *community* and *society*. For Tönnies, there was a strong sense that community was rapidly being transformed into an impersonal and fragmented social world: a move from the traditional to the modern. Importantly, Tönnies' work defined social change theoretically rather than dealing with empirically real social entities.

Gemeinschaft and Gesellschaft connote different social relations (and forms of relationship), inevitably leading to different senses of self and identity. In Gemeinschaft, relations are local and primary, and often based on family and personal ties: the social world is shaped by consensus and custom. In Gesellschaft, by contrast, association is instrumental, based on rational means–ends calculations, shaped by individual self-interest and governed by centralized authority and contract.

In both these models, *place* is very significant but perhaps in different ways. Tönnies didn't suggest that Gemeinschaft-type community had been swept aside by Gesellschaft; rather that it persisted *within* it. For him, Gemeinschaft represented the lived experience of real social life. The forces of late modernity seem to militate against Gemeinschaft-type community in industrial and post-industrial settings. Family, friendship, work and leisure patterns may no longer be interwoven in the context of place in the way that was represented in the 'classic' community studies of the 1950s and

1960s (Day, 2006: 27). However, that is not to say that community identity and belonging is no longer meaningful. For those who have the appropriate cultural and economic resources, locality, place and belonging still engender attachment and identity and people continue to live in places where they feel 'at home'. For example, in the UK durable local identities and strong attachment to place persist through forms of 'elective belonging' in which identity is more or less self-consciously adopted and *performed* (Savage, Bagnall and Longhurst, 2005: 207). The literature on social capital shows how community in the form of solidarity and belonging can be protective of young people's developing sense of identity (Johnston, 2011).

Tönnies was writing as massive social upheavals were occurring across Europe (the rapidly disappearing peasant population and associated urbanization and industrialization) and his work was influential on Durkheim, who was preoccupied with similar changes. It is easy to see Bauman's point about the search for safety and security emerging in this context, suggesting an atavistic sentiment in the quest for community. Perhaps this is an integral feature of a community always more imagined than real.

Thinking of Durkheim's distinction between mechanical and organic solidarity as constituting different social worlds (the first based on similarity and the second characterized by difference), perhaps caution should be exercised in assuming that community might exist in the present. Following Bauman, community could be understood as nothing other than a kind of a *longing* or *yearning* for something that is experienced as lost in some way. Benedict Anderson (1991) suggests that community is always an act of imagination as, at the level of the nation at least (the archetypal community), individuals can never have complete face-to-face contact with fellow members. Community, thus, has to be imagined and re-imagined and as Anderson points out, communities can be distinguished by the different styles in which these imaginings are undertaken. Most sociological definitions incorporate a combination of the elements described in Table 3.2.

The literature on community suggests it is increasingly likely that people belong to different kinds of communities, consistent with a complex and perhaps fragmented social world, with which they engage at different points of their lives resulting in multiple identifications and loyalties: for example place, politics, pastimes (Day, 2006: 213). Globalization has increased the possibility of faith communities appearing in new locations and settings and becoming influential in providing ties and affiliations that shape young people's lives. Understanding the role of religion and its future necessitates taking account of young people's engagement with faith and religious communities. Religious affiliation is a 'core dimension of personhood, an important source of values, life purpose and communal belonging, and a vehicle for marking the transition from adolescence to adulthood' (Collins-Mayo, 2010: 1).

Table 3.2   Dimensions of community

Dimensions	Examples from lived experience
Common space or place: being somewhere	This might be physical place (a village or a housing development, for example); virtual place (Facebook); the local and the global
Common interests, shared goals and activities: aspiring/desiring/doing in a similar way, social practices become recursive	Social position (poverty or exclusion from certain facilities or resources); sense of common disadvantage/advantage/perspective
Collective action: working together for the common good	Political agitation or action: perhaps environmental action of some sort, faith-based campaigning groups, civil disobedience, or simply doing similar things together: restoring a narrowboat, repairing a historic building or opposing a supermarket or housing development
Shared history, collective memory and identity: a sense of 'we'	The foregoing might lead to a sense of identity constructed over time and that forms the basis to shared or collective memory lodged in stories and other acts of imagination; the presence of some kind of affective bond; self-defined as belonging to the community (a sense of being part of a minority, for example): the community is greater than the sum of its individuals and greater than different identities; indeed, it is a primary form of identity

Over to you...

Research, read and critically reflect

Can you identify any actual communities to which you belong? What kind of community/communities are they, what makes them communities and what precisely makes you a member? Is community a 'good thing' as far as you are concerned and why?

Some authors have been critical of the very idea of community. Richard Sennett is one. Here is his view on community as common identity.

> The feeling of a common identity ... is a counterfeit of experience. People talk about their understanding of each other and of the common ties that bind them ... But the

lie they have formed as their common image is a usable falsehood – a myth – for the group. Its use is that it makes a coherent image of the community as a whole ... The image of the community is purified of all that might convey a feeling of difference, let alone conflict, in who 'we' are. In this way the myth of community solidarity is a purification ritual ... The enterprise involved is an attempt to build an image or identity that coheres, is unified, and filters out threats in social experience. (Sennett, 1996: 9 and 36)

What is Sennett saying here and do you share his position that there is something suspect about the idea of 'community'?

Table 3.3 Forms of new community

Type and examples	*Characteristics*
Network community: people that you 'know', connections and 'mates of mates'	Emanates/radiates from individuals; loose, open and mediated connections often through new technologies; compresses space; low solidarity
Lifestyle community: leisure identities of different kinds, fashion, music	Shared cultural codes and values; locale as marker of identity; collective identity often achieved through consumption; belonging through identification with others having similar tastes; the shopping mall
Tribal community: sports fans, music fans, fashion followers	Affiliation based on affective ties (feelings) as much as interests; warmth and companionship
Social movements: anti-capitalists, eco-warriors, the 'gay community', the 'Black community'	Centred on political mobilization, loosely structured and networked; express identity and values through affiliation
Virtual community: Runescape or World of Warcraft gamers, social networking, educational groups	Compresses space: contact/interaction can be from anywhere to anywhere; participants can assume limitless online identities, e.g. through the use of avatars; questions about authenticity of relationships and transactions

Source: Adapted from Day (2006)

A number of analysts suggest that community has proliferated in the contemporary world and is constituted in networks and elective associations of varying kinds. This leads to the view that it is necessary to bring community into the twenty-first century and to consider its contemporary pluralist manifestations: the new communities. As Day points out, these are characterized by their voluntary nature and membership is invariably chosen according to their members' particular interests and dispositions. Table 3.3 suggests that a number of these communities have particular relevance to young people.

Table 3.3 suggests that these forms of community could overlap and the exact boundaries between forms are unclear. The *degree* of community varies from one form to another. Virtual community may exhibit a very *thin* sense of community (weak social ties or obligations, for example) whereas lifestyle communities and tribal communities may incorporate a *thicker* sense of community with stronger affective and interpersonal ties, obligations, norms and values. These may also be incorporated into *friendship*.

Personal Relationships: Friendships, Peers and Intimates

Over to you...

Critical reflection

Before we look at friendship from a sociological perspective, it is worth looking at what friendship means. Think about your own friends from, say, the age of about eight or ten. Map out your friendships from then onwards. How did these change over time? Which friendships were long lasting, which faded or disappeared and can you work out why? (You might think about the changes in your life that shaped your changing friendships.)

Thinking about friendship is a reminder that young people can be located in a network or constellation of different kinds of personal and interpersonal relationships (indeed, youth work and other professional practices with young people focus much of their interventions on these). Figure 3.2 shows one way of thinking about this and it may be possible to include other important relationships here.

These different relationships provide the settings in which young people construct their personal and social identities. These relationships are important in various ways and at different times but they provide (at least, ideally) social recognition and affirmation to young people. To understand young people's lives and experiences, it is important to understand something of how these relationships shape young people's conduct, permitting them to

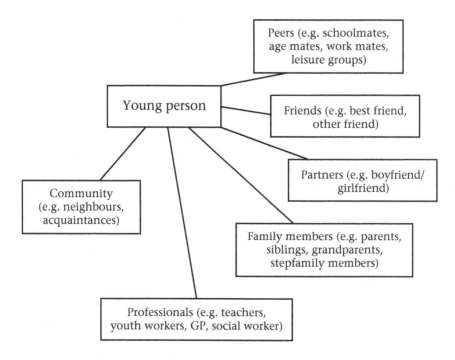

Figure 3.2　Young people's networks of relationships

adopt different positions and roles at various times and gain feedback through the relationships they have with others. The relationships imply at least some agency and choice by young people as well as imposing various structural constraints on those choices. In that sense, young people (like others) have some capacity to make decisions about themselves and their lives, but not always in the circumstances and situations that they would choose. One way of understanding the nature of the relationships identified here is in terms of the levels and types of *intimacy* that define them. Morgan (2009: 2) defines three dimensions of intimacy that are helpful in understanding this.

1. Intimacy that is either physical or *embodied* in some way. This might be sexual but the category might also include a range of physical caring or nurturing that signifies an interpersonal bond of some sort (holding hands, touching in particular ways or putting arms around someone).

2. Intimacy that is *emotional* and entails the sharing of feelings, anxieties or passions, for example. This emotional intimacy may also include the recognition of another's emotional needs or circumstances and may entail appropriate responses to these.

3. Intimacy that is constituted in particular forms of *knowledge* that are shared between people and that is denied to those outside the relationship of intimacy or the circle of intimates. These knowledge-forms construct boundaries between public and private domains.

It is evident how these dimensions shape relationships that might be defined as intimate.

The remainder of this section reflects on the nature and importance of peers, friends and partners in young people's lives. As Pahl puts it, 'The social convoy that we associate with as we go through life – our fluctuating and ever-changing personal community – defines us, reflects us, supports us and so much else besides'. Friendship could be seen as a kind of social barometer: each era constructs friendship in its own terms, shaped by prevailing economic, social and cultural factors. Late modernity emphasizes choice, individualism and individuality and these characteristics are reflected in contemporary discourses of friendship, shaped by social difference (Pahl, 2000: 166–7).

In general, *peer* relationships are with others of similar age, status or position of some kind. They assume potentially common interests and concerns (for example by virtue of shared position or status), but no necessary physical proximity (consider peer-to-peer file sharing networks: no real proximity but shared interests or position). Despite the absence of material closeness, peer relationships may be very influential. That is something that adults (perhaps parents especially) are often anxious about and so-called peer-pressure is invariably understood in negative terms (it may be quite the opposite in situations where young people take care of each other or look out for each other's interests in some way). In other ways, for example, similar subcultural groups in London, Birmingham and Berlin may be mutually influential. Haywood and Mac an Ghaill's work on school-based peer cultures and their impact in constructing masculinity is important here. Haywood and Mac an Ghaill (2003: 69–70) do not make any absolute distinction between peers and friends (the two may or may not overlap) but they point out the significance of these cultures in creating and policing what counts as appropriate masculinity. Their argument suggests that gender – in this case masculinity – is something that is *practised* rather than a static property that an individual has or doesn't have.

Haywood and Mac an Ghaill identified four distinct peer group affiliations that marked out specific cultures of masculinity in the school settings that were researched.

1. The *Macho Lads:* working-class young men who rejected formal schooling and resisted attempts to co-opt them into it.

2. The *Academic Achievers:* working-class young men who affirmed the value of study and upheld the practices and processes associated with that.

3. The *New Entrepreneurs:* working-class young men who took an instrumental view of schooling and who used technical and vocational knowledge to position themselves as high-status achievers.

4. The *Real Englishmen:* middle-class young men whose version of masculinity accommodated individuality, autonomy and being different and who simultaneously rejected schooling.

It was within these class-based peer cultures that normative and contrasting masculinities were constructed, regulated and contested. Barron and Bradford (2007) identified the significance of peer groups in producing and regulating similar masculinities in Irish schools in relation especially to those whose sexual identity is seen to transgress normative heterosexuality. There is a strong sense in this literature of how the routines and practices that constitute male peer group cultures in schools shape discourses of masculinity. School becomes a 'space of opportunity' for some and a place of danger for others. It is worth reflecting on how youth practitioners are involved in creating such spaces of opportunity or oppression.

The rejection of or resistance to schooling is not restricted to male peer groups. 'Time and again girls ... told me that it is not "cool" for girls to be seen to work hard on school work' (Jackson, 2006: 23). Jackson convincingly demonstrates that the 'uncool to work' discourse is often a powerful influence on girls and young women and is identified as a means of gaining social acceptance and popularity for some girls. Perhaps that aspect of peer group relations is shaped not only by gender but by other dimensions of social difference and by some of the institutional practices of schools themselves. As Jackson suggests, fear of academic failure in contexts where academic credentials and success are seen as very important and combined with robust testing regimes can lead to defensive strategies (what she refers to as 'laddishness') that deflect attention from students' poor levels of ability in order for them not to appear stupid in the context of the peer group.

Valerie Hey's work on girls' friendships provides important comparisons with and extensions to Haywood and Mac an Ghaill's work. Interestingly, Hey refers to *friendship* in contrast to Haywood and Mac an Ghaill's references to *peers*: does this signify that the terms friend and peer are themselves gendered? Can girls be members of peer groups?

Hey, like others, sees friendships (and the same could be said about peer group relations) as *practice*, something that young people 'do' rather than something they 'are' or 'have'. By looking at these relations as entailing practices, the active nature of friendship, young people's choices and the constraints that mediate those choices are emphasized. Inevitably, this raises important questions about how power is implicated in these circumstances, particularly through race, class, ability or disability and, of course, gendered positions. Hey challenges the assumptions that are made about girls' and young women's relationships, namely that these are characterized exclusively by an essential and intensively emotional content. She suggests that this view is predicated on a very specific view of what counts as 'natural' femininity and whose conduct is consistent with being a 'good girl'. Girls' friendships, she argues, must be understood in the wider context of gender inequality and should be seen as sites of 'power *and* powerlessness' on which young women work out their sense of identity and belonging (Hey, 1997: 19). Most importantly for Hey, as for Haywood and Mac an Ghaill, this performative view of friendship must be understood in terms of the immediate institutional context in which friendships are developed and contested: in both these instances, schools and the broader societal setting in which established power relations work through existing structures (gender, class and race, for example) to shape the agency of individual young people.

In general, it has become recognized that friendship is something that is chosen and has value in and of itself. Bauman points out that friendships 'do not serve any purpose other than being mysteriously satisfying in themselves ... as soon as you have friends for your fun and amusement you've got some new kind of friendship as well – a friendship in which it is the friends who are for you, instead of you being for them' (Bauman, 1993: 184). The point here is that for Bauman and others, friendship is an elective affinity based on an 'ethical' stance in which a degree of self-sacrifice is entailed and through which the 'rituals of friendship create and recreate the basic norm of friendship, which is the readiness to sacrifice oneself for one's friend. Just as a believer is willing to sacrifice all for [faith], so is a friend ready to give all for the friendship, but the "faith" of friendship is faith in a friend, rather than faith in a deity or another abstract moral force' (Wallace and Hartley, 1988: 102).

The selflessness referred to by Wallace and Hartley contrasts with a more instrumental view that friendship (and intimacy generally) can be seen as part of a modernity in which the self becomes the focus of intensive work: self on self in the production of what has been referred to as a 'choice biography' (Woodman, 2009). This is a view that suggests the importance of *detraditionalization* associated with a declining belief in the pre-given authority and 'natural' order of things (for example according to traditional gender or class relations). So-called detraditionalization results in a form of individualization in which the self is required to exercise authority (choices and decisions) in the face of contingency and disorder that emerge as traditional structures, arrangements and practices decline (Heelas, Lash and Morris, 1996: 2). In such a world, one is enjoined to '*make* something of oneself' rather than expect that things will 'fall into place' in a natural way.

Giddens (2000) makes three observations in this respect. *First*, he suggests that globalization introduces an almost unlimited diversity of 'lifestyle choices' that become the core of identity. *Second*, late modernity signals the decline of tradition ('the local'), and has less capacity to ground interpersonal relations. These processes of detraditionalization have shaped personal relationships: friendship and intimacy generally are things to be worked on, chosen and cultivated as part of the developing project of the self. *Third*, the influence of 'expert systems' (particularly psychotherapeutic discourses) and feminism has encouraged new dimensions of emotional communication, and the questioning, exploration and development of emotional well-being. Indeed, it is quite easy to see how some of those practices have influenced professional interventions with young people. Many youth workers in particular would see personal relationships and their development as the principal rationale of their work.

The 'democratized' relationship is seen by Giddens as:

> ... a relationship of equals, where each party has equal rights and obligations. In such a relationship, each person has respect and wants the best for the other ... [it] is based upon communication, so that understanding the other person's point of view is essential. Talk, or dialogue, is the basis of making the relationship work. Relationships function best if people don't hide too much from each other – there has to be mutual trust ... Finally, a good relationship is one free from arbitrary power, coercion or violence. (Giddens, 2000: 80)

Giddens' account indicates the extent to which personal relationships – including friendships – have become subject to individual choice. He argues that these 'pure relationships' are no longer strongly anchored in external economic and social conditions (class and gender, for example) and are initiated for reasons of gaining personal emotional satisfaction. However, McCleod's study (2002) of young Australians' friendships suggests that Giddens is overly optimistic and utopian. While reflexive modernity demands that individuals live out some degree of personal autonomy, McCleod's research participants showed just how much their choice biographies were shaped by social and structural difference (particularly class, race, gender, place, dis/ability). This research-based work poses an important challenge to theoretical work like that of Giddens'. Clearly, in late modernity people *are* expected to be active, reflexive and responsible in their life choices but the choices that are made continue to be taken in circumstances that are structured by social difference and structural inequality.

This discussion of friendship suggests links between friendship (and other personal relationships), the idea of *social capital* and community. Social capital is a contested concept that, in some ways, has been over-used and under-defined but basically refers to networks of personal relationships

(Pahl, 2000: 147; Spencer and Pahl, 2006: 26). However, social capital is also a term that is used in relation to services for young people and its capacity for supporting learning and personal development. Much of the literature has considered social capital with reference to community and from the perspective of interpersonal networks that generate trust, reciprocity, social solidarity and emotional support (Coleman, 1989; Putnam, 1995; Field, 2003). Bourdieu's more critical conception of social capital defines it in terms of a resource for achieving and maintaining social position and power (Bourdieu, 1986). Much of the more accessible literature on social capital has identified three principal forms of social capital shown in Table 3.4 (adapted from Johnston, 2011) below. Johnston undertook a detailed ethnographic study of the social capital generated by disabled young people and on which they drew in their transitions through further education but its significance could be generalized across education.

Table 3.4 Types of social capital

Type of capital	Social capital resources in learning settings	Effects on learning
Bonding capital: dense bonded networks, high trust, reciprocity and homogeneity of membership	Support and guidance from peers, friendship groups; group identity, values, norms and practices	Exchange of information, 'hot knowledge', influence on identity construction, but poor access to new knowledge and low trust of information gained from 'outside' the network
Bridging capital: open-ended networks, shared norms and common goals, more limited reciprocity, heterogeneous membership	Inter-peer group and support from professionals, membership of clubs and organizations, access to range of services (counselling, PA, mentoring, etc.)	Exchange of a range of possible knowledge and skills including a range of resources for identity development and renewal; relations with education system context-dependent
Linking capital: more open-ended networks even more limited reciprocity and non-member relationships	Connections to and relationships with links with materially/socially more distant groups	Access to resources (knowledge, skills, etc.) that might promote contingent advantage in various settings

Source: Adapted from Johnston (2011)

Johnston's work on young disabled people's peer relationships shows how these relationships (construed as different forms of capital) had a bearing on their life experiences and educational potential. Johnston draws some very important conclusions about young disabled people's relationships: their *peer* relationships, their *friendships* and the importance of both in gaining a sense of identity and value (Holt, 2010). He identifies how *bonding* social capital may be (relatively easily) established in closed groups with tight boundaries, but asks how this enables young people to move *beyond* relatively limited social and cultural horizons. Bonding capital has considerable potential: criminal groups, terrorist cells and political extremists of various kinds demonstrate this. Johnston asks how young people can be enabled to move into negotiating and generating forms of social capital that might permit them to realize potential that could form resilience and capacity in the face of inequality. Johnston suggests that *bridging* and *linking* social capital is crucial in enabling young people to participate in relations beyond immediate peer and friendship groups to increase social and economic opportunity. On the other hand, Reynolds (2007) shows how central the social resources developed in peer and friendship groups are for young people when they face generalized mistrust, hostility and exclusion in the wider society, conditions which are characteristic of the liminal state of transition. Reynolds, like Johnston, points to the fundamental importance of these resources in supporting the development of a resilient identity during youth.

Research like that of Johnston and Reynolds draws our attention to the vital role of 'the social' in understanding young people's friendships and peer group relations especially in offering personal choices. However, multiple contexts, circumstances and forces over which they have very little individual control embed and shape young people's relationships.

Relationships with partners have been seen as principal components of young people's transitions to adulthood. Youth transitions have, at least until relatively recently, been understood in linear terms, and cultural understandings of young people's intimate relationships (that is, relationships with partners) have mirrored this. The linear transition associated with partnering has followed a familiar path, predicated on a normative heterosexuality:

- being 'single'
- meeting a potential partner
- developing a relationship: 'going steady'
- engagement
- marriage
- having children.

Although each or any of these stages may be important, it is the process described that is less linear and, for some, more complex in contemporary worlds. This argument draws on the 'Inventing Adulthoods' project that researched young people's experiences of achieving adulthood in the early part of the twenty-first century (Henderson et al., 2007: 139–43) and explored the pathways into adulthood taken by a range of young people. As part of that, the place of personal (partnering) relationships in those path-ways was investigated. The project identified three broad tendencies in the ways that young people approached their close relationships, represented in Figure 3.3. Because of underlying shifts in patterns of transition and a departure from the view that adulthood is constituted in marriage and family formation synchronized with transition into the labour market, it is difficult to know at which age young people will make choices about their intimate relationships. Henderson suggests that any one of the three tendencies could apply at any point. Indeed, they may not only apply to young people but might also characterize other people's experiences of the life course, given the kinds of changes identified in relation to family life and the significance of personal relationships to contemporary identities. The three tendencies in young people's intimate or personal relationships might be (but are not necessarily) part of a potentially two-way continuum in which young people can move from one state into another and, perhaps, back to the original state: from 'uncommitted' to 'fusion', for example.

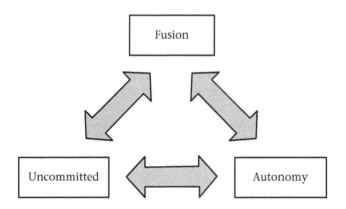

Figure 3.3   Young people's relationships

Fusion designates close partnerships that are based on trust and security, understanding and acceptance, closeness and intimacy. Being part of such a relationship means that opportunities for new friendships (with each partner's previous friends, for example) may arise, or new friends may be made together, perhaps with other couples. Intimacy is important in these relationships, and as Robb suggests (2007: 333), intimate relationships are one domain in which young people can express aspects of adult identity. This is significant when transitions to adulthood have been protracted through difficulties in entering the labour market and the associated periods of education and dependency on parents.

Autonomy describes an instrumental approach to the life project in which young people wish to remain unencumbered by relationship commitments, where the rational is privileged over the emotional and the future is prioritized over the present (attention perhaps being devoted to education, for example).

According to Henderson et al., those young people who are *uncommitted* are more interested in extending a pleasurable, and perhaps liminal, youth without allowing relationships with a partner to obstruct this. They may be single or involved in casual relationships and may resist relationships characterized by fusion because of their own perceived emotional vulnerability, a view that such relationships would lead to tensions with family or friends or that plans would be compromised because of the loss of freedom or independence.

Henderson et al. argue that their research reveals no simple conformity to existing gender scripts, no particular differences in terms of sexual identity. Any of the three approaches could, they suggest, apply to gay or straight young people, but their research suggests young people's relationships are shaped by normative discourses of masculinity and femininity. Underlying and 'traditional' inequalities remained present in these relationships despite young people's aspirations towards equality. Overall, young people's futures were envisaged in terms of partnership, yet tensions between commitment and independence were evident. This reflects broader strains between traditional relations and what Giddens referred to as detraditionalization.

Summary and Conclusions

Chapter 3 has explored aspects of the concept of identity and its relevance to understanding youth. As the chapter indicated, identity only becomes significant when identity itself comes into question. In other words, identity is a consequence of the changes that led to modernity and, especially, *late* modernity in which social difference such as class, gender or race, retains enormous significance yet, paradoxically, individual lives and experiences seem to have become disembedded from these structures. The role of sociology is to analyse these processes.

The concept of youth transition has also been explored as relevant to identity questions. Several transitional processes were identified as marking out young people's experiences: bodily and cognitive transitions, knowledge and skill transitions and a range of shifts that materially and symbolically constitute the acquisition of adult status in Western societies including attachment to the labour market and family formation. As suggested, there have been changes in the synchronicity of these, and transitional pathways have become increasingly unravelled in the UK as elsewhere. These changes have fundamentally problematized the concept of youth as a transitional status.

Transition is a metaphor that has underpinned much youth sociology in recent years but there has been a tendency to understand transition as a linear process designating a normative shift from dependence to growing independence. As the youth labour market has become riskier for young people, moves to independence have become acutely problematic for many young people, some more than others. Some analysts have argued that youth has no uniquely transitional qualities (as all life stages are transitional) and that the concept is, therefore, unhelpful.

The concept of liminality was used to suggest that young people are located in anomalous social space, neither children nor adults. Their liminal status renders them symbolically dangerous and powerful and explains their consistently problematic historical social status. Street disturbances in Europe and across the world in 2011 and 2012 seem to support this. Liminality can also be understood as a period of preparation for incorporation into a new adult social status that, the chapter has argued, is increasingly individualized.

The sociological concept of individualization has been understood with reference to the underlying processes of *detraditionalization* and *disembedding*. It has been suggested that as modernity has developed, young people (and others) have become emancipated from the ties of tradition, religion and locality, forcing them to make individualized decisions and choices. Indeed, identity itself can be considered an aspect of reflexive choice, a 'project' that unfolds through the life course. However, the chapter has also suggested that despite the 'individualization thesis', the categories of class and gender (and social difference generally) continue to be resilient predictors of life chances. Knowledge and understanding of these processes and their consequences is, clearly, vital for policymakers and practitioners with young people.

Finally, recognizing the social context in which young people make transitions, Chapter 3 has considered family, community, friendship and other personal relationships as major institutional sites of identity formation and construction. The chapter pointed to the decline and fragmentation of 'lived communities' in which relations of family, work and intimacy were interwoven and assumed importance as clear signifiers of future identity. These have, arguably, been supplanted by more *reflexive* and performative identities.

Further Reading

● Day, G. (2006) *Community and Everyday Life*, London: Routledge.

Day's account of community is thorough and scholarly. It provides important theoretical frameworks for understanding the concept of community in terms of history, ideology and futures.

● Martin, B. (1983) *A Sociology of Contemporary Cultural Change*, Oxford: Basil Blackwell.

Chapters on youth culture, rock music and 1960s counterculture provide a critical and complex framework in which the emergence of the helping professions – social work and youth work, for example – are analysed as an element of modernity.

● Smart, C. (2007) *Personal Life. New directions in sociological thinking*, Cambridge: Polity Press.

This contains important chapters on families, family life and personal relationships.

● Thomson, R. (2009) *Unfolding Lives. Youth, gender and change*, Bristol: Policy Press.

This book includes case studies of contemporary youth transitions and shows how social difference (class, race, gender or sexuality, for example) shapes patterns of opportunity and disadvantage in the contemporary UK.

4

Being Similar and Different

Youth and Social Difference

Introduction

This chapter explores aspects of social difference. The term *social difference* implies that people occupy different social positions and that these could be considered to entail different levels or degrees of social power. In contemporary modern societies these difference are organized in terms of distinctions such as age, social class, race, gender, sexuality, disability, faith affiliation, geographical location and so on. Chapter 4 will suggest that to understand young people's experiences in contemporary societies, it is vital to have a clear picture of those aspects of the social world that differentially shape and structure their experiences. As suggested in Chapter 2, the argument here is that it is on the basis of age that youth is organized into a meaningful social category. Mizen points out that the 'simple fact of possessing a biological age brings with it differentiated access to social power' (Mizen, 2004: 9). The sociologist Karl Mannheim was the first to outline a sociology of generations and of youth in the 1920s, arguing that during times of rapid social change (like that shortly after the First World War when Mannheim was writing) youth becomes a 'revitalizing agent ... a kind of reserve which only comes to the fore [in] quickly changing or completely new circumstances' (Mannheim, 1943: 34). Evidence of this can be seen in recent changes such as those that took place in North Africa and the Middle East during 2011. In Tunisia, Egypt, Libya, Syria and Bahrain young people – including young women – have been in the vanguard of change.

Although Mannheim's position may seem dated and optimistic it points to significant differences between youth and older generations. For example, one distinction that continues to exist is a cultural distance between youth and older or ageing generations. Young people's familiarity with digital technologies today, for example, gives them access to knowledge and practices that are not regulated by (adult) elites. Although one should be cautious in overestimating the significance of this accessibility, and it might not be so important for future generations, it has led to the decline of adult control over some aspects of contemporary cultural life. Inevitably, it means that present-day young people will have to create lives for themselves that are quite different in some respects from those of previous generations. They will do this – especially in the context of post-recessionary late modern societies – in a world where the youth labour market has declined markedly. Many young people in such societies have been propelled into extended periods of education. However, financial crises and changing relationships between the state and individuals mean that access to continuing education will not be possible for all. In England and Wales for example, aspirant working-class and lower-middle-class young people will be hard hit as tuition fees are shifted to individual 'consumers' of higher education.

While age differentiates young people – youth – from other social groups (children, adults and elderly people, for example), it is also crucial to understand how youth is *internally* differentiated as a category by other structural factors. To some extent, youth is a shifting identity that, insofar as its features become a reference point, is likely to become generational. Its substantive identity becomes associated with the youth (sub)cultures of a particular generational cohort. Chapter 4 examines some of these structural aspects of difference and, implicitly, explores the relationship between those factors that differentiate young people *from* each other and the single factor that they share: age. Social difference is constituted in a range of factors including class, gender, sexuality, race, ethnicity, place, (dis)ability, and religious or faith affiliation. It is crucial to acknowledge that these intersect to create different social spaces in which young people's lives and identities are shaped. Sometimes, these are spaces in which opportunity can be created, but at other times, inequalities and disadvantage are played out (Thomson, 2009). In Chapter 4, social class, gender and sexuality and race and ethnicity are discussed as specific examples of social difference.

Youth Social Difference and Inequality

In Chapter 3 the concept of identity and its significance for sociology of youth was discussed. In short, identity is relational and concerns belonging, what one individual or group has in common with others and what differentiates them from others.

Whatever the underlying reality, it is clear that as a distinct social category, youth changes across time. For example, the experience of 'youth' has undergone important changes since the 1980s in the context of shifts in global manufacture, involving different experiences of transition from education into the labour market in East and West, and between generations. Throughout Chapter 4 youth is considered as a concept that encapsulates diversity and differing representations of the young, and the duality of 'targeting and absences' which 'problematize' youth as a category and young people themselves. There is little doubt that in its early history, the sociology of youth (a little like youth work) concentrated primarily on working-class white heterosexual males rather than other groups of young people: young women, ethnic minority youth, gay and lesbian youth.

The very process of constructing identities, as suggested in Chapter 3, is made in the context of community, families, friendships and peer groups. Identities are shaped – constructed – both personally and in the practices of social institutions where relations of privilege, inequality and disadvantage are central. Youth provision tends to be funded with reference to the question of youth as a problem or young people with problems, through a set of dominant assumptions about youth in general, and targeting particular groups of young people through racialized, gendered and class-specific perspectives. Until relatively recently, few sociological studies were conducted into the lives of white middle-class youth because they are not perceived as problematic. Ironically, despite their relative invisibility in research or policy, this group has implicitly served as the (imaginary) norm against which other young people are judged. Historically, this group has had access to comparatively better education and training, career prospects and leisure opportunities. However, as inequality and disadvantage have become more visible in modern societies, and different youth groups have been perceived as socially and politically problematic, sociology and sociologists have increasingly researched and theorized the lives and experiences of these relatively advantaged young people (see, for example, Reay, 2008; Reay, Crozier and James, 2011). As social difference has become central to the sociological imagination and its work so the range of groups researched and analysed has extended.

Social Class

This section considers the approach to social class taken by two of the 'classical' sociologists, namely Marx and Weber.

Over to you...

Critical reflection

What is your own view of class? What would you identify as the main 'markers' of class where you live? Which class do you belong to and what exactly signifies your belonging: what makes you a member of your class?

There are several possible class markers here:

- **material resources:** wealth, property of different kinds, money
- **work situation:** occupational location (for example manual work, professional work or skilled technical work)
- **education and qualifications:** what kind of school someone attended, university, degree, no formal qualifications
- **social position and status:** participation or membership of recognized groups or societies
- **lifestyle:** owning or renting a house or a flat, spare time interests, patterns of consumption (for example cars, fashion, holidays).

These are the sorts of indicators that come to designate social class and are structured or patterned in relation to specific groups. There is significant evidence that the UK, for example, is geographically marked by and segregated according to social class (Dorling et al., 2007). Dorling's work shows that it is possible to literally 'map' class in the UK.

Marx's view of social class is important particularly because he argued the inevitability of social class divisions in all existing and previous modes of production including slave societies, feudalism and capitalism. In Marx's analysis, capitalism inevitably gave rise to the emergence of two antagonistic classes. Class could only be understood as a *relational* concept that designated the *positions* of the producers of commodities and the owners of the means of production. Capitalism is characterized by the production of commodities in the context of 'free wage labour' in which the working classes who, although free in the sense that they could sell their labour power to the highest bidder, were never free of those who sought to profit by their labour: the capitalist owners. Marx saw this capitalist class division as structured in terms of the continual exploitation and domination of one class (the proletariat or working class who sell their labour power) by another (the bourgeoisie or capitalist class who own the means of production and make profit from labour) and through which the capitalist class acquired its wealth. For Marx, class position in capitalism represented a *shared interest* that would lead to *class-consciousness*. In his analysis, how people thought about themselves and the world was fundamentally shaped by the nature of the world in which they lived, and the underlying economic organization of society, such as in capitalism, shaped the totality of life: its social, political and intellectual aspects. As Marx put it, it is not 'the consciousness of men that determines their existence, but, on the contrary, it is their social existence that determines their consciousness' (Marx and Engels, 1968: 181).

By this, Marx means that it is real *material* conditions of life that produce the categories and boundaries of thinking that make life what it is in any particular circumstance. This was not a reality that could be wished away through idealism or religion. A changed world could only come about by changing the material reality of that world. For Marx, the inherent tensions between the class of producers (the working class) and the capitalists (those who exploited the working class for profit) could not be contained indefinitely and would lead to revolution whereby the workers would seize ownership of the means of production and in so doing create the conditions for an equal society. Class-consciousness would, according to Marx, override other forms of difference (age, gender or race, for example) and lead to revolution. In that sense, capitalism contained the seeds of its own destruction and it was only a matter of time before the revolution occurred. Until then, the dominant class would use all its resources to retain its position. Here, the resources and institutions that enable control of ideology, for example media and education, are especially important. As Marx puts it, 'The ideas of the ruling class are in every epoch the ruling ideas, i.e. the class which is the ruling material force of society, is at the same time its ruling intellectual force' (Marx and Engels, 1970: 64).

Over to you...

Critical reflection

Marx's ideas about the way in which 'ruling ideas' support powerful elites are important. It is not difficult to see how this might be understood through control of the contemporary mass media by large corporations. Have a look at the arguments and ideas that are put forward through, say, CNN or some of the Murdoch media. Watch them and work out on whose behalf they speak, which groups benefit from the positions they adopt and who is disadvantaged?

Marx's analysis foregrounded the importance of two classes: the proletariat and the bourgeoisie. Contemporary society is more complex and class positions more ambiguous than this analysis suggests. As the activity above indicates, there is more to class than one's position in the *mode* of production or one's relation to the *means* of production. Marx was aware of this and certainly acknowledged the existence of other residual classes. The peasants and landlords, for example, who characterized feudal societies and who remained in parts of capitalist societies, and the so-called 'petit-bourgeoisie', the shopkeepers and small businesses that thrive in capitalist and other societies but who don't exploit labour in the way that Marx indicated the capitalists did. If the example of media corporations (let's say, CNN or Sky) is taken, it is clear that capitalists might own them but there are others who are part of their dominance. Managers, technocrats and professionals are key to retaining their power and position and are vital to the practices of control that Marx so persuasively outlines. In the twenty-first century a simple division between capitalists and workers cannot fully account for the contemporary world.

There is an important argument here that *the state* acts to support the interests of capital while simultaneously mediating the most extreme effects of capitalism. Claus Offe, for example, in developing Marx's analysis in relation to theories of welfare states, identifies the paradox that 'while capitalism cannot coexist *with* the welfare state, neither can it exist *without* the welfare state' (Offe, 2006: 71). Offe's point here is that in the absence of welfare in the form of state subsidized education, housing and health services, which a 'pure' capitalist market cannot provide, it would be impossible to run a modern industrial economy.

In this context, Max Weber's nuanced analysis of social stratification is useful. Central to Weber's analysis are hierarchical relations of domination and subordination and the significance of power in organizing, sustaining and reproducing these relations. Power can be understood as any resource that can be held and to which access is limited. Broadly speaking, power exists in three forms:

1. **class power** (property owners and property-less)
2. **social power** (status held by those who are respected or recognized as superior in some way)
3. **political power** (the consequence of being able to influence decision-making in order to advance interests in some way: political parties, pressure groups, professional associations).

Although Weber shares some of Marx's arguments (particularly the emphasis on competing interests) he points towards social class existing in the intersection of several dynamic factors. For Weber, the market (as both metaphor and material institution) is key to determining class position. The relationship between a group and the market determines their shared position – their 'market situation' – as a class and it is, thus, their economic circumstances that locate them in social space. For example, manual labourers share the same economic relation to the means of production and therefore an identical class position. In that sense, Weber shares some of Marx's argument on class position: *having property* and *being property-less* are the fundamental class positions that characterize capitalist society. However, Weber recognizes that within those two positions 'class situations are further differentiated: on the one hand, according to the kind of property that is usable for returns; and on the other, according to the kind of services that can be offered in the market' (Gerth and Wright Mills, 1967: 182), and he looks *within* each of the two fundamental classes identified by Marx to acknowledge a range of other positions: occupational groups, managers, technicians, clerks, for example. Weber points out 'the kind of chance in the *market* is [always] the decisive moment which presents a common condition for the individual's fate' (ibid.). This quotation suggests that Weber's interest here lies in the factors that determine the capacity of individuals to achieve position through the exercise of power as members of status groups or social classes. Weber suggests a kind of internal heterogeneity within classes where, for example, particular status groups seek to protect their position by effecting social closure, engaging in practices through which their power position is sustained or advanced.

Over to you...

Critical reflection

One way of thinking through the struggle for scarce resources discussed by Weber is to consider how occupational groups in the UK have achieved 'social closure'. This is defined by Parkin as 'the process by which social collectivities seek to maximise rewards by restricting access to resources and opportunities to a limited circle of eligibles ... its purpose is always the closure of social and economic opportunities to outsiders' (1982: 175). A very clear example of this lies in the occupational strategy of professionalization that leads to privilege and reward for members of professions. We are familiar with the way that medical doctors and lawyers have, over the last century, managed to gain substantial control over entry into their professions and the rewards that accrue from this. Both professions have, as a consequence, become very powerful and exercise influence in a range of ways.

In considering the position of youth practitioners of different kinds, is it possible to identify any attempts over recent years to effect closure or restrict entry to the occupation (profession)? Have professional representatives also tried to claim privilege and reward as part of achieving social closure? If so, how?

In an increasingly globalized world, Weber's arguments are also suggestive of questions about citizenship and who is able to acquire citizenship entitlements (to welfare benefits, for example) that accompany the status of citizen.

For young people (and others), labour market position is of key importance in sustaining their identity as citizens. Labour market position confers status and it is no accident that asylum seekers are denied the right to paid employment until their claims are formally approved by the state. In thinking through the social significance of work, individuals' sense of 'participation' and status is likely to depend on the nature and quality of their work. One of the principal labour market changes of the last couple of decades has been the growth of temporary, low-grade, unskilled work and it is important to ask about the extent to which this is likely to contribute to the individual's sense of personal value and fulfilment. Ruth Levitas has suggested that if inclusion in the labour market is taken as *the* measure of 'social inclusion', then inequality and subtleties of class *within* the labour market become obscured, as well as the contributions of people *outside* the labour market to social life and cohesion (usually women but also old and young people) being ignored or undervalued (Levitas, 1996, 2004). Le Roux et al. make a similar point in arguing that the terms *inclusion* and *exclusion* are used to distinguish between a mainstream population and marginalized minorities. This, they suggest, fails to take account of the 'complex inter-play between economic, cultural and social capital' that animates class divisions (2008: 1066).

It is worth asking here about what supports or enhances social participation and citizenship status. Arguably, ideas of fairness and justice are important in this. Nancy Fraser, arguing partially from a Weberian position, suggests that injustice is rooted in practices of *distribution* (referring to economic wealth) and *recognition* (matters of one's identity being acknowledged as legitimate). She argues that demeaning cultural representations of particular groups, of disabled people, black people or young people, for example, underlie perceptions of injustice as an absence of proper recognition. Cultural practices such as racism or sexism are often combined with patterns of economic distribution in which groups are economically disadvantaged (consider here the evidence of young black men's labour market position). Fraser points out that contemporary 'identity politics', through which people take identity as the basis for political activity and campaigning, are one response to the problem of recognition (and perhaps to economic disadvantage), but she suggests that these can obscure the roots of inequality that lie in political economy (Fraser, 2000: 119). Fraser's response to this, acknowledging the importance of 'recognition', is to argue for what she refers to as a 'status model', an alternative politics to that implied by 'identity politics'. In this, the important thing is to ensure that people are able to participate as full members of a society (rather than somehow *separate from* society), and that institutional practices (in the law, policing, social policy, education and so on) must take account of this by de-institutionalizing 'patterns of cultural value which impede parity of participation and ... replace them with patterns that foster it' (ibid: 115). Fraser later argues that political *representation* is also a central aspect of social justice as it too creates important dimensions of social belonging and membership (Fraser, 2009: 18). It is worth considering how these dimensions might apply to the position of young people and asking which policies might secure such status, recognition and representation.

Social Class, Identity and Youth

Arguably, social class is the principal and most emotive mark of social distinction in the UK and is the main form of social stratification in capitalist societies. In recent years, politicians in late modern societies have become slightly more comfortable and accustomed to talking about gender or race as social markers, but class often remains unspoken as a dynamic identity relating directly to questions of social conflict and the distribution of wealth. By its conspicuous absence, of course, it becomes very much present. Class can be considered from two main perspectives (both of which emerge from our discussion of Marx and Weber): the *economic* and the *cultural* (including aspects of identity).

The connection between class and identity derives from Marx's ideas about *class-consciousness,* which refers to the idea that different classes had conflicting interests and that these were expressed in distinct cultural and political forms. Much of the current literature on class, culture and identity has been influenced by the work of Pierre Bourdieu who worked in a broadly Marxian framework (1984). In particular, his concepts of *habitus,* *capital* and *field* have been intellectually generative. *Habitus* can be understood as a set of lasting dispositions (views, values, sensibilities, appreciations, taste and understandings that form a structure of mind) deriving from a specific class position and which are acquired through processes of primary socialization. *Capital,* and especially *cultural capital,* is, for Bourdieu, a form of social power that acts as a resource for achieving and sustaining a position in the social world. For example, middle-class cultural capital is a precious resource that some young people can 'trade' for success in education, career or social position. Bourdieu identifies three forms that this cultural capital might take:

1. **embodiment:** forms of speech, bodily dispositions, for example 'fit or fat' bodies, particular ways of dressing or decorating the body, for example piercings or tattoos. Embodiment may be classed, gendered and racialized
2. **cultural goods:** for example art objects, cars, and designer goods
3. **institutionalization:** for example membership of prestigious bodies or qualifications.

The important thing about cultural capital is that it operates in a relational way; it establishes position *in relation to* other positions and thus contributes to patterns of opportunity and disadvantage. It is in the context of a particular *field* that the struggle to mobilize and trade these resources operates. A profession might be such a field and is characterized by a system of social positions in which those involved, say, in the field of medicine or law, engage in great competition for recognition of achievement. Reward structures reflect that. Youth workers, teachers, and health and social workers could be seen similarly. In the youth professional field there are struggles to define young people in specific ways, to have particular approaches, relationships and qualifications recognized and rewarded.

Bourdieu represents society as fluid, as different actors seek to sustain or advance their social positions by trading or deploying their capital in various ways. He describes a view of class in which capital of different kinds is located and more or less mobile within social space that is structured over historical time: wealthy families retain their wealth over generations by having the capacity to use their capital and poorer families have little or no capacity to do this. Children are born into families that occupy these social spaces and inherit positions 'from which comes access to and acquisition of differential amounts of capital assets' (Skeggs, 2002: 9). As Skeggs points out, class, gender and race are not in themselves capital but they open up social space in which particular *dispositions* become organized as capital and used to advantage.

Over to you...

Critical reflection

What kinds of cultural capital can you identify in relation to the identities given below? Use the categories of embodiment, cultural goods and institutionalization referred to above.

The prime minister or president:

A working-class young man with whom you work:

A world-class footballer:

A working-class young woman with whom you work:

A black and female member of parliament:

Using the categories of cultural capital defined above it is quite easy to complete the table above. A simple example might be to consider the capital available to working-class young men and the consequences of that for their transitions. What legitimate forms of capital do they have access to? Their embodied capital (perhaps physical strength or hardness) might have value in some parts of the labour market but not in others. For work requiring *emotional labour* (the capacity to manage, display and control particular emotional responses) perhaps some forms of working-class masculinity or femininity might be disadvantageous. On the other hand, the institutionalized forms of capital typically the outcome of middle-class educational pathways (for example a degree or professional qualification) have high legitimacy in labour markets associated with knowledge economies. Importantly, in this analysis of class, accounts of other aspects of social difference, and how particular *aspirations* are classed, gendered and racialized are significant (Bradford and Hey, 2010). Cultural capital of other kinds is *embodied* in slim, beautiful and fit bodies that are able to achieve status in different social settings.

In the list above it is noticeable how social class, gender and race combine in various ways to produce 'subject positions'. This refers to articulations of self and identity that are made possible by virtue of class, gender, race or other structural and individual differences, and that are shaped and given meaning by those factors. For example, as a young woman, a mother, a sister or a work colleague, someone can assume a variety of identities that acquire meaning in different settings and at different times. Identity thus has some fluidity rather than being fixed or unchanging. The idea of being *positioned* refers to the dynamic and often subtle ways in which practices of social categorizing (through discourses of class or gender, for example) make some positions possible to some people and less so for others. Think about what it means to be a 'man', or a 'woman' in your own society: there are certain ways of thinking and talking about masculinity or femininity that make some ways of being a man or woman more or less tenable.

Over to you...

Reading

Annette Kuhn's book *Family Secrets, Acts of Memory and Imagination* (2002) provides an evocative account of family memories and their place in creating a sense of identity and self. The book is worth reading from cover to cover. In Chapter 6, Kuhn reflects on family life at the time of her gaining a scholarship to the local grammar school. This is an account of the intersection of social process, social institutions and social difference:

▶

class and gender (implicitly and unspoken, race), family and school. Kuhn raises questions about how memory deals with authenticity, place, belonging and identity. She shows how memory of family life (everyday pleasures and family troubles) is sedimented through memory into Kuhn's sense of her class identity and social place. Interestingly and importantly, she shows how a sociological imagination can open up questions about self and one's place in the world. As Kuhn puts it, 'Happily, once embarked upon, there is no end to critical consciousness, to the hunger to learn and to understand.'

Class is frequently an underlying theme in popular culture and is understood through the representations of class contained in films, TV and media advertising, for example. In British popular culture, class is a perpetual, although often unspoken, presence. Television soap operas are predicated on implicit understandings and identifications with class and class positions, *Eastenders* or *Coronation Street* being good examples.

From certain, particularly dominant, positions of power, certain groups are positioned as 'other'. Classically, women are seen as the 'other' of men (Weedon, 2004), black people as the 'other' of white, and the process of 'othering' can be also considered from the perspective of social class. Arguably, in the UK there has been considerable intensification of middle-class preoccupations with class in the last two or three decades. Skeggs (2002) suggests that this is a consequence of middle-class insecurity and the fear of losing what (for them) is a potentially precarious position of power. This preoccupation with the 'other' from a classed perspective takes on many forms and is expressed through various class practices. The rise of neoliberal economics as part of Margaret Thatcher's reforms of the welfare state in the 1980s resulted in spiralling inequality. New experiences of class inequality characterized by marked divisions between winners and losers in the context of powerful ideologies of individualism characterized the last two decades of the twentieth century in the UK. These experiences contrasted strikingly with those of the post-war years of austerity in which, to some extent, the welfare state mediated collective experiences of poverty (Rogaly and Taylor, 2009: 93).

Through the research that Valerie Hey and I completed on a Surestart programme in one area of an English town we named Westfield, we came across many examples of what Skeggs refers to, in extreme versions, as 'class hatred', the antagonisms that emerge in imagining the characteristics of the 'other' (Hey and Bradford, 2006). The 'chav' phenomenon could be read as an expression of such hatred. For example, we spoke to one professional in Westfield who was concerned about children's diets and potential obesity, and blamed working-class parents:

'It's as much to do with sometimes not understanding how to cook properly ... maybe too much sugar or salt and not too much fruit ... it's a lifestyle choice.' (Health Promotion Worker, Westfield)

Most parents we interviewed were positive about professionals but there were some who sometimes found the family support workers' implied judgements of them difficult to take:

'They're ok, like, but they give you crap sometimes ... think they know it but don't ... they come in your home and you can see them looking round and thinking "oh yeah" another poor family ... can't cope and not looking after the kids properly.' (Westfield mother)

These are examples of positioning and a middle-class condemnation of what are seen, or imagined, as working-class irresponsibility and negligence.

There are many contemporary examples of these practices of defining lifestyle as either acceptable or not. Importantly, this is a power practice and an attempt to demarcate what counts as appropriate, and is often constructed around arguments about working-class excess: diet and obesity, alcohol consumption, public behaviour, fashion and clothes. Young people, who are anyway judged as threatening by virtue of their liminality, are often a particular focus. Judgements are often made on health or aesthetic criteria (reflecting Bourdieu's account of the importance of cultural capital). Arguably, there is a radical shift in the way that (specifically white) working-class culture is now viewed, and this is expressed through popular culture. Recent television representations of white working-class life have included *Shameless*, set in a fictional Manchester social housing estate. The programme works by referencing (albeit in extreme form) what are seen as white working-class conduct and lifestyles. To some extent, *Shameless* (and similar representations: *Little Britain*, *The Royle Family* or talk shows on which working-class people have high profiles) trades on a moral panic focused on the underclass – the so-called undeserving poor – that confirms a middle-class stereotyped view. The, grudging, respect accorded working-class culture in popular representations of the 1950s and 1960s, which traded on ideas of community, solidarity, loyalty, warmth, hard work and good humour, has arguably diminished considerably.

For young people, class is a major element in individual and collective lives and particularly in relation to so-called 'choice biographies' referred to in Chapter 3. Despite the individualization that has accompanied Giddens' and Beck's accounts of detraditionalized late modernity, that is not to argue that class, as a collective category, is no longer significant. Class shapes young people's pathways to adulthood, in terms of education, access to labour markets and careers, for example, because the individual choices they make – the *agency* they exercise – are made in contexts shaped by class and the opportunities and cultural capital it offers or denies. That means, for example, that young people from middle-class families may have access to very different levels and types of resources than those from marginalized or disadvantaged backgrounds. In the UK, in comparison to other parts of Europe, these differences are often more extensive (Wilkinson and Pickett, 2009: 15–16) and the processes of individualization that were identified in Chapter 3 (processes of disembedding, diminishing security and reintegration) are likely to be experienced particularly acutely by those in marginalized positions. While class is central to these arguments about structures of opportunity and disadvantage, it intersects with other aspects of social difference including gender and sexuality.

Gender, Sexuality and Youth

The distinction between *sex* and *gender* is the starting point here. Sex refers to the biological or physiological characteristics that differentiate men and women (for example, women menstruate and men have testicles). Gender, on the other hand, defines the social and cultural characteristics, expressed as femininity and masculinity that are considered appropriate (behaviour, conduct, roles, and so on) to specific cultures, times and places. For example, women are usually expected to undertake more domestic work than men and domestic work is considered feminine. In that sense, gender is usually regarded as socially constructed. The first question that needs to be asked about gender is connected with *difference* and *inequality*. Men and women *are* different but the important questions concern how and why these differences become expressed or structured in relations of social inequality. Importantly, when the distinctive meanings of sex and gender become confused or conflated, questions of difference and commonality between male and female also become confused or exaggerated.

Perhaps the most basic point that can be made about the sociological study of gender is that it explores the differences between masculinity and femininity and the extent to which gender differences constitute social inequalities. Are men and women equal but different, or do these differences constitute inequalities? There are many forms of contemporary feminism (including liberal feminism, Marxist feminist, eco feminism, black feminism, second wave feminism), but all have in common an interest in countering gender inequality and promoting women's rights. Such feminism has generated activism campaigning for women's votes, equal pay and access to reproductive health, in addition to feminist theoretical work exploring the cultural constructions of sex–gender. One way to think about gender divisions is to ask whether feminism, where it has been influential, has served its purpose. Are late modern societies now in an era of post-feminism? It may be the case that feminists and feminist political activity are not as visible in Europe, the US and Australia as they were in the 1970s, for example. But does this mean that women have achieved gender equality? Are women now treated equally to men in these states? Has feminism achieved its goal? To what extent are class and race (as well as other indices of difference) implicated here? The evidence remains clear about continuing inequality between men and women in UK and other European societies (Walby, 2004).

In relation to the labour market it is true that in the UK since the Second World War many more women have participated in paid work. However, this has invariably been 'feminine' work that is less well paid and less secure than that of men. It is worth asking how many senior women managers are employed in services for children and young people, for example. In general, men dominate in the high status, high paid and senior sectors of the economy. Women tend to be located in retail, service and clerical work and, in professional work, lower status positions. It is worth thinking about how young women's improving rates of education performance and success may suggest that the future could be different. While, superficially, the gender divide may appear to have narrowed, the evidence suggests that the answer to the above questions remains a resounding 'No!' While women have increasingly participated in paid work, since the early 1970s, they have taken up the lower-paid and more insecure type of work. Men remain dominant in the higher paid, and more prestigious, managerial sector of the economy. More women work part-time than men. Women predominate in selling and personal service work and in secretarial and clerical jobs. In the UK, South Asian women participate much less in paid work than white and black women. The recent, relative educational underachievement of boys, reversing the circumstances of previous generations when girls underachieved, may be related to working-class boys considering educational achievement to be irrelevant to the opportunities available to them locally for skilled work. Gender and ethnic differences in educational achievement of young people are important indicators of the specific views of young people about their opportunities, identities and future potential (Foster, Kimmel and Skelton, 2001).

Hegemonic Masculinity and Emphasized Femininity

An influential work theorizing gender is that of Connell (1987) who, in exploring gender construction and performance, argues that there are multiple ways of 'doing' or performing masculinity or femininity, but some are more valued than others. In this, Connell argues that *hegemonic mascu-*

linity, a dominant masculinity that has become most valorized and valued in the contemporary West, has involved an emphasis on 'toughness', heterosexual virility and rationality. Conversely, the equivalent, 'emphasized femininity' is performed in contrast to this masculine 'ideal'. For example, this kind of femininity may highlight passivity, frailty, kindness and heterosexual attractiveness. This is not to say that Connell argued that other ways of doing masculine or feminine performances were not possible, but just that they were evaluated in comparison to normative ideal forms. These ideals would also be shaped by local cultures, and would thus be 'raced' and 'classed'.

Recent interest in the situation of lesbian, gay, bisexual and transgender (LGBT) young people has led to a growth in the literature in this area. Barron and Bradford (2007), for example, discuss the concept of corporeal (bodily) capital in their exploration of young gay men's experiences in education in Ireland. They start their analysis by considering the *social construction* of the body of young people and young gay men in particular. What Barron and Bradford are suggesting here is that the human body has to be understood as a social entity as much as it is biologically defined. They argue that identity, self and difference are *embodied* and that to understand identity, it is important to recognize how identity is 'contained', partially at least, in the body (Shilling, 2005: 231).

Over to you...

Critical reflection

Can you identify how your own identity is, at least partially, embodied? The fact that you have a sex/gender is itself expressed bodily, as Barron and Bradford suggest. You can probably identify a range of other ways in which bodies are modified in order to change identity: surgery, tattoos, piercings, fashion and hairstyle are some of these.

Can you connect any of these to your own sexual identity: your identity as a man or woman, straight or LGBT?

Bodily pleasure and pain assume enormous significance for young people and adolescence is constituted by bodily transformation from child to adult. Specifically, adolescence signals expectations on the individual young person to become a competent agent marked, in part, by the (deeply gendered) capacity to sustain continuous bodily control and discipline (Aapola, Gonick, and Harris, 2005: 32). Youth – often expressed bodily – is sometimes spectacular and, in a culture in which visual images are paramount, the gendered body is key to the construction of a visualized and recognized self (Frost, 2003: 54). In late modern consumer capitalism, the body as a key bearer of identity has become central to the acquisition of cultural capital based on image, style and fashion. A number of commentators have pointed to the potential for 'identity damage' (Frost, 2003: 59) in circumstances where social difference – principally class, but also gender, race, sexuality and disability – prevents young people from participating fully in practices of consumption and in developing a sense of wellbeing and recognition (Henderson et al., 2007; Holt, 2010).

As Barron and Bradford argue, for gay young people, as for others, the body has a continuous, but changing, material presence in their lives. The gay body is central to the accomplishment of gay identity, which is 'a "production" ... never complete, always in process, and always constituted within, not outside, representation' (Hall, 1990: 222). Thus, gay and other identities are formed in the ways by which young people construct and acquire a sense of who they are and how that is presented and represented through the deployment of bodily capital. This means that identity should be understood as an outcome of the repertoire of cultural practices and meanings (perhaps effeminacy or camp, for example, in relation to gay young men) in its ongoing production. An example from Barron and Bradford's work (2007: 244–7) shows the extent to which sexuality, difference and identity are tied up in the practices of embodiment. Some young men interviewed by Barron and Bradford had devised careful defensive strategies of self-representation as a means of fitting in at school and resisting hostile school cultures. Their responses to the common violence they had experienced as gay young men emphasized the importance of the visual codes constituting sexuality, and entailed their engagement in complex reflexive work on the body and on their own 'talk repertoires'. The idea was to pass as straight and to minimize the sense of perceived difference that would lead to violence.

> 'There was stuff written about me in school, I was slagged going down the street, there was stuff thrown at me. I had to go to hospital in 4th year because someone pushed me off the stage. I had to move from that school to another one ... I had to stand on my own, no one would talk to me unless they wanted a cigarette, or they wanted money.'

Different ways of performing gender and sexuality have become increasingly significant in understanding how young men and women might accomplish their gender identities and the effects that this may have on academic performance in school. Carolyn Jackson's work (2006), for example, explored boys' and girls' performances of a 'laddish' anti-school identity, where hard work had to be hidden in order to uphold an acceptable gender identity. Being 'laddish' was not linked only to boys, but for young women and young men in Jackson's study it was important not to appear too diligent in schoolwork, and to participate in rough play and banter in order to sustain an 'anti-school' ethos. Such research highlights how the performance of gender within a social setting can shape young people's experiences of school and future life direction. It is, of course, important to take account of how class and other indices of social difference combine with gender in settings like that explored by Jackson.

Over to you...

Critical reflection

You might like to reflect on Jackson's work in relation to young people in your own work setting. What significance does the anti-school culture she refers to have for the young people with whom you work? *Is it related to difference and identity?* Do youth workers and similar professionals have any particular role here?

Gender Relations, Divisions and Young People

The sociology of youth subcultures has demonstrated the importance of leisure in constructing specific youth identities and subcultures and in understanding the impact of class, gender and race in these. There are important historical accounts of young women's leisure in the pre-war period. Clare Langhamer (2000), Penny Tinkler (1995) and Selina Todd (2005), for example, show how expanding commercial leisure provision shaped gender relations and the experiences of young women during the interwar and immediate post-war periods. David Fowler offers an analysis of the 'flapper cult' in the 1920s and suggests that this might be seen as a proto-youth culture (2008). However, from a youth culture and subcultures perspective, Bill Osgerby (1998) examines the idea that young women have been *hidden* from post-war accounts of youth in Britain. The concept of youth subcultures in particular focused on the spectacular displays of masculinity during this period, mods, skinheads and punks, for example. Young women were largely ignored, or viewed as relatively passive participants in some of the male-dominated subcultures, for example skinheads, mods and motor bikers (Willis, 1978).

While women were central to the post-war economic boom, both as producers and consumers, it wasn't until the mid-1960s that researchers began to pay attention to the changing social and economic status of young women. After 1945, young women began to take positions in consumer industries, business services, retailing and the clerical sector. In growing numbers they worked in factories and offices and this broadened their economic and cultural horizons, compared with the pre-war period. They drove the teenage consumer boom of the late 1950s and 1960s, purchasing clothes, records and cosmetics although, as Todd suggests, this was prefigured by similar growth in the 1930s and 1940s. Magazines such as *Valentine* and *Jackie* were produced specifically for teenage girls. It was in the fashion sector that young women had the largest post-war cultural influence, with Twiggy representing this in the most dramatic way as 'The Face of 1966'. The appearance of the teenage girl image also manifested itself in popular music, and film, with Cathy McGowan, Helen Shapiro and Rita Tushingham all achieving fame in the late 1950s and early 1960s. What linked these and other female icons of the time was their so-called 'girl next door' image, which seemed accessible and proximate to the experiences of white young women in the 1960s.

Osgerby (1998) examines the influence of young women in the punk rock movement of the late 1970s as they embraced more assertive and rebellious forms of feminine identity. Osgerby cites the punk bands, The Slits and Siouxsie Sioux as high profile examples of this. Madonna continued this assertive female identity through the 1980s, 1990s and into the 2000s.

In *Feminism and Youth Culture* (2000) Angela McRobbie presents seminal arguments on young women and subcultures. McRobbie was herself a member of the Centre for Contemporary Cultural Studies at Birmingham University that was at the heart of the youth culture debates in the 1970s and 1980s. She draws our attention to the apparent absence of girls in subcultural accounts, while also suggesting that girls' interactions actually create a distinctive (and feminine) culture of their own. If that is so, the presence or absence of girls in male subcultures is not really the issue. McRobbie focuses on girls' comics and magazines as a manifestation of this cultural distinctiveness. Her studies included pre-teenage girls as well as those in their teens. She concludes that so-called late twentieth-century 'teenybopper' 'subcultures could be interpreted as ways of buying time, within the commercial mainstream, from the real world of sexual encounters while at the same time imagining these encounters, with the help of the images and commodities supplied by the commercial mainstream, from the safe space of the all-female friendship group' (McRobbie and Garber, 2005: 112). Chapter 5 looks specifically at youth subcultures.

O'Donnell and Sharpe (2000) used a combination of questionnaires and interviews with boys to investigate young men's attitudes to gender, race, families, work, and culture in four south London schools in the mid-1990s. Theoretically, their book employs various typologies drawn from the literature on the construction of masculinity. The seminal work here is Paul Willis's *Learning to Labour* (1977) and it is Willis's conception of the culture of 'the lads' upon which these authors draw. Through a very sophisticated empirical and theoretical investigation, they came to the conclusion that a big divide continued between formal schooling and informal peer activity. The main manifestation of this was that the boys accepted (perhaps passively) in school the anti-racist and anti-sexist educational regime but, outside of school, showed a strong tendency to be racist and sexist: 'the lads' culture. O'Donnell and Sharpe suggested that girls were the main beneficiaries of sex-discrimination legislation in relation to academic performance and increased understanding of life choices, and they also noted that some of the boys were not racist or sexist. As highlighted earlier, Carolyn Jackson explores how 'lad and laddette' culture (which included racist and sexist attitudes) shapes the experiences of young people in many schools and concludes that behaviour may be motivated by different factors, including fears of failure and the acquisition of 'popularity points' from peers. For some young people, 'laddishness' is cool but creates real challenges in balancing the demand to be both socially and academically successful (Jackson, 2006).

The alleged absence of men as 'role models' in many boys' lives has led to a construction of male youth culture as separate from the world of adults. This is a position challenged in the case of black young men (the absent fathers debate) by Tracey Reynolds (2006) who suggests that this argument is a diversion from looking at the inherently racist institutions that young black men experience and the consequences of these on their sense of identity. Reynolds' work reminds us that social difference has to be understood as a series of intersecting dynamics that *in combination* shape young people's lives. Despite this, there is a perceived 'crisis in masculinity' that is promoted by some academics. O'Donnell and Sharpe went in this direction as does Tony Sewell (1996, 2009). This is apparently supported by men's visibility in unemployment figures, young men's declining educational performance, the alarming rates of male suicide and hidden forms of self-harm.

Over to you...

Critical reflection

Do you recognize the 'crisis of masculinity' picture painted by O'Donnell and Sharpe and others? What is your own experience of this in your life or that of the young people with whom you work?

▶

How would you account for this? Is this a problem of absent fathers? Are there other explanations or contributory factors? Perhaps it is a mistake to use the term *crisis of masculinity* to account for a range of issues that may have no underlying connection?

Sociology does not provide us with off-the-shelf answers to social problems, concerns and issues of the kind that we refer to here. Social policy should develop ideas that are based upon sociological investigations. Social reality and social relations are complex and fluid and it is important not to jump to conclusions. One significant debate here concerns the extent to which there is actually a crisis of masculinity, either new or otherwise. O'Donnell and Sharpe's and Jackson's work suggests a continuity with and persistence of older male attitudes and outlooks. So, is the so-called crisis a new phenomenon at all? While labour market patterns have and are clearly continuing to disadvantage some young men, perhaps sexist attitudes remain a residual but embedded core component of male identity?

Race, Ethnicity and Youth

Race and ethnicity are important markers of difference and power inequalities but they are also unstable categories whose meaning is contested, perhaps even more than gender and class. It is therefore important to start by thinking about the meaning of these terms.

Over to you...

Critical reflection and reading

Take a moment to consider the terms *race* and *ethnicity*. Quickly jot down what the terms mean to you. What are the distinctions that you would make between them?

Both refer to marking distinctions between people and categorizing them in various ways. Sometimes, race is understood in biological terms and ethnicity is understood to refer to cultural differences. However, the important point is that although these distinctions are in one sense arbitrary, they are historically and socially formed. Categorizations in terms of race or ethnicity are invariably used in ideological ways in the sense that they support particular relations of power by relying on (usually negative) representations of particular groups (for example young black men, Islamists, East European migrants) in the form of racism. Racism can be understood as ideology (and thus as containing knowledge and ideas) and its consequences have real material force (that is, people's lives are shaped by the effects of racist ideology).

Read Monica Ali's book *Brick Lane* to explore how race, gender and class have real consequences for people's lives. Ali's protagonist Nazneen's transition from Bangladesh to London's East End is marked by events that point up the recurrent significance of race and ethnicity. Ali's narrative shows how intersecting aspects of similarity, difference and division mark out individual biographies.

Looking again to Osgerby's (1998) *Youth in Britain Since 1945*, the emphasis is on cultural responses to race and racism. That immigration has often been met with racist attitudes is accepted as a given. In the UK and Ireland in recent times, for example, migrants from Eastern Europe have been subjected to new forms of racism, as were Irish migrants to Britain in the 1950s and 1960s. Kate Stanley (2005: 198) argues that the language used in relation to migrants and asylum seekers in the UK represents them as a 'threat that must be contained'. In the British election in 2010, for example, immigration, particularly *Eastern* European immigration, was a topic that caused great concern and controversy, reflecting a conflict-ridden history of migration into the UK in the post-war period.

Despite the fact that Caribbean music played a vital part in the 'rude boy' and ska cultures of the 1970s and 1980s, racism and racist violence has continued. While 'Two Tone' and politicized musical expression such as 'Rock Against Racism' in the 1970s and 1980s attempted to bring black and white young people together there have also been various cultural and political expressions of racism. The skinheads, emerging in the 1970s, were one instance. Support for the British National Party (BNP) or the English Defence League is a political example of this racism. In recent years formations of racism have moved from the language of 'race' to anti immigration and, in particular, Islamaphobic sentiment. This changing emphasis means that debates centred on immigration may also focus on (white) Eastern Europeans as targets for Far Right groups. The English Defence League's anti-Islamic racism (denied by them as racist) includes campaigns against mosques and the presence of Islam in the UK. Such shifts highlight how formations of racism (the structure, relations and organization of racist discourse) shift across time and space, but often focus on supposed differences in values, and the castigation of an 'othered' and often marginalized group such as asylum seekers, economic migrants, refugees, Travellers, Muslims, as a threat to the continued social stability and job security of the so-called 'host' communities (Hetherington, 2005).

Ethnicity is sometimes conceived in terms of shared culture, including language, customs and religion and therefore can acknowledge a positive sense of cultural identification. 'Race' is a social categorization enforced, for example, by governments relying upon (discredited) attempts to identify distinct racial types. *Race* relations are often hierarchical and exploitative while *ethnic* relations may not always be understood in such terms. However these terms are construed, they are ways of classifying or categorizing groups and sections of populations and, through their use in different circumstances, are thus implicitly tied to relations of power.

Ethnicity and race in the form of racialized identities can be seen as *enacted, performed* or even *imposed*, rather than being fixed properties of some kind that someone 'has'. For example, the enactment of and engagement in particular kinds of rituals or practices confers specific ethnicity. Other aspects of identity intersect with ethnicity and race. In that sense, everyone has *multiple identities*, yet the ways one may choose *to identify* shift in relation to context and situation. Work by Ali (2003) and Tizard and Phoenix (1993) with mixed-heritage children and young people questions notions of *essentialized* (fixed or immutable) racial identities. They highlight how people from mixed-heritage backgrounds may choose to identify in different ways at different times. Indeed, some people simply identify themselves as 'black' or 'Asian'. This has led some sociologists to use the term race/ethnicity as a kind of either/or.

None of these issues and the questions they encourage are settled; they are matters that are often contested. Indeed, white Europeans may have given very little thought about how and with what they identify nor considered in any depth how their 'whiteness' or 'Britishness' forms part of their racialized and ethnic identities (Knowles and Alexander, 2005). There may be important generational aspects to such identity questions, and migration, for example, may be very significant here.

These points may be summarized:

● Race and ethnicity are constructed through *attribution* by external sources (for example other groups, media, policy documents, professional practices) and practices and therefore set in relations of power.

● Race and ethnicity are *asserted* or claimed through identification and membership, for example Black Power, black, white, Asian.

● Racism is an ideology based on the claim that one category of people (a 'race') is superior to another and that inferior treatment can be justified on that basis; apartheid South Africa and the treatment of black people in the post-war United States were based on ideologies of racial superiority, and racism was socially and politically *institutionalized* in those countries as it was in some welfare entitlements in the UK in the 1960s and 1970s. There are many contemporary examples of racism in Europe: treatment of the Roma people in Hungary, anti-Semitism in France and racism on black footballers in England.

Whatever terms are adopted, ethnicity and race remain important (and often emotive) forms of social difference. The link between 'labelling' and *power-knowledge* to which Foucault (1980) draws attention is evident here. If a person is labelled by the state or by a dominant group as 'non-white', this has potentially significant implications for that person: entitlements, autonomy, security and so on. Both race and ethnicity are socially produced through governments' power-knowledge practices and are potentially divisive and abusive (nationality and immigration legislation are examples of this). As such, they are located in the power relations of difference and division that characterize late modern societies.

Race and ethnicity are thus forms of social knowledge that organize social relations at the micro level of how individuals relate and identify with others, *and* at macro (political, ideological and structural) levels to create patterns of opportunity or exclusion for particular groups. It is important to recognize the instability of racial or ethnic categories, as they are socially and historically contingent, neither 'natural' nor 'inevitable'. Instead, race and ethnicity (and even the social or political concern with them) are the products of particular social processes that characterize societies at particular historical times. The emphasis and focus upon 'non-whiteness' might constitute a need, desire or unconscious 'drive' to control and regulate a particular section of the population. In many official questionnaires on race or ethnicity, the category 'white' seems to be treated as unproblematic and uncontested. After all, so-called 'white' people are often a complex combination – 'hybrids' – of different ethnic groups. Why, therefore, is 'whiteness' hardly ever the focus of official attention?

This discussion raises questions about the assumed homogeneity of social groups. Clearly it would be a mistake to assume that whiteness secures social power. Returning to the example of Westfield, it was plain that there were distinctions between white groups on the estate, and different economic positions marked out ways of understanding and imagining others. White migrant families from Lithuania, for example, were subjected to processes and practices of categorization in which their ethnicity (or race?) was constructed by the everyday practices of life on the estate, and often understood by others in competitive and conflicted terms. The social power of migrants (capacity and capital) seemed very limited. However, it would be equally mistaken to think about *blackness* as a universal category of meaning. For example, one of my black students recently visited her grandparents in Barbados for a month and she was made very aware that Bajans saw her as distinctively *different*, despite her own Bajan heritage. In that sense, identity is subtle, complex, often ambiguous and implicated in producing positions of advantage and disadvantage.

This discussion highlights the potential fluidity of young people's social and cultural identities which are shaped by various racialized and gendered discourses that often suffuse shifting notions of 'beauty' and 'cool'. Some writers have understood these marginal *hybridized* spaces as 'in-between the rules of engagement' (Bhabha, 1994: 193), settings in which young people are able to exercise agency by challenging fixed notions of what it means to be black, white or Asian (Song, 2005: 72). However, this destabilizing of essentialized identities (for example the simple binary of *black–white*) sometimes reifies hybridized identities as inherently progressive, thus potentially occluding the 'the wider processes of power relations, appropriation and exploitation that occur in the production and consumption of youth culture' (Alexander, 2000: 239). This means that the celebration of complex identities and new spaces of youth culture might simply conceal processes that lead to inequality and the marginalization of some young people.

Summary and Conclusions

Chapter 4 has continued the exploration of the concept of identity. In particular it raised an implicit question about whether the factors that make young people *similar* to one another are as significant as those that make them *different*. As part of this discussion, the idea of generation was discussed, thus specifically identifying age factors in constituting similarity and difference. Age clearly differentiates individuals' and groups' access to social power. For young people, that is a major factor in their life experiences.

The chapter considered social difference, initially social class, from the perspectives of Marx and Weber, broadly corresponding to economic and cultural perspectives on class. For both Marx and Weber, social class is identified as a key determinant of power relations: class and power are intimately interlinked.

Social difference was then considered as a vital aspect of creating *subject positions*, articulations of self and identity – personal and social – that are produced in a combination of factors of social difference: class, gender or race, for example. In that sense, identity is shaped and given meaning by social difference and becomes complex. Someone might assume a variety of identities that acquire meaning in different settings and at different times: as a man, a father, a brother or a work colleague. More theoretically, class, gender, race, sexuality and ability, for example, can be understood as forms of social knowledge: what is known *about* people and what people know about themselves. These knowledge forms organize micro-level social relations in day-to-day life *and* are crucial factors at the macro level (the level of society) in structuring relations of opportunity and disadvantage. This sociological perspective helps to explain the reality of face-to-face racism and its structured and institutionalized patterning that creates obstacles for many young people, and emphasizes the importance of recognizing the conjunction of individual and social factors in shaping young people's lives.

Further Reading

- Lawler, S. (2008) *Identity. Sociological perspectives*, Cambridge: Polity Press.

  Chapters in this book deal with the main sociological questions about identity: those of *similarity* and *difference*.

- Aapola, S., Gonick, M. and Harris, A. (2005) *Young Femininity. Girlhood, power and social change*, Basingstoke: Palgrave Macmillan.

  The authors look at the historical development of girlhood and femininity in the context of social change, taking account of feminism and the sociology of youth.

- Knowles, C. and Alexander, C. (eds) (2005) *Making Race Matter: Bodies, space and identity*, Basingstoke: Palgrave Macmillan.

  This collection offers case studies of race and ethnicity, including aspects of youth cultures, using embodiment, space and identity as key theoretical tools. Chapters on young people, belonging and gang cultures are especially relevant.

5

Being Social

Complying and Transgressing

Introduction

Chapter 5 will explore the emergence of distinctive youth cultures in modern societies. It also considers the institution of leisure, so important in post-war Western societies. A discussion of young people and their capacity to breach social boundaries is included: to what extent can youth culture be seen as 'transgressive'?

Over to you...

Critical reflection

Have you ever adopted a particular style or 'subcultural' identity? Why and what do/did these identities mean to you and/or your friends? What do they signify? Does this suggest you adopt (or 'have') a multiple identity in any way? What are these identities and what do they signify for you?

Youth Culture in Modernity: Youth and Subculture

The first serious studies of youth and youth culture were conducted in the United States in the interwar years by urban sociologists Robert Park, Fredrick Thrasher and William Foote-Whyte at the University of Chicago (the so-called *Chicago School*), who argued that the social environment of the city, like the natural world, had to be understood as a kind of ecology or equilibrium. These studies retain a real quality and deserve re-reading. Foote-

Whyte's account of Boston's street gangs in the early 1940s resonates with current circumstances in the UK where the interest in gangs seems no less acute (see Alexander, 2000, 2008). American patterns of urban development, characterized by repeated inflows of new migrants, disrupted the perceived equilibrium of US society. The result, the Chicago sociologists thought, was social disorganization, a loss of normative social control and the emergence of gangs that passed on delinquent traditions or subcultures through generations of young people in the marginal areas of American cities. Contemporary studies of youth have inherited this tradition by pointing to the importance of the social and cultural practices of *labelling* for understanding youth deviance and delinquency. Claire Alexander's (2008) work on youth gangs, written for the Runnymede Trust, offers a critical account of the contemporary use of the term *gang*. Alexander wants to argue that the gang is more an idea or a fiction than it is an empirical or objective reality and that it works to marginalize certain young people more than support them.

Research into teenage gangs in the US spanned the first half of the twentieth century and the work of Albert Cohen (1955), in particular, is relevant to youth subculture research as it later developed in the UK. Cohen's argument about youth gangs (drawing on the theoretical work of Robert Merton) was that they provided a compensatory source of identity and self-esteem for working-class young men who underachieved in education. Cohen's work raises important points about youth subculture that have shaped much of the recent and contemporary work on youth culture and subculture in the UK.

● Youth subculture is expressed in values that are counter to or that invert 'mainstream' (adult) culture, primarily hedonism, the search for instant 'kicks' and resistance to authority.

● Subculture is a source of social bonding and solidarity.

● Subculture is located in the context of *leisure*.

● Thus, the concept of subculture focused on leisure, pleasure and resistance.

Other US sociologists in the 1950s and 1960s explored the role of youth gangs but identified not only gangs and groups characterized by resistant or 'subterranean' values but youth groups that expressed values similar to their parents (Miller, 1958; Matza, 1964). Matza, for example, argued that young people 'drifted' in and out of delinquent activities both reflecting and challenging the values and norms of their parents. Thus, youth was seen as both mirroring and potentially transformative of the social world.

The second major sociological position in the interwar period and beyond was *structural functionalism*. In this perspective the study of youth was approached from two quite different starting points: the *macro* (large scale) as opposed to the *micro* (small scale) social system, and the *functionality* rather than *dys-functionality* of that system. Youth was understood by structural functionalists as a central element in the socialization process and thus as a mechanism for maintaining social stability rather than bringing about either disruption or social change.

Talcott Parsons (1942) envisaged youth as being at the maximum point of tension between two value systems of traditional and modern society, a state of anomie or normlessness. In modern societies, the roles the child learns in the family no longer match the adult roles that must be adopted in wider society. Youth subcultures, according to Parsons, usually had important positive functions in easing the transition from the security of childhood (in affective relationships) to that of full adult in marriage and occupational status in complex modern societies characterized by self-interest and the pursuit of status.

However, it was Eisenstadt (1956) who most consistently developed the functionalist approach to youth and youth cultures. He argued that leisure-based youth culture played a major role in the preparation ('socialization') of young people for the world beyond the family because these cultures created a set of values, attitudes and behavioural norms that engendered a sense of empowerment otherwise lost by young people because of their marginal socioeconomic and cultural position in modern society. Young people were understood to be seeking a collective cultural solution to a socioeconomic status problem but the precise form that solution took was viewed as more or less irrelevant. Hence an important implication of the functionalist approach is that the specific *forms* of youth culture are of marginal importance. Structural functionalists argued that youth culture was a singular rather than plural notion, because whether skinhead, punk, mod or rocker, participation in youth culture was interpreted as having both psychological and individualized aspects as well as social functions.

British Youth Research

Youth became especially visible in the UK post-war years in which full employment and relative affluence created the conditions in which leisure and consumption-oriented youth cultures could emerge, although as pointed out, embryonic youth cultures existed in the pre-war years (see Fowler, 2008; Todd, 2005). Others have argued for the existence of youth culture in the late nineteenth century and into the early twentieth century (for example Davies, 2008). Perhaps crucially, the growth of post-war mass media (especially television) ensured the high visibility of youth and young people.

Since the 1970s, British youth research has reflected shifting sociological paradigms. It has moved from neo-Marxist analyses of youth culture and subculture, and representations of the transition from school to work as a critical moment in the reproduction of the labour force, to more recent concerns about citizenship, gender inequality and socioeconomic polarization in the transition from youth to adult status. The changing circumstances of youth and the perceived inadequacy of earlier theory for explaining contemporary developments have led to theoretical re-formulations aimed at exploring the consequences of economic restructuring for the experiences of youth and the patterning of transitions from youth to adult lives.

The 1950s, 1960s and early 1970s were years of relatively full employment in the UK, and processes of class continuity and reproduction in the transition from school to work are generally understood to have been relatively unproblematic, although there are criticisms of this assumption (Vickerstaffe, 2003). Forms of socialization, through family, school and work relations, were seen to underlie smooth transitions between these life course stages.

Concerns with *culture* (reflecting the rapid growth of consumerism, especially among young people) drove the British youth studies agenda through the 1960s and 1970s, as increasing attention was paid to how mass cultural forms might secure the reproduction of (unequal) social relations in late capitalist society. In other words, the positive 'socialization' talked about by the structural functionalists was seen by those on the critical Left as just *incorporation* into the inequality generated by capitalism. Moreover, as youth and student political activism grew in the 1960s, young people were increasingly identified as key agents of potential subversion of existing social relations. Prior to this, Parsons' picture of a conformist, increasingly middle-class youth culture reflected the climate of the post-war period in Western Europe and North America, characterized by the affluent society, the right to leisure and expression of self through consumption. Central to this Western affluence, in the 1950s and 1960s particularly, was the *teenager* who rapidly became identified as a new economic actor with distinctive patterns of consumption involving particular products, media forms, services and entertainment.

The development of the concept of subculture by the Centre for Contemporary Cultural Studies (CCCS), particularly through the book *Resistance Through Rituals* (Hall and Jefferson, 1976), draws on Phil Cohen's (1972) interpretation of subcultural conflict at a community level. In the UK, the concept of subculture (originating in the work of Albert Cohen in the US) was applied theoretically as a device within the Marxist base (economic relations) and superstructure (cultural relations) problematic. The work of Marxist theorists such as Althusser and Gramsci, and structuralist theorists such as Levi-Strauss and Barthes redefined the concept of subculture as a potential space for youth to engage in creative agency (Blackman, 1995). In building on their elaboration of the base and super-structure metaphor, the CCCS created a macro theoretical model for the general reading of youth cultural styles (Hall and Jefferson, 1976).

The Concept of Youth Subculture

The term *subculture* designates a separate entity within a larger society. Graham Murdock offers a seminal definition:

> Subcultures are the meaning system and modes of expression developed by groups in particular parts of the social structure in the course of their collective attempts to come to terms with the contradictions of their shared social situation. (Murdock, in Brake, 1985: 27)

Murdock's analysis suggests that membership of a subculture necessarily also entails membership of a *class* culture and he indicates that the subculture may be an extension of, or exist in opposition to, the class culture. According to Brake, the significance of subcultures for their participants is that they offer a solution to structural dislocations by opening up social space in which an identity can be achieved beyond the ascribed identity offered by home, school or work. He further suggests that the majority of youth pass through life without significant involvement in (deviant) subcultures. The role of youth subculture involves offering symbolic elements that are used by youth to construct an identity outside the constraints of class and education (Brake, 1985). Cohen suggests that subcultures offer a 'compromise solution between two contradictory needs: the need to create and express autonomy and difference and the need to maintain identifications to the culture within whose boundaries the subculture develops' (P. Cohen, 1972: 26).

Over to you...

Critical reflection

It is interesting to explore the extent to which the subculture thesis can be applied to young people of the early twenty-first century. Can you think of any groups of young people that equate with the 'mods and rockers', skinheads or subcultures of the 1970s? What are the similarities and differences? Can the contemporary groups be described as subcultures?

▶

Clearly, young people do form groups and these may, in some instances, be thought of as 'subcultures'. Perhaps 'ravers', 'clubbers', and so on might come into this category. One interesting phenomenon is the persistence of 'old' subcultures such as skinheads, punks, goths and so on, alongside the newer groups (some members of these old groups are, themselves, older as well). However, today's groups don't appear to be quite as homogeneous and distinct – certainly not as spectacular – as the 1970s subcultures. Do you agree?

Thinking about what we said about class in Chapter 4 and reflecting on the quote from Mike Brake above, do you think that contemporary youth groups (as subcultures) represent attempts to resolve youth's marginalized position (the 'structural contradictions rising from the wider societal context' that young people find themselves in), as Brake suggests? A good example of this in the literature is John Clarke's piece, 'The Skinheads and the Magical Recovery of Community', in Hall and Jefferson (1976).

The CCCS approach was characterized predominantly by Marxist cultural studies, with its emphasis upon the centrality of social class (reflecting the arguments considered in Chapter 4), culture being an expression of class difference and subcultures representing a variant of the 'parent' class culture. It adopts the Italian Marxist Gramsci's idea of the cultural *hegemony* of the most powerful groups within society (Bennett, 2005: 23–5). Hegemony refers to the power that a dominant class exercises over subordinate classes in ideological forms (through language, beliefs, culture and so on) and the extent to which that is unquestioned by the subordinate classes. The *dominant culture* is that practised by the *dominant class* and culture is defined as the realization or objectification of group life in meaningful forms (art, literature, music and so on). This means that cultural events and objects represent the commonality within groups and culture expresses what particular groups share. However, culture is a 'two-way street' in that it provides a set of meanings for individuals as group members. Culture shapes the social relations of a group, its structure and the means by which membership is acquired (socialization).

Expressed in these terms, culture is clearly an enormously important concept for sociologists. In class terms, youth subcultures have generally been perceived as 'resistant', 'deviant', challenging or problematic in various ways and understood as the most visible, direct and unmediated responses to class subordination. Hence the importance placed upon them in the 1970s. This becomes very clear when the CCCS writers turn their attention to middle-class youth subcultures and argue that they should be theorized in a different manner: as part of the 'contradiction' of being members of the *dominant* culture.

The variations on the theme of subculture and its functions are summarized in Table 5.1.

Table 5.1   Youth subcultures

Compensatory source of identity and self-esteem (see Cohen, 1955)	Youth subculture as a response to underachievement in the institutions of mainstream America: subcultural values subvert the 'American Dream' by stressing hedonism, immediacy in leisure; bonding and solidarity
Natural transition from childhood to adult status (see Eisenstadt, 1956)	The 'modernist' view of subculture: youth groups act as transitory points on the journey to adulthood; they provide psychological support for surviving in a hostile social world and for managing the tension between child and adult identities
Resistance and working-class struggle expressed through distinctive youth subcultural groups (see Hall and Jefferson, 1976)	Youth subculture as the expression of working-class values in resistance to dominant bourgeois culture and institutions (e.g. school or employment)
Expression of class experience and attempt to achieve 'relative autonomy' in the context of multicultural society (see Hebdige, 1979)	Class experience encoded in youth subculture that uses the vehicle of 'style' to express that experience
Spaces for new identity construction based on individualization (McRobbie, 1994)	The late/postmodern view of subculture as a lament for the collective identities of modernism and a response to the loneliness of late modern culture and individualization; this trend affects all classes and generations

The assumptions underlying these concepts of subculture are very different, so much so that they are almost completely different entities. However, the perspectives that are summarized share some fundamental characteristics. They are based on youth as an *age category*, they focus on broad questions of *leisure-based identity* and they include a *collective* aspect that entails social bonding and solidarity. As such, subcultures describe a primarily social phenomenon that incorporates specifically *psycho*-social aspects such as identity, identification, investment.

The concept of *style* (in fashion and dress, language and conduct) has been a central feature of the subculture literature and of ethnographic work in the sociology of youth beyond that. Style has a number of functions in relation to youth subcultures (Hebdige, 1979). Style can be read as a kind of practice; something that is performed or achieved, rather than a static property that is attributed to a group or individual. The adoption of style signifies boundary, it acts as a language of inclusion and as a public statement creates visibility, spectacle and drama, thus also generating solidarity.

In summary, a number of key characteristics are evident across the subcultures literature.

- Social difference (age, generation, gender, race and class) forms the basis to subculture.

- Subcultures form a kaleidoscope of visible and sometimes spectacular groups (although it is argued that the spectacle of 1970s and 1980s subcultures has diminished and later groups have been less conspicuous: ravers and dance cultures, for example).

- Subculture can be seen in *instrumental* terms as a response to shared problems (marginality or subordination, for example, in education or the labour market) and seemingly to provide a resolution to the marginalized position.

- Subcultures can be seen as *expressive* entities: they make sense of lived and shared experience by offering creative opportunities to forge identity by using a variety of cultural resources: fashion, music, literature, and so on. In this sense, they may pose a symbolic challenge to the 'old order', and resolution may be illusory as nothing changes at structural level.

- Subculture creates the opportunity for exercising *agency* in a setting where young people experience powerlessness.

- Subcultures project in a way that makes identity seem *beyond* and *independent* of structural position (educational or occupational position, for example): hence references to 'magical resolution' of structural contradictions.

- Subculture mainly appeals in young people's *leisure lives* (other than in unusual cases, members of subcultures are 'part-time'; exceptions might be Travellers or eco-warriors, see Hetherington, 2005).

- Leisure space is the site upon which creative subcultural activity has occurred; much of this activity has centred upon 'bodily pleasure' (alcohol consumption, drug use, sexual activity, and so on) and the consumption of experience as a consequence of affluence among young people.

Criticizing Subculture

Subculture theory in the UK (and elsewhere) has been markedly influenced by the work of the CCCS. However, it has been criticized for romanticizing working-class culture and subcultures. The groups the CCCS identified were predominantly male. They also formed only a small section of working-class young people, as Clarke and others acknowledge (Hall and Jefferson, 1976). Therefore the issue of the *representativeness* of youth subcultures must be raised. Alongside this consideration is the question of how 'permanent' subcultures are, and therefore how *structural* is their existence? Are youth subcultures a permanent and significant social phenomenon or are they more transient and somewhat superficial?

Some writers have been critical of the use of Gramsci's concept of hegemony, central to subculture theory (Hebdige, 1979: 15). Hegemony means that domination and conformity are achieved ideologically rather than through force or violence, for example by the control of education, the media and cultural production generally. Critics argue that the concept ignores the possibility of individual agency and reflexivity (that is, individual young people making decisions and choices about their lives and futures themselves regardless of youth subcultures), and suggests an almost robotic conformism to dominant cultural forms.

There has been considerable criticism of the subculture approach too from the point of view of it being difficult to verify in research terms. Critics have suggested the absence of supportive empirical work and even Dick Hebdige (a prominent member of the CCCS) cast some doubt on the validity of the subcultural theorists' work, suggesting that 'It is highly unlikely, for instance, that the members of any of the subcultures described in this book would recognise themselves reflected here' (1979: 139).

The British (specifically CCCS) literature on youth subcultures therefore raises many questions. Three critical points are considered here:

- youth subculture as leisure culture
- feminist views: social difference
- exaggerated and distorting: subculture as 'moral panic'.

Youth Subculture as Leisure Culture

Some analysts raise questions about tensions between *generations* rather than classes (Edmunds and Turner, 2002; Mannheim, 1952: 288). This asks about the extent to which youth values *are* any different to those of their parents: are society's central institutions really the focus of rebellion or resistance? Perhaps post-war teenage culture has been more a reflection of changing structures of working-class life and adult authority than any fundamental shift of values?

In prosperous societies, young people's leisure opportunities have widened, become more accessible and become increasingly part of commercial markets. Thus the post-war UK was characterized by relatively full employment and the expansion of service and commodity markets aimed specifically at young people and creating opportunities that released *some* young people from the imperatives of duty and responsibility. Drawing on Durkheim, Victor Turner and Mary Douglas to consider youth's 'liminal' status, Bernice Martin suggests that prior to the post-war revolution in consumption, this (truncated) status was traditionally managed through rituals of class boundary control interspersed with 'pockets of *framed* and licensed liminal excess' (1983: 138). Adolescence or youth is one such pocket. Martin's analysis draws on ideas of social boundary and category as offering a symbolic order that shapes cultural experiences. Classes, she argues, as antagonistic categories, structure different views of the world that cannot be mixed. Post-war working-class youth culture developed its characteristic cultural patterns of activity based on strong group commitments in which the individual body symbolized clear boundaries to the *social* body, thus suggesting that the 'body is a model that can stand for any bounded system' (Douglas, 1966: 142).

John Clarke's (1976) analysis of skinhead culture referred to above offers a clear example of tightly drawn bodies with exceptionally short hair, boots and jeans, football affiliations and community all marking the symbolic boundary of the group itself. Contrast the skinheads with middle-class youth cultures, classically the hippies or *grungers* and *emo* groups, and a very different body symbolism is evident: long hair, flowing and almost borderless clothes and music. This is a much more individualist and less group-oriented culture that reflects middle-class values.

The point to be made here is that these cultures have 'enlarged the site (time, place and resources) in which liminality prevails' (Martin, 1983: 149). This has, of course, applied not only to young people but also to adults. It is through the serial examples of youth culture and excess represented in the popular media that adults have become inured to this, and many adults have welcomed opportunities to engage in liminoid excess and expressiveness.

Yet can subcultures be considered as anything more than leisure-based peer or friendship groups? Leisure is a complex and paradoxical concept that is generally understood in the binary relation of 'work–leisure'. It designates an apparently inexhaustible range of practices, activities, and material and temporal spaces whose sole commonality is constituted by being defined and – *apparently* freely – chosen by participants as leisure. The paradox lies in leisure's potential for, and claims to, freedom; in leisure time being invariably understood as non-work time. Yet, it has a simultaneous designation as a setting in which young people, who have become commonly construed as a troublesome social category, are subjected to increasingly invasive adult surveillance. In societies where the individual is constantly expected to 'make something of him or herself', leisure also becomes a space (both material and temporal) in which intensive work occurs on the project of the self. As Rojek points out, leisure is no longer to be understood as 'free time', but as yet another domain in which people acquire and develop social and cultural capital (through developing their capacities, performance, physical bodies, knowledge and expertise, for example) and in which they are encouraged to cultivate their 'emotional intelligence and enhance [their] emotional labour capacities' (Rojek, 2010: 188). In that sense, leisure has become crucial in constructing late modern identities.

One of the characteristic features of late modernity is that the logic and certainty of social solidarity fostered by class identity have been supplanted by the much less certain, yet seductive, power of (individualized) consumption, which confers a sense of identity and status. As *consumed commodities*, leisure activities, fashions, and technologies may have real significance to young people as a source of stability, identity and a sense of wellbeing. There are, of course, many questions about inequitable access to leisure as consumption. Nevertheless, Bauman (2007) points out that, increasingly, Western societies are becoming characterized by *consumption* rather than *production* and that identities are formed more in the practices of consumption (organized, for example, in youth groups and subcultures) than in production (in the solidarity of work experiences). The 'leisure industries' are, of course, crucial in this as they have the capacity to create a fantastic range of leisure possibilities while simultaneously also apparently diminishing traditional associations between class and leisure activity (as suggested in the subcultures literature). For Bauman, and others, this raises interesting questions about the role of leisure as an institution of social control.

Figure 5.1 suggests a historical change from mass class-based leisure opportunities (which characterized the immediate post-war period) that mirrors shifts in youth transitions during the same period. Essentially, this is a much more fragmented view of leisure that apparently relies more on individual choice and agency although this is, inevitably, socially mediated (Ball, Maguire and Macrae, 2000; Bradford and Hey, 2007).

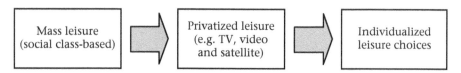

Figure 5.1 Changes in leisure processes

The leisure industry demonstrates aspects of both *seduction* and *repression*; in other words it creates new *opportunities* for consumption while also *constraining* choices (Bauman, 2007). Seduction relies on incorporating young people into proliferating markets that become highly significant as part of identity construction in the context of delayed or extended transitions. Bauman argues that seduction relies on a *willingness* to be seduced, similar to the ideological power that characterizes the *hegemony* that the subcultural theorists attribute to consumer markets. Aspects of a more repressive tendency might be identified through the shaping of choices, socialization into consumption, as well as questions of access to these markets. This might be connected with economic and class position (some choices are financially out of range), gender (some leisure spaces are highly gendered: young women, fearful of male violence and domination, retreat to 'bedroom culture' within domestic space), race (the threat of racialized violence which creates 'no-go' areas for some young people), disability (broad questions of physical access). Inevitably, these factors shape the formation of youth groups or subcultures.

The leisure industry has carefully commercialized 'resistance', 'outrage' and 'difference' in youth subcultures, using these to promote a range of commodities. This has frequently placed youth culture in liminal spaces: on the margins of illegality in the context of dance and club culture, the use of recreational drugs, alcohol, and sexual experimentation. Arguably, risky behaviour has become normalized in youth culture (Parker, Williams and Aldridge, 2002), yet it is this world that has created and sustained a multi-million pound Western market for fashion and music.

Feminist Views: Social Difference

The essentially *masculinist* slant in much of the subcultures literature from the CCCS (and the US literature before that) has been remorselessly criticized for ignoring not only gender relations but all social difference other than class.

Over to you...

Critical reflection

Think about the leisure lives of young women that you know or work with (perhaps in a youth project or club). What could you identify as examples of their own sense of agency within the broad cultural realm? You might think here of how they use or appropriate cultural artefacts (music or fashion, for example) to create identities, belonging, position and relationships. How do they see their own 'cultural practices' and how would they compare these to young men? Are girls' leisure practices and spaces simply different from those of boys? If so, does this have implications for professional work with young women?

Feminist sociologists discussing the male-dominated terrain of subcultural forms such as the teddy boys, mods, skinheads, and Rastafarians argued that girls and young women were rendered invisible in much of this sociology because gender as a social category was also hidden, as were women as a group. As early as 1975, Angela McRobbie began to critique youth subcultures literature as androcentric, as concentrating almost exclusively on the experiences of young men and marginalizing the experiences and activities of young women who were understood as peripheral to youth subcultures, playing only bit parts in male dramas. Critiques of the masculinist slant of many subcultural studies stimulated a range of studies on the experiences of young women, from McRobbie's work on secondhand fashion and girls' bedroom cultures (McRobbie, 1998; McRobbie and Garber, 1976, 2005) to work on similarly excluded groups such as black and minority ethnic young people (Alexander, 1996). Sheila Rowbotham made the general point in a succinct way some forty years ago.

> It is as if everything that relates only to us comes out in footnotes to the main text, as worthy of the odd reference. We come on the agenda somewhere between 'Youth' and 'Any Other Business'. We encounter ourselves in men's cultures as 'by the way' and peripheral. According to all the reflections we are not really there. (Rowbotham, 1973: 35)

The point here is not just that the subcultural theorists didn't 'spot the girls'. It is more the case that theory failed to read and understand young women's relationships to and position within popular cultural production and consumption. Perhaps young women are located on a different cultural and personal terrain and their lives, although deeply penetrated by class experiences, less preoccupied by opposition and class resistance. In short, girls' leisure spaces are different from those of boys'.

Exaggerated and Distorting: Subculture as 'Moral Panic'

From the 1950s onwards, in the UK at least, there was a proliferation of youth styles that were associated with distinctive subcultural groups. These were often interpreted as symbolically and materially threatening to the existing social order. Youth became a metaphor for change and a source of considerable social anxiety. However, it is important to acknowledge that this anxiety was already becoming established in the interwar years.

Over to you...

Read, watch films and critically reflect

There are many examples in novels and films of the 1940s and 1950s of a growing sense of anxiety and fear of young people, often focused on young men in particular. I have chosen to look at two here. First, Graham Greene's novel '*Brighton Rock*', published 1938 and made into a film in 1947 can be read as reflecting contemporary social anxieties about the association between crime and youth in classic 'good and evil' terms. Green's character Pinkie Brown is the introverted 17-year-old leader of a Brighton racetrack gang whose protection racket involves violence and extortion. In the classic film noir version of *Brighton Rock*, Pinkie is a tragic, nihilistic yet stylish, figure who seems to represent the essence of 'otherness'. He reflects much wider fears about what can happen if young men are not properly absorbed into respectable working-class life.

The second example comes from a film made in 1953, *The Wild One*, starring Marlon Brando who appears as Johnny Strabler, the leader of motorcycle gang (prefiguring the rockers, who emerged into public consciousness a little later in the UK). There are lots of classic lines in the film but the following sums up a particular representation of youth:

'Hey Johnny, what are you rebelling against ...?'
Pause ...
'What've you got ...?'

Since the interwar years, style has been crucial in thinking about youth culture. By this we mean:

▶

- Image and appearance
- Demeanour, expression and posture
- Vocabulary

Can we see Pinkie and Johnny expressing style ... proto-teenagers heralding the proliferation of youth styles that emerged a few years on?

You might also like to think about these two characters: what kind of young men are they and what do they have in common? To some extent they both appear tormented and brooding, inward looking and troubled. You should also look at how young women are represented here. Both films have important female characters; again they have some aspects in common. At least in their cinematic representations, young women are seen as a kind of 'civilizing force' a kind of counterweight to male transgression (look at Kathie, for example, in *The Wild One*). What does this tell us about the discourse of youth?

Post-war anxieties about youth and youth culture should be understood as constituting an important social process that has, broadly, shaped public views of young people since the 1950s and which led to youth being regarded as a social problem. Indeed, youth services in the UK were revitalized in the early 1960s partially as a consequence of the process in which youth became highly visible in the mid and late 1950s, partially through media obsessions with transgressive youth.

Figure 5.2 suggests the basic elements that form the process in which youth becomes increasingly understood in problematic terms as a consequence of adult reaction to young people rather than the nature of young people's activities specifically. These reactions and responses to youth have shaped a broad (and often negative) discourse of youth (Griffin, 1993; Bradford, 2007).

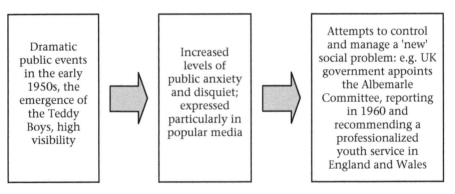

Figure 5.2   Moral panic as social process

The process outlined here is classically referred to as 'moral panic' a term coined by Jock Young in his work on drug users in the 1960s (Young, 1971), but associated in particular with Stan Cohen's seminal work *Folk Devils and Moral Panics* (S. Cohen, 1972). In this analysis, the *folk devil* is evocative of the scapegoat, a kind of 'blank figure', onto which a range of anxieties (invariably about social order) is projected (Hetherington, 2005: 247) and which are carried on behalf of the community. Arguably, young people (in countless guises) have become *the* folk devils of our times.

Cohen suggests that the popular media were responsible for the creation of these social groups by successfully *labelling* them and focusing on their activities as a particular form of working-class *deviance*. Labelling theory contains two basic component ideas. First, deviant conduct is not simply the violation of a norm but conduct that can *successfully be defined* as deviant by others; it thus entails a power *relation* (the definers and the defined). Second, this act of labelling produces or potentially amplifies deviance. The overall point here is that deviance is *relational*; it is not a quality or characteristic of a particular act (such as jostling or congregating on the street), rather it is the consequence of effective labelling by others (those in a powerful position, media or politicians, for example) whose definitions are likely to stick. This approach defines actions as part of *process*, rather than simply as *events*.

On mods and rockers in the 1960s, Cohen suggests that the popular media actually *created* them as social groups:

> At the beginning of the decade, the term 'Modernist' referred simply to a style of dress, the term 'Rocker' was hardly known outside the small groups which identified themselves this way. Five years later, a newspaper editor was to refer to the Mods and Rockers incidents as 'without parallel in English history' and troop reinforcements were rumoured to have been sent to quell public disturbances. Now, another five years later, these groups have all but disappeared from the public consciousness. (Cohen, 1972: 10–11)

Rather than suggesting that the mods and rockers existed somewhere 'out there' as social groups, Cohen suggests that they are a construction of the media and its reporting practices. He goes on to look at how the media actively intervened and engaged to exacerbate – to *amplify* deviance through the processes and practices of identifying and reporting events – tensions and violence in the bank holiday outings of scooter and motorcycle groups to places such as Clacton and Brighton.

More recently in the literature of moral panic, Critcher points out that moral panics 'are ostensibly about new forms of troubling behaviour which society appears unable to control … a reaction to changes: bad things are happening which didn't used to' (Critcher, 2006: 7). The media, politicians, pressure groups, and other 'moral entrepreneurs' (those who believe they are the right people to define the public interest) often foment moral panics. There are lots of current examples, including young people wearing 'hoodies', young Muslim men and teenage parents, all exemplifying contemporary *folk devils*. The important point here is that the moral panic may begin with a genuinely new topic or circumstance; a key event that generates media and public interest or concern. It can rapidly take on a life of its own, fanned by publicity, which itself generates public anxiety, feeding further concern and anxiety and so on (another example of the way in which the spiral of amplification works).

Goode and Ben-Yehuda (2009: 49) offer useful criteria for identifying what might count as a moral panic. First, they point to five elements that characterize most moral panics:

1. concern or fear about the conduct of an identified group
2. expression of hostility towards that group
3. generalized view or social consensus on the nature of the threat posed
4. disproportion between the concern and the threat
5. volatility surrounding the concern: moral panics are quick to erupt and to die down.

Within this framework, the demand that 'something should be done' receives a response in the event of successful labelling of the phenomenon causing concern. Goode and Ben-Yehuda go on to identify the settings and social actors around whom moral panics coalesce and by whom they are expressed:

1. general public
2. media
3. social movements
4. politicians and legislators
5. law enforcers.

Although clearly an engaging and generative concept, the idea of the moral panic has had its critics, mainly focusing on the question of disproportionality, which has always been central to the concept. Some critics have argued, for example, that issues considered to be moral panics (those associated with drug or excessive alcohol use, for example) are matters of *real* concern and that social responses are not disproportionate. Other commentators have suggested that globalized risk societies generate new and unanticipated threats: global warming, HIV/AIDS or nuclear 'meltdown', for example. These unanticipated and almost anonymous conse-quences of the new technologies and their faceless agents are argued to be quite different from the concerns that underlay the original moral panics, such as the mods and rockers of the 1960s and 1970s. They were associated with *known* threats and concerns and were temporally and geographically bounded. The argument here is that unbounded global threats have supplanted the older delimited concerns that drove moral panic.

Other critics have suggested that the *moral* aspect of moral panic has changed and that late modern risk societies no longer demonstrate the collective morality that underlay earlier sensibilities, therefore specifically *moral* panics cannot exist.

However, and despite these criticisms, even a casual reading of some of the tabloid press (*The Sun* or the *Daily Mail* are excellent examples) shows that the older forms of moral panic persist in addition to these wider globalized threats that allegedly generate so much social anxiety. Goode and Ben-Yehuda point out how public perceptions of risk are dispropor-tionate in comparison with the calculations made by technical experts. There seems to be a tendency here, as in the 'traditional' moral panic, for disproportionality.

Over to you...

Critical reflection

Using Goode and Ben-Yehuda's criteria, try to identify a moral panic that has emerged over the past year or two (there are lots of examples that you could use here: the so-called 'legal high' users, binge drinkers or video gamers and social networking). Use the framework suggested to identify how the moral panic emerged and who was involved. What were the various stages of the moral panic and which social actors were involved and at which points? Make some notes on each aspect of the moral panic itself and the social actors who were part of it. You could try to draw a timeline to map out the panic and that should help you to see the process involved. What can you learn about the particular concern or those on whom the concern is focused? Does the analysis help to clarify what's going on, put things in a better perspective or simply offer a new way of looking at the world? What might this all mean for practice with young people?

This part of the discussion began by looking at criticisms of the concept of subculture. Subculture can be linked to the concept of moral panic and some critics of recent sociology of youth have argued that the subcultures literature has too easily confirmed a negative discourse of youth. Davis (1990), for example, has suggested that this literature has a number of deficiencies. First, most young people have never belonged to subcultures and even where they do, it is methodologically inappropriate to characterize them solely on that criterion; this entails the *reification* of subculture. Second, the literature tends to focus on the exotic and the problematic, thus contributing to the idea that young people are 'other'. Third, the literature overgeneralizes from specific subcultures to the totality of youth.

What is important, however, is to acknowledge the powerful symbolic role that young people and youth have in Western societies. Youth has reflected a social ambivalence, becoming a kind of 'screen' (Davis, 1990: 22) onto which hopes and anxieties have been projected, youth being either national asset (the positive view) or the folk devil already referred to (the negative view). Youth is also, as Martin (1983) suggests, a liminal status that has expanded enormously since the Second World War and around which moral panics have absorbed and channelled recurrent waves of adult anxiety that have accompanied the rapid social changes occurring since. It is noticeable that the terms used in relation to many of these folk devils, seen as the source of disorder (real or potential), rely on vocabularies of *purity* and *pollution*. Consider, for example, how in recent times, young Travellers, 'chavs', young migrants to the UK, drug users, benefit scroungers ('the underclass'), teenage mothers (the exemplar here is Vicky Pollard in *Little Britain* but it is easy to identify a gallery of grotesque young people in popular culture) have been clearly regarded as outsiders, undesirables and, as Mary Douglas (1966) might put it, as *dirt*: 'matter out of place'. The point of that argument is that transgression is constituted in the breaking of boundaries or taboos, of polluting by crossing a symbolic boundary. Such transgression threatens the coherent and socially established categories that maintain social order. Youth as a symbolic category so often appears to be cast in the role of pollutant by virtue of its liminality, its 'between-ness' and capacity to overstep boundaries.

A more recent criticism of subcultural theory comes from Jenks who suggests that youth subculture is 'an idea that has run its course' (Jenks, 2005: 145). Subculture, he suggests, reflects a preference for the exotic or 'other'. The concept has an underlying and paradoxical inclination to *reaction* and, as such, is a form of containment, 'a kind of cognitive wrapping paper and string with which to bundle up clusters of deviance, criminality, ethnicity, poverty or just generations' (Jenks, 2005: 144). Sociology's great value lies in its acknowledgement of the ordinariness of transgression and the absolute embedded-ness of the unusual (or the irrational) within society. Perhaps there is something about the concept of subculture that resists this.

Nevertheless, as Bennett points out, subculture theory, and the work of the CCCS in particular, was important in sensitizing sociology and sociologists to the cultural processes that have characterized late capitalism. This has led to 'progressive understandings of everyday life' (2005: 29). Whether such understanding is generalized beyond sociology is a moot point. However, the work has drawn attention to the capacity of young people – as active agents – in shaping their everyday and cultural experiences rather than passively accepting 'culture from above'. Shildrick and MacDonald (2006) argue that the legacy of CCCS work and in particular its attention to difference and inequality still has much to offer the sociology of youth. They are critical of what they refer to as 'post-sub-cultural studies' (for example Bennett, 2005; Hodkinson and Deicke, 2007) because by 'focusing in on the most obviously stylistic forms of contemporary youth culture (whose adherents might be argued to be predominantly drawn from more advantaged social positions) these studies are less likely to be able to uncover evidence of how class, and other social divisions, delimits youth cultural possibilities' (Shildrick and MacDonald, 2006: 136). Shildrick and MacDonald believe that aspects of the CCCS project should be rejuvenated because of its explanatory power and capacity to point towards the inequalities of capitalist society and its implications for young people. Having considered subcultures as transgressive entities, the following section briefly explores the broader sociology of deviance.

Deviance, Youth and Transgression

In a very simple and straightforward sense, deviant conduct is anything that departs from a set of social norms accepted by a significant number of members of a community or society. From this starting point, it can be assumed that some kind of *boundary* exists that is somehow crossed, breached or transgressed in certain circumstances that become understood or labelled as 'beyond the pale'. In other words, the deviant or transgressive act breaches accepted values or norms. Without a *socially defined* boundary, no such act can occur. For example, in most places and at most times, murder is seen as a crime although what counts as murder may be difficult to define. It is likely to depend almost entirely on historical, social and cultural positions and who is defining what for whom. Drinking alcohol may well be regarded as a serious crime in one country or culture, as a possible crime for *some* people in another but socially expected in yet another setting.

Ideas of what counts as 'deviance' can take many forms then, including drug-taking, particular sexual behaviour, unusual lifestyles, political perspectives, even fashions, as well as the more obviously *criminal* behaviour such as theft, burglary and so on. The American sociologist Howard Becker pointed out that societies 'create' deviance by establishing rules whose infringement constitutes deviance. He argued that deviance is not a qualitative characteristic of particular actions; rather it is the consequence of the successful application of those rules.

[S]ocial groups create deviance by making the rules whose infraction constitutes deviance, and by applying these rules to particular people and labelling
them as outsiders ... deviance is not a quality of the act a person commits, but
rather the consequence of the application by others of rules and sanctions to
an 'offender'. The deviant is one to whom that label has successfully been
applied. (Becker, 1963: 9)

It is important to establish, from the outset, that deviant behaviour,
defined as above, is (potentially, at least) *quite* different to criminal behaviour. It can *include* crime but this is only a very small part of a range of
activities and practices that include all acts that deviate from, or transgress,
social boundaries of some sort. This is the key point. It is highly likely that
many people engage in deviant or criminal behaviour at some time in their
lives, if not on a regular basis. To give some relatively trivial but commonplace examples, using work stationery for personal purposes and using the
work telephone for personal calls or the desk computer for accessing a Facebook page or football team homepage may be, technically, infringements of
law and could be classified as criminal behaviour. However, many people do
these things on a regular basis and many people probably see them as
'normal'. The use of drugs such as cannabis is widespread but clearly illegal.
However, in some groups, cannabis use might be the norm and *not* to use
cannabis could be considered deviant in some circumstances. Therefore,
the same practice (using cannabis) can be illegal, deviant and normal simultaneously, depending on the perspective taken and the social groups to
which one belongs. Durkheim (1982: 102) made the point that a complex
relationship exists between deviance, difference and crime and that deviant
conduct and deviants sometimes exist in a kind of 'edge' space, somewhere
on the borderlands of 'normal' society, not always attracting sanctions
specified by law but probably subject to other forms of social control (either
successfully or ineffectively applied).

Becker suggests that deviance is constituted in the *successful* definition of
certain conduct or behaviours as deviant and in making this point he draws
attention to the significance of power. In one sense, deviant acts or behaviour only exist by virtue of power relations. It is worth having a look at
some of Becker's work. His book *Outsiders* (1963) is an accessible and fascinating account of his approach to understanding deviant behaviour and
practices. Becker's seminal paper *Becoming a Marijuana User* (1953) can easily
be accessed online (http://www.soc.washington.edu/users/brines/becker.
pdf). As Becker points out, powerful interests can often manipulate what
constitutes deviance. It is worth considering how black young people in
Western societies have become subject to 'stop and search' procedures
simply for being on the street – 'in the wrong place at the wrong time'.

There is frequently a racist assumption of deviance – or criminality – in their very being (Delsol and Shiner, 2006; Bowling and Phillips, 2007).

Social norms are usually accompanied by formal and informal sanctions intended to promote conformity. These include the (formal) law, but can also entail (informal) social disapproval. In some ways the latter can be a more powerful social 'police force'. There are lots of interesting and important examples of where this works. Two forms of social control are suggested here.

Over to you...

Critical reflection

First, reflect on the phenomenon of 'gossip'. In societies that are characterized by close face-to-face relationships (often defined as traditional societies), gossip can have real importance as an informal mechanism of social control. It can confirm or destroy reputation and lead to people modifying or changing their behaviour because of the fear of humiliation or shaming in the public domain. Have you ever been the subject of gossip? What did it feel like and did it affect your conduct?

The second example concerns the way in which gender is 'worked out' in educational settings. You might think about your own experiences here or those of young people with whom you work. How do peers or teachers police masculinity or femininity in the classroom? What are the consequences for those who transgress the sometimes unspoken but powerful norms of sexuality and sexual identity that prevail in these spaces?

To get a sense of the consequences of these forms of social control (gossip and gender discourses), you might look at Bradford and Clark's work (2011) on the identities of LGBT young people's experiences growing up in Malta. This is a society characterized by dense networks of close face-to-face relationships and a relatively 'traditional' world view influenced by a still powerful Church.

Childhood is a period in the life course when people are socialized into the norms that characterize their societies. Most of this is unconscious and transmitted by parents, teachers, siblings and peers. However, in the period of youth, young people challenge some of these social norms often in a licensed and legitimate way: a kind of socially sanctioned deviance. Overall, this challenge is mounted in a wide variety of ways, from the relatively innocuous bedroom cultures characterized by online gaming or music, to overt criminal behaviour, with many different forms in-between (this is Durkheim's point that there are degrees of divergence from the norm). In this sense, adolescence, or youth, has often been characterized as a period of almost *natural* deviance or transgression of which subculture is just an external expression. Interestingly, and controversially, current work in brain science seems to claim that young people are somehow 'hard-wired' to behave in these ways (Bessant, 2008). As Martin puts it, post-war youth in the UK became 'a vastly expanded *frame* within which all the contractual, instrumental and constricting disciplines of societas held no sway – it was one long "evening of masks and freedom"' (Martin, 1983: 150).

The apparent synonymy between youth, adolescence and deviance is highlighted in authoritarian and liberal literatures on these subjects. Hence, there is consensus that young people are *deviant* in some manner and to a greater or lesser extent, and that position characterizes the dominant discourse of youth and adolescence in Western cultures (see Bradford, 2004, for an account of this). The highly influential work of the nineteenth-century American psychologist G. Stanley Hall, which set the terms of reference for understanding the meaning of adolescence at the beginning of the twentieth century, considers adolescence as pathologically deviant. Hall's work can be found online (http://www.archive.org/details/adolescenceitsp00hallgoog).

Despite this dominant and negative view of youth, deviance in youth can include colourful, expressive behaviour, creative musical and theatrical work, body manipulation and art and other practices that make positive contributions to cultural life. Hence, deviance (as constitutive of difference) can be a positive and powerful force. Challenges to social norms can also take the form of exciting and stimulating creative expressions that provide a glimpse of desirable alternatives that contrast markedly with experiences of everyday life (some analysts characterized the 2011 street disturbances in London and elsewhere in this way). During the last 40 years or so, there has been a tendency to continue this manifestation of (deviant) youthful behaviour into later, adult life. One historian has labelled this phenomenon a hedonistic 'modern immaturity' (Cross, 2008).

Before Chapter 5 is concluded, we refer to one aspect of cultural life that is not usually considered deviant as such: individualism and consumerism. It has already been suggested that in the post-war period the UK and other similar societies were shaped by an era of strong and increased individualization. Zygmunt Bauman offers an important discussion of what he sees as the increasing 'absence of society' in this context and in one sense, Bauman points towards this as being transgressive or betraying of the social.

Over to you...

Critical reading and reflection

Download Bauman's paper on http://www.jrf.org.uk/publications/absence-society or read it in Utting (2009).

Paradoxically, and reflecting a position that Durkheim would have recognized, Bauman suggests that the social ills currently afflicting Western societies derive from the diminishing of the social bond (society) rather than its increasing demands. In other words, individualism has created a range of tensions for late modern societies. See what you make of Bauman's arguments and if you want to pick up on similar discussions, look at chapters by Neil Lawson or Stephen Thake, in Utting (2009).

The position taken by Bauman and others seems strongly oppositional to political trends that have been influential since the 1980s. You may feel, however, that the way in which the so-called Big Society in the UK has been invoked by the coalition government as the solution to contemporary ills is highly ideological (for example, its celebration of volunteers and voluntary activities may be a way of justifying cuts to public services). What do you think? Will some of the ideas proposed here create the renewed social bond that Bauman and others argue is important?

For many young people, discourses of individualism (tied up in a range of exhortations to 'make something of yourself' in education and the labour market) have, arguably, been very important influences. An overemphasis upon 'the self', one's self-interest, appearance, and individual wellbeing can be understood as a kind of 'transgression': a form of deviance. However, it might be suggested that this preoccupation with self as a kind of narcissism, sometimes to the point of excess, has become the norm. Fin Cullen's research, for example, on young women and alcohol shows the extent to which young women's leisure drinking cultures are understood in terms of transgression, excess and a kind of deviant femininity (Cullen, 2010), often reflecting middle-class perceptions of working-class lifestyles. The sociological questions here are to do with the practices and mechanisms in which excess becomes defined – by whom and in relation to whom?

Much sociological research demonstrates that young people's access to the social, economic and cultural resources to become successful varies enormously and is shaped by social difference (Bradford and Hey, 2010; Johnston, 2011). However, individualism itself *could* be characterized as departing (*deviating*) from social norms embodied in various concepts of 'community' or from the demands of collective life and shared responsibilities (Day,

2006). The often quoted (perhaps apocryphal) comment of Margaret Thatcher, the British prime minister in the 1980s that 'there is no such thing as society' appears particularly pertinent to young people who were growing up at that time and those who are currently in transition to adulthood. While welfare benefits were (and are) being cut, jobs were (and are) harder to find and youth training schemes of various types were (and might be) introduced for young people who were not incorporated in education or the labour market, there appeared an unprecedented scrutiny of young people's lives in many and various ways. The experience of 'community' and 'society' arguably left some young people's lives untouched during this period. While parents and others often accuse young people of selfishness there seem to be generations (adults and young people) for whom individualism and consumerism are far more powerful motifs than conceptions of and investments in *collective* society. Arguably, the patterns of consumption that grew during the 1980s and 1990s continue to resonate, although the post-recessionary economies of Europe and the world (some parts and groups more than others) will no doubt influence this enormously.

Summary and Conclusions

Youth culture and youth subculture are central themes in the sociology of youth. The origins of these concepts have been explored in Chapter 5. As suggested in Chapter 1, youth culture is a consequence of the processes leading to modernity, although there is evidence of aspects of youth culture of sorts existing in pre-modern times. Broadly, youth cultures emerge in modern capitalist societies – nation states – in which youth is marked out as somehow separate from other age groups, through institutions of education, training or the labour market, for example. Sociologies of youth culture arose in the United States in the first half of the twentieth century and reflected a preoccupation with young people and youth (often young men) in that society. Seminal work in the US in the 1940s and 1950s considered both youth culture and subculture. Subculture was seen as largely compensatory, providing a sense of identity and self-esteem for youth who had not achieved through education and was characterized by aspects of *leisure, pleasure and resistance* (this is a very familiar perspective in current times). More functionalist accounts of youth culture emphasized its institutional importance in socializing young people into the world beyond the family. Leisure as a principal cultural site and institution of modernity was central to both these perspectives.

In the UK, from the 1960s, the sociology of youth subculture was greatly influenced by Marxist sociology through the pivotal work of the Centre for

Contemporary Cultural Studies at Birmingham University. This concentrated on the centrality of class from a *cultural* rather than economic perspective, again emphasizing the significance of leisure as a site for cultural expression. It meant that the sociologists of youth became especially interested in aspects of youth style, its symbolism and capacity to express class values as a resistance to bourgeois culture and institutions: school or work, for example. Although largely focused on working-class youth and subculture, studies of middle-class youth and its collective resistance through protest movements or drug use, for example, as *counter-culture* were part of the literature on subculture. Thus, *resistance* was a central idea in this literature, whether focused on working-class or middle-class youth.

Sociologies of youth culture and subculture share an interest in both *instrumental* and *expressive* dimensions. Subculture can be understood instrumentally as a response to circumstances shared by youth: its subordinate social position or marginality in the labour market, for example. Subcultures can also be seen as expressive entities offering social spaces in which creative responses can be made to shared experiences through music, fashion, literature and so on. Chapter 5 touched on critiques of subculture theory and referred to its apparent gender-neutrality, its leisure-oriented approach and the tendency to generalize across youth from the experiences of spectacular or deviant minorities. The sociology of youth subcultures remains influential along with the sociology of youth transitions discussed in Chapter 3.

Youth as a source and focus of social anxiety was a central theme of Chapter 5 and the concept of *moral panic* defines the social processes in which young people come to be seen as problematic and deviant. Youth in modernity has become something of a screen onto which broader anxieties about social change (specifically *adult* anxieties) have been projected and through which they are symbolized. The media have been especially culpable in exaggerating young people's propensities for deviance or crime.

Policymakers and youth practitioners should remember that good sociology indicates that most young people do not belong to subcultures, gangs or similar groups and most do not commit crime or become involved in drug use. Through rigorous research and theorizing, sociology can point out these facts. However, it is also important to acknowledge that some sociology has, perhaps, failed to be sufficiently reflexive. It has contributed to interpreting the experiences of *particular* young people to account for the *general* category of youth; sociologists should always take account of their own appeal to deploy a sociological imagination.

Further Reading

- Fowler, D. (2008) *Youth Culture in Modern Britain, 1920–1970*, Basingstoke: Palgrave Macmillan.

  Fowler's book contains chapters that show the importance of youth cultures in pre-war Britain and Ireland and the cultural significance of the 'cult of youth' in the early part of the twentieth century.

- Jenks, C. (2005) *Subculture. The fragmentation of the social*, London: Sage Publications.

  Jenks is critical of the whole concept of subculture, suggesting that it places youth outside of the mainstream of society and thus of sociology itself.

- Hodkinson, P. and Deicke, W. (eds) (2007) *Youth Cultures, Scenes, Subcultures and Tribes*, London: Routledge.

  This collection of studies raises questions about the coherence of youth as a concept in late modernity and its meaning in the light of apparently fragmented youth cultures and subcultures.

- Gelder, K. (ed.) (2005) *The Subcultures Reader* (2nd edn), London: Routledge.

  A collection of classic readings on the theme of subcultures.

- Khosravi, S. (2008) *Young and Defiant in Tehran*, Philadelphia: University of Pennsylvania Press.

  This is a fine ethnographic study of youth in contemporary Iran and the significance of identity, generation, opposition and defiance in a country where change and constancy are both important.

6

Being Somewhere

Youth, Space and Place

Introduction

Chapter 6 considers the significance of space and place in relation to youth. Young people's lives should be understood in the context of the spaces and places in which they are located, or to put it another way, young people's identities (like those of others) are always *emplaced* in social, material, discursive and, increasingly, virtual spaces and places (connected with the internet). Biographies and life histories are fundamentally shaped by the experiences associated with different spaces and places: the home, the classroom, the street or the workplace, for example.

Youth Space and Place

First, the terms space and place and their significance for young people are defined. Formally, *space* can be understood as a three-dimensional environment where things happen and objects exist and in which they have both direction and are positioned (Harrison and Dourish, 1996). On the other hand, *place* is an aspect of space invested with particular cultural meaning, which becomes significant at particular times and for particular participants. For example, young people's presence 'on the street' at particular times, mainly after dark, sometimes transforms it into something menacing and intimidating for others. Elderly people can experience a small parade of local shops as a lifeline in the daytime but at night, it can be entirely out of bounds because of the presence of young people.

Over to you...

Watch, reflect and research

Watch the film *Harry Brown*, with Michael Caine as Harry. The film exploits the visceral anxieties that are sometimes generated by urban landscapes, in this case the streets of south London. The film illustrates very effectively how particular spaces in the urban landscape become understood in specific ways and associated with certain groups and experiences. We shouldn't imagine that it is only urban landscapes that are amenable to such imaginings. James Watkins' 2008 horror movie *Eden Lake* evokes similar anxieties but partially sets these in a rural lakeside location. Indeed, you could see the symbolism of the lake itself (fluid and constantly moving) as reflecting the liminal status (their betwixt and between character) of the young hoodies who terrorize Jenny and Steve, the leading characters in the film.

Harry Brown and *Eden Lake* seem to reflect social anxieties about the state of Britain and British society, focus these on young people and locate the narratives of both films in very clearly imagined places that contribute to the sense of menace invoked both by place and characters. It's probably worth considering who finds these films disturbing. Does everyone experience similar anxieties or particular sections of the population: might gender or class be important in shaping how these films are watched and understood?

Have you ever felt frightened in a public place? Where and when did this occur and what was it that frightened you? Would this place be different at a different time of the day, and what would make it different? You might explore some of these questions with young people. What are their views of their own neighbourhoods and the safe or scary places that exist?

Let us return to the idea of place. One way of thinking about place as a concept is to see it as a space 'which people in a given locality understand as having a particular history and as arousing emotional identifications, and which is associated with particular groups and activities' (Watt and Stenson, 1998).

This definition points to the distinctively social nature of place: place is constituted or constructed through the meanings attributed by those involved. The quotation also suggests that *place* is much more than simply a location in space; it becomes place through the social and cultural meanings that are attached to it.

Many of the spaces and places that are experienced in everyday life are associated with different things by different people and may even be contested in some way or another: for example how Iraq or Afghanistan is spatially contested in the context of war, the sectarian designation of neighbourhoods in Belfast, a controversial planning application for the development of 'green belt' land, and family disputes over the use of particular rooms in the home. At a micro level, the emergence of bedroom cultures in which young people (mainly in the relatively prosperous global North) are able to develop aspects of lifestyle or communicate with peers from all over the world means that domestic space – the bedroom – has, for some relatively privileged young people, been completely reconfigured in the last few decades. For some, bedrooms are spaces of opportunity (and possible risk and exposure to unknown dangers), of entertainment, fun, intimacy and relationship (Lincoln, 2004).

Space and place are, then, subject to definition and, as the examples above show, those definitions can shift around. As with the concept of *labelling* discussed in the previous chapter, power relations may be very important and the definition that sticks may be a consequence of these. Different participants may have different views of what characterizes particular spaces at particular times. In Table 6.1, some of the spaces that contribute to young people's experiences of the world are identified.

Table 6.1 Space and place

Spaces and places	Young people's lived experiences
The home: domestic space	How gendered is this? What about the domestic division of labour: who does what? What kind of regulatory regime prevails and does this lead to intergenerational tension, for example? Opportunity shaped by economics: size of dwelling and partitioning of space. Privacy?
The school: educational space	Safe and dangerous spaces: corridors and playgrounds; classrooms and school gates? How are these spaces regulated and watched formally or informally?
The club, park or football ground: leisure space	Safe and dangerous spaces: How are these spaces regulated and surveyed? How are they formally and informally organized and by whom?
The street: public space	Autonomous space: hanging around, hanging out, messing about, having a laugh; young people often seen as a polluting influence in shopping malls, for example; surveillance and spatial or temporal curfews as means of regulation. How do age, gender and race and disability shape these spaces?

The first point that can be made from Table 6.1 is that space and place both matter in shaping ideas of youth. Two further examples will show this. There has been recent speculation (and some evidence) in the media that the UK government's housing benefit cuts will mean that 'the poor' will, in the next 15 years or so, no longer be able to live in southern England, and will be confined to areas of cheap housing north of a line drawn roughly between the Wash and the Severn. In that sense, space matters initially from an economic perspective and the other aspects of life deriving from economic position.

The importance of space and place for young people also becomes evident by Googling 'post code wars' and listening to young people's views about place on YouTube clips. Issues of identity, rivalry, territory and, above all, space (real or imagined) are clearly matters, sometimes, of life and death. Some of the young people on the clips (and on various blogs) seem to have 'mental maps' of the areas in which they live (see Brent, 2009). There is also an understanding that location in a certain space creates all sorts of expectations about how to behave, how to conduct yourself, who to talk to and not to talk to, and how to talk. The sociological point here is that space and place constrain or enable different kinds of social practices. Chapter 3 discussed young people's sense of self in public and private worlds and, in one sense, the public and the private can be understood in a distinctively spatialized way. The private is often thought as being constituted by intimacy and the public as somehow existing 'out there'. These worlds, at least in the West, are clearly demarcated in spatial terms. Home and work are, for example, generally very different spaces. However, prior to the Industrial Revolution, the domestic world was the centre of both production and consumption. Clearly, space matters.

Over to you...

Critically reflect and research

There are several ways in which you might think further about questions of space and place as they emerge in Table 6.1. These questions are especially important to young people and to those who work with them. Young people are acutely aware of issues of safety and danger and how these are linked to space and place. So, you might want to think about the relations between friendly space and hostile space and how particular places become understood as friendly or hostile. You might explore this with young people you work with or who you know. There are several important factors here.

● Space is fluid: different groups form place in different ways and at different times so a place is probably not *essentially* hostile; it may become so at different times.

- Space is gendered: so domestic spaces may be safe or dangerous and we know that gendered violence invariably occurs in such spaces rather than in public space.

- Space is often racialized: local areas become associated with specific groups and may be 'no-go' areas for others. This may be because of political groups such as the English Defence League or the BNP being active in particular locations.

- Space may also embody aspects of class: middle-class and working-class young people may understand particular spaces in quite different ways.

- Space and power are linked: it may be possible to identify strategies of control and influence in particular areas. These may be based on aggressive or defensive practices.

Whether a person comes from the global North or the South, northern or southern England, a rural or urban setting, or whether they live in a house or flat, these are all factors of space and place that are likely to shape their life and experience of the world.

Space and place should be understood as fundamentally sociological in the sense that the capacity to constrain or enable social processes, practices and relations is always spatialized. A good example of this can be found in the work of the sociologist Erving Goffman. Goffman wrote prolifically about how identity and self are constituted in ritual performances and displays in everyday settings. His work draws on the metaphor of social life as a drama and he points out that identity performances can often be thought of as having both *front-stage* and *back-stage* aspects, a little like a theatre performance. What Goffman is suggesting here is that social life occurs in different sociological spaces: the *front stage* demands a performance that is understood in a particular way by a particular audience and is constrained and enabled by specific cultural factors. On the other hand, the *back stage* is a space in which other cultural norms may prevail, encouraging different kinds of performance and presentations of self and identity (Goffman, 1959). It might mean, for example, that in these back-stage spaces people are more relaxed, disclosing, or more willing to express intimate aspects of self.

Over to you...

Critically reflect

Thinking about Goffman's distinction between front stage and back stage, identify examples from your own experience of front and back-stage identities that you might perform.

Consider how you present yourself in a professional meeting when senior managers might be present, and how different this might be from the times when you are together with a few close colleagues. What is important here is that there are no 'absolute' back and front-stage spaces in our lives. For example, when a university lecturer is front stage with students in the lecture theatre she presents herself in a way that is constrained by the requirements of the occasion and the rules and norms that are familiar to everyone present. However, in the Senior Common Room afterwards, the lecturer may also be front stage and unlikely to say too much about the gaps in her knowledge to which a particular student was able to draw attention. The constraints in that space may be different from those in the lecture theatre but nonetheless important.

For Goffman, these presentations (construed as individual and collective attempts to maintain social coherence) are always to be located in sociological space.

Chapter 3 referred to family and community being *imagined*. The 'family imaginary', or the 'imagined community', for example, are representations that are born of our capacities and practices of imagination. That, of course, doesn't make them any the less real in their power to shape how people think about themselves and who they are. Space and place are similarly imagined.

I was recently reminded of the power of imagined place to invoke strong and sometimes negative feelings and responses when I undertook the research evaluation of a local Surestart project located on a large 1930s local authority housing estate, referred to earlier as Westfield. As part of this I met with local residents, young people and a range of professionals and service providers to get their views and perspectives on the area and the services that were provided and needed. I was immediately aware of the varying imaginations that were at work in constructing representations of this estate in particular ways. Different people spoke of the estate as 'home', 'friendly and familiar', 'deprived', 'dangerous', 'outlawed' and 'no-go'. For young people who lived there, the micro-spaces of the estate were understood in great detail: there were areas that were too dangerous to traverse at specific times while at others, there was little threat; there were special places where they could meet with friends, undisturbed by anyone outside of the group and there were other places that only came alive at specific times of the day or night. For older people, parts of the estate could be marked off as 'safe', 'open' or 'dangerous' depending on the time of the day. Most people who lived on the estate, young and old, were able to categorize different streets, pubs and shopping areas on the basis of a complex and, often, nuanced symbolic order.

However, it is also important that estates such as Westfield are recognized as *home* for many people who live there and are held by them in some affection. We were reminded on numerous occasions that the estate represented security and stability for many. One of the members of the Surestart project's steering group, Sally, had lived on the estate since she had been a small child. She described Westfield in one interview:

> 'It has changed but there is still a sense of community around and people look out for each other. You know that when you've been into town and you come back ... there's a sort of feeling of "well, you know where you are here" and that you know people around you. Mostly, I know everyone in my street and though they can be a bit nosey they also keep an eye on what's happening ... I wouldn't really want to live anywhere else in (town).'

Another member of the steering group, Jen, had moved out of Westfield for a year to another part of the town but had come back:

> 'It was terrible ... people didn't want to know us when they knew that we'd been in Westfield ... that was it ... we never really settled there and we couldn't wait to get back.'

It was also clear from some of our interviews that once one goes beneath the surface, the everyday taken-for-granted of any particular place, it becomes evident that all sorts of claims and counterclaims emerge about who 'belongs' and who is 'outsider'. In Westfield, long standing residents who originally came from Ireland, the Caribbean or South Asia saw more recent arrivals from Poland and Lithuania as outsiders and with little real claim to being in the area. Families whose antecedents had moved into Westfield when it was originally built considered their claims to belonging far more authentic than those of others. As this suggests, place is deeply layered and shaped by the stories told about it and the imagination and memory invoked by it. As Price points out (2004: xxi), without such stories place is literally *unthinkable.*

A palpable sense of belonging to and in Westfield shaped many residents' experiences and as the interview with Jen suggests, this mediated the hostility from others that some people experienced when they went out of the estate. However, for professionals the essential view was that the estate was generally deprived and threatening and that the people living there were very much of a 'type'. It was as if the estate and its residents had become mythologized and most people associated with the area – practitioners and some residents – were able to tell lurid tales of occurrences in the area.

What was clear was the extent to which both real and imagined aspects of Westfield influenced the ways in which people who lived there thought about themselves (often as deprived, labelled, poor) and how the 'space/place imaginary' shaped professional perspectives. Very specific representations of the estate and its people were embedded in the culture and practices of some of these professionals. The prevailing reputation of the area and its residents seemed to shape policy and practice responses as well as everyday understandings of those living there.

Over to you...

Read and critically reflect

The following quotes, the first from Beatrix Potter describing the area around St Kathryn's Dock in east London in the late nineteenth century (Potter was a rent collector for the Charity Organisation Society), and the second from Percy Alden, a settlement worker in Canning Town at the turn of the century (and later MP for Tottenham in 1906 and again in 1923), show how vivid the imagination can be in creating representations of place.

> Alas! For the pitifulness of this ever-recurring drama of low life – this long chain of unknowing iniquity, children linked to parents, friends to friends ah, and lovers to lovers – bearing down to that bottomless pit of decaying life. (Beatrix Potter, in Garnett and Matthew, 1993: 240)

> The City to some reformers, is no longer the objective embodiment of the higher life of man, but a terrible maelstrom of degradation into which men and women are being rapidly sucked, and in which they are finally engulfed. Those of us who have lived in such districts have seen the process of demoralisation and destruction. (Alden, 1904: 20).

These potent evocations of a particular kind of London show how the association of certain ideas and groups (in this case late nineteenth-century ideas of underclass, decay, demoralization and menace) with place – in this case, the 'East End' – can have a powerful effect on mobilizing imagination and constructing people and place in very specific ways. In turn, this can inform policy and, in the case of work with young people, practice itself. In the nineteenth century, London's East End was seen as 'alien' and 'foreign' and, for the middle-class reformers, as much in need of missionary work as any overseas setting. Young people and the problem of regulating and integrating youth into a capitalist economy were central to this. You might try to identify how similar acts of political imagination have influenced policy and practice in your contemporary world.

Space and inequality are often linked. In the discussion above, it was suggested how, at a very local level, some spaces and places are accessible to some people and not to others. The street, for example, may present particular dangers to some people (gender and race might be very important here). Moving up in scale, it is possible to think about inequality in the context of Britain as a whole and to understand how inequality can be understood as spatialized. The work of Dorling et al. (2007) and Thomas and Dorling (2007) is illuminating, particularly in relation to poverty.

Dorling suggests that poverty has tended to be considered *aspatially*. By this, he means that attention has been focused on the proportions of households that fall into particular categories at any given point in time: how many are poor or wealthy, how poor are the poor and what share of wealth do the wealthiest own. When this is considered in terms of space, questions about the geographical mix of populations, the spatial polarization of the poor and the wealthy and the actual location of different groups become important and begin to give a much more nuanced picture of inequality (Dorling et al., 2007: 84). The example above of nineteenth-century east London is particularly relevant here. Interestingly, when the sociologist Charles Booth 'mapped' poverty in London at the end of the nineteenth century, he discovered great differences of wealth and poverty existing side by side (Englander, 1998).

Dorling's work shows the extent to which internal population movements – migrations – increase geographical inequality across Britain. So, for example, Dorling suggests that poorer places become poorer and wealthier places become wealthier because it is more likely that people with qualifications and other forms of capital move to places with opportunities for good jobs and incomes than those with poorer stocks of social and cultural capital (for example educational attainment, knowledge and skills). There is evidence for this in London and the South East, where graduates and others with good incomes become concentrated. As Dorling suggests 'internal migration will have inevitably displaced other groups who could no longer move in, in similar numbers to the past, to the areas now seeing increasing concentrations of the young and affluent' (Dorling et al., 2007: 85). Thomas and Dorling's work (2007) shows in great detail how advantage and disadvantage constitute distinctive geographical patterns of inequality across Britain.

The structural changes of the past decades have produced an intensely skewed geography of employment and unemployment in the UK (Thomas and Dorling, 2007: 96–7). The often highly remunerated and prestigious knowledge-based service industries, for example, are clustered disproportionately in the South East of England (interestingly, Westfield, discussed earlier, is located in one such town that has benefited from the expanding knowledge economy in the South East) while de-industrialization has blighted the older industrial areas of Wales, Scotland and the North and Midlands of England. This is particularly acute in cities such as Liverpool, Newcastle, Stoke and Glasgow, despite intensive work in regeneration over past decades (although these cities have their own sectors that are based on the knowledge economy). High rates of persistent structural unemployment characterize these areas, especially among male manual workers. While in Britain as a whole the unemployment rate has been between 7% and 10% since the early 1980s, in the areas of the most acute de-industrialization such as Liverpool or Tyneside the population has experienced rates that are more than double the average and in some localities as high as 50% among unskilled young males.

A further factor that aggravates economic problems in areas of de-industrialization is that professional and managerial workers are more mobile and can function in *national* and *international* labour markets, but unskilled and semi-skilled people – young people particularly – are invariably trapped in *local* labour markets, limited in terms of where they can seek employment. This renders the structural, long-term unemployed much more unable to escape the effects of de-industrialization in their home areas.

In the example of Westfield, the spatial distribution of wealth and poverty was evident. The estate was located in a town centrally placed in the South East's knowledge economy and which is home to many global businesses, attracting a well-qualified and experienced labour force. Westfield itself is situated in close proximity to other parts of the town that would be considered wealthy, and the contrast between these and Westfield is extremely marked. In the research, the boundaries between these areas were deeply symbolic, and many of those living in Westfield would never think of crossing them even though they might simply be a road or a narrow stretch of land. Effectively, Westfield residents *knew* that they were excluded from neighbouring areas and presumably people living in those areas would avoid Westfield. So, Dorling's analysis of the geographical distribution of advantage and disadvantage should alert us to the various levels at which this occurs. There is a national distribution that privileges specific areas of Britain (the South East, especially) and elsewhere, but this has to be understood at the local level as well. Westfield residents and their wealthy neighbours exist in proximate space.

Youth, Identities, Virtual Space and Place

Digital technologies and practices (especially social networking and gaming) have become enormously significant in opening up new locations in which young people engage in the processes of transition and identity work. Virtual, online space should be understood as real but in a different way from material space such as the street, the park or the youth club. Young people are becoming increasingly accomplished in the occupation and use of these different spaces: they make friends online, sustain those friendships in a variety of ways *and* build friendships in school, on the street and at the youth club. Sometimes these spaces overlap and what goes on in one domain spills into the other. However, it is worth asking what kind of space such technologies create. Perhaps the best way of thinking about this is to see it as *networked space*. The network metaphor has become dominant in some sociology at the present time and a number of theorists have developed the idea of societies that are characterized by *networks* of different kinds. For this discussion, Manuel Castells provides a helpful starting point.

Castells' argument is that twenty-first century Western societies (European, North American or Australasian) are characterized by five broad changes that constitute *network society* (see Table 6.2 below). Although interesting, Castells' work raises several important critical questions. For example, does Castells' focus on networks (and the horizontal relations through which they are constituted) ignore *vertical* power relations? Which groups have political agency in this networked world? Who is included (and excluded) in the network society? Who has mobility in the global world and who is stuck in specific places? On a global level, are some parts of the world out of the network? What about North/South relations? And, locally, who has access to the internet and to virtual space and who is excluded? Questions might be asked here about how social differences and inequalities shape digital opportunities. Young people's position here is crucial, particularly as there are prevailing assumptions that young people as a group are identified almost inevitably as major beneficiaries of these technologies. The final report of the project 'UK Children Go Online' shows the extent to which access to the internet is shaped by socioeconomic factors (Livingston and Bober, 2005: 3). Practitioners might reflect for a moment on the young people who are the object of their work, and their place in all of this. To what extent are they empowered by aspects of networked society?

Characteristic of Castells' argument is that place as a fixed and self-contained physical location that has a stable identity and meaning, such as one's town or street, is erased by what he refers to as the 'space of flows' (2009: 33). By this, Castells means the networked shifts that characterize the new society that he wants to elaborate: shifting populations (the experience of migration), resources (the flow of capital and knowledge across boundaries), and cultural artefacts (mobile culture such as rap music or video game characters). Castells seems to suggest that fixed space (perhaps local neighbourhoods, the town or city where someone lives: essentially *places*) have somehow become undermined or even annihilated by the *global*, almost, he suggests, by *space* itself. This is an abstract and complex argument but Castells' idea is that the space of flows is constantly shifting and makes the fixity of place impossible to sustain because of the raw power of circulation and flow. One example that might be drawn from Castells is the ubiquity of global architectural forms that, literally, *displace* local ways of life. Local town centres or regional centres invariably contain standard forms of shopping malls, airports and out-of-town supermarkets with their standardized consumer goods of all kinds that could be purchased in China, the US, France or the UK.

Table 6.2   The network society

Type of change	Characteristics	Implications for young people
Technological paradigm	Pervasive deployment and embedding of information technologies; information and data are the raw material of this paradigm; convergence of digital technologies	Development of new forms of social organization and social interaction: e.g. Facebook, Bebo, and game worlds. The question here concerns access: who can and who can't?
Globalization	All systems work on a planetary scale, facilitated (not caused) by information technologies	New risks and opportunities: new cultural artefacts and practices become available to those who can access them; routes to economic independence become constrained for some as capital becomes increasingly mobile
The internet	The emergence of interactive, electronic hypertext that becomes the means of managing all forms of communication	Virtual worlds and virtuality (game worlds, education worlds and social networking) become part of young people's environment and communication capacities
The demise of the nation state as a consequence of expanding global information and economic networks	Power is shifted from concentration in nation states to networks of shared sovereignty: e.g. EU, NATO, UN	Political decisions taken through global frames of reference, growth of social movements in which some young people are involved: environment and sexuality, for example. Local and specific affirmation of primary identity become increasingly important: religion, ethnicity, locality, for example
Redefining the relationship between nature and culture	A shift from modernity's industrialization of nature towards strong forms of environmentalism	New cultural movements in which (some) youth is ideologically engaged

Source: Adapted from Castells (2002a, 2002b)

Over to you...

Critically reflect and research

Castells' argument (and it is an argument that seems common in so-called postmodern sociology), put simply, is that place no longer matters. The uniqueness that is signified in place, he suggests, of towns and cities has been erased by the influence of global networked forms. The examples we gave above of shopping malls and supermarkets suggest something of a critique of Castells. These apparent 'non-places' with their standard forms invoke powerful responses and feelings: desire or revulsion, perhaps, for the goods on sale or the people that shop there. In this way, they share great similarities with other places (your local park, the youth club or the corner shop) that are also identified in specific ways.

Talk with young people about the places that they find important in their lives. Try to identify a list of three or four of these and work out the extent to which these have fixity and permanence, and the extent to which they are influenced or changed by the 'flows' that Castells identifies. Think about flows of population and cultural artefacts in particular here. How do these affect young people's sense of places to go and places to belong?

In this argument, according to Castells, place and space have to be understood in new ways. It is important that proper account is taken of the so-called Information Revolution whose pervasiveness has shaped the lives of the majority of the planet's population in one way or another (in different and unequal ways, inevitably): the creation of common digital languages, the shrinking of space and time and the establishment of networks of all kinds are key features of this revolution.

Over to you...

Research and critically reflect

If not already familiar with it, visit the Youth Work Online website (www.youthworkonline. org.uk). This will give you a clear idea of the extent to which some youth workers have taken up the idea of using virtual spaces to engage with young people in different ways. Try to find out as much about this as you can from the site. You might even decide to sign up!

You should also reflect on the extent to which this site has become a place in which youth workers have built their own space for undertaking certain kinds of social activities. You might want to reflect on how the virtual and the material link here, how what happens online and offline 'join up'. Considering what we said in Chapter 3 about identity, you might also want to look at whether anything on this site is part of online identity construction. Some of the personal pages are very carefully crafted to create certain kinds of representations. What do we learn sociologically about these people and who they are from how they present themselves?

The first thing to recognize is the extent to which Western and other societies have become *digitized*. Digital technologies and computing are ubiquitous. Computers, as a key element of this, are everywhere; they are invariably interconnected, accessible, cheap and incredibly mobile (through laptops, phones, tablets and watches, for example). For many young people in late modern societies there is little doubt that the internet plays a central role in their lives and some analysts, perhaps a little extravagantly, have referred to young people as 'digital natives' whose sense of agency and identity is being reconstructed by the growth of digital technologies (see Prensky, 2001; Livingstone, 2009). Young people's digital participation increasingly defines youth as a separate and distinct social category by virtue of their access to knowledge.

However, different people use these technologies in different ways: keeping in touch with friends, families and acquaintances, making arrangements and creating new social spaces and activities and making economic or commercial transactions. In the latter case, business and commerce have been quick to recognize the potential of these tools. As well as linking people together, social networks open up new forms of space. A little later, this chapter looks at some of the game worlds that have emerged in recent years and that, for an increasing number of young people, have become alternative play spaces in their leisure time.

These technologies have provided platforms (places?) on which young people are able to present and represent themselves in particular ways to the world through social networking sites such as Facebook, I-pals, MySpace, Bebo, or Friends Reunited; online gaming areas such as World of Warcraft and virtual worlds such as Second Life or Twinity. As well as creating opportunities for self-presentation, digital technologies offer the capacity to link up with others in relation to personal and collective interests of all kinds (from hobbies to sexual and political interests).

Over to you...

Research and critically reflect

Do you have a Facebook page? (If you don't have a page, see if you can get access to someone else's). Reflect for a few minutes on what you have included on the page:

images, information, links, lists of friends, music you like, food that you cook and so on. What does this say about you? What kind of 'you' is presented to the world and in what sense does it accurately represent who you are and how you would like other people to see you? If you were thinking about this in terms of the question of identity, what sort of identity does your Facebook page make of you? It would be worth sharing your reflections with a close friend and a course colleague (someone who might know you less well). What do they think of your page and what it says about you? Is this the 'real' you? Indeed, is there such a thing as the 'real' you? Try to extend this activity to include some of the young people with whom you work. Open up some discussion about Facebook and get them to reflect on their own pages and what they say about their sense of who they are. How do they choose what to include and what to leave out? What does this tell you about young people and identity?

The example of social networking technologies such as Facebook or Bebo raises very interesting and important questions about the concept of identity and how and where identities are made and remade in late modern societies. One of these questions concerns the extent to which anyone using Facebook and the like is 'free' to represent themselves in whatever way they want. To put it another way, can Facebook construct any kind of identity that its users want? Remember Bauman's argument (see Chapter 3) to which attention was drawn earlier. Bauman (2004) suggested that people in late modernity are no longer 'born into' an identity and that they have to make of themselves what they can. Perhaps the use of technology can also be seen as part of Giddens' idea of the 'project of the self'? Superficially, it seems as if that could be the case. Surely young people construct a sense of themselves on Facebook in a freely chosen way: they decide on the images, the friends, the favourite movies and the music, including what they want and omitting things that they think might not give quite the right angle on who they are. This argument suggests that identity is partially constructed online and through the spaces and places that young people and others inhabit. This is an interesting position to take but perhaps one that confuses *presentation* of self with the *actual* material self or as the 'whole' self when it is only one part of complex contemporary ways of being? This also raises interesting questions about how archives of digital and cyber 'stuff' (all the text and images that are placed online at different times and circulated or combined with other cyber-stuff in different ways by different people) constitute identity. There are clear differences between this kind of archival material and the sort of 'first person narrative' that the individual constructs online. The question of authorship also arises here: it seems pretty straightforward in relation to the first person narrative but who *authorizes* the archive construction of identity online? In effect, *whose* identities are these?

Social networking technologies such as Facebook and Twitter are also, literally, tools for *networking*. They have enormous capacity to link people in different ways to produce new forms of social life and activity. For example, by Googling 'Scumoween', websites can be found describing the parties and social activities that constitute Scumoween. These, apparently, involve large numbers of young people and as well as the parties themselves (held in real life places at real times!) there is a mass of cyber discussion around the idea of Scumoween.

Over to you...

Research and critically reflect

Take a look at partyvibe.com and you'll find lots of (presumably) young people engaging in cyber talk about their escapades on the way to parties, at parties and trying to locate parties that are happening. It is almost as if the discussion itself becomes as significant to them as the parties that they go to.

Have a look at some of the web pages that come out of the Scumoween phenomenon. Try to get a real understanding of what this is all about. In thinking about Scumoween (in the context of young people's production and use of space), where do you think the boundaries lie between virtual (online) and material (real life) space? Can you find evidence of one leaking into the other? What do you think the significance of this might be for understanding young people, space and place?

Scumoween is an interesting example of how the boundaries between online and offline social worlds are (at least sometimes) erased and one category or space merges into the other. The internet clearly has considerable capacity to facilitate offline cohesion and solidarity in subcultural groups (Wilson and Atkinson, 2005: 305). Scumoween is one example of this.

Sherry Turkle, who is something of a cyberspace utopian, has lots to say about identity and online communities. She argues that, online, people enter spaces in which, according to one of the gamers in her study, 'you are what you pretend to be ... you are what you play' (1997: 192). For this gamer, the boundaries between self, game and online avatar (the character they become in the game world) seem to be completely blurred. Turkle's position suggests that there is a transfer of online experiences to 'real life' and that the two come to be seen as aspects of one reality. It is almost as if the gamers that Turkle studied no longer acknowledge substantive difference between online and offline realities: they become just different windows on the world and the material world or day-to-day life becomes just one of many possible worlds. Turkle claims that the role playing that goes on in game worlds is somehow transferred into real life and that subsequently becomes an ongoing play of surfaces and fictions, real life intersecting with game worlds. She suggests that potentially, at least, one's sense of self (identity) becomes an amalgam or multiplicity of fleeting or transitory elements self-projected through or onto various cyber locations such as Google Buzz or Windows Live Spaces, along with those that might have a more sustained presence and existence including Facebook.

Turkle argues that one of the consequences of the networking technologies is that the idea of the fixed and individual notion of self (a kind of 'modernist' self) vanishes, to be replaced by a self characterized by multiplicity, cultural relativism and dispersion across the web and throughout cyberspace (a typically 'postmodernist' self). The proposition here is that identity (as self) can be understood as formed in the spaces that constitute cyber networks and linkages. Identity is, thus, transitory, unstable and the outcome of network relationships and association with various online groups. Turkle suggests that the web opens up opportunities for the elaboration of new forms of *public* identity that are somehow almost autonomous or independent of any pre-existing self. She implies that self and *presentation* of self are synonymous.

These arguments have been criticized by a number of analysts. Bauman, for example, is pessimistic about what he sees as the pretence of virtual community (he is, however, pessimistic about community as a whole!) and its tendency to thwart 'spontaneous interaction with real people' (2004: 25). The other critique that might be made of the utopian position is that it tends to ignore the political context of gaming. As Stallabrass, for example, suggests, video games are a 'capitalist and deeply conservative form of culture' as gamers are tricked into imitating 'idealized markets' and 'sweatshop labour' through repetitive manipulation of game objects and numbers (1993: 104). As Stallabrass points out, it is easy to become seduced by the fantasy world of the game without asking whose interests might underlie its pixelated narratives.

The work of Crowe and Bradford (2006) offers a contrast to that of Turkle and the other 'cyberspace utopians'. Crowe and Bradford explored young people's use of the gaming site *Runescape* and came to the conclusion that gaming *is* important in young people's ongoing performances of leisure time identity. Cyberspace offers a range of opportunities to define or shape identity, conceal parts of identity and develop or narrate identity in various ways. However, Crowe and Bradford take the view that cyberspace (like Runescape or World of Warcraft, another popular online gaming site) can be understood as *another* form of space (different from but also like everyday *material* space) and it is used by young people at different times just like other spaces and places. For example, one of their research participants discussed her use of Runescape in the following way.

'Last year my dad lost his job, he's ok now but we didn't have money so we couldn't go on holiday and I spent the six weeks playing Rune. I used to go down to Cathaby and hang out on the beach, when the sun came through my window it was nearly like being at the seaside ... lol this is sooo stoopid I know but guess what ... I used to go to the gnome village for cocktails in the evening, it was well good, I would meet up with my friends and we would all put the same beats on and pretend like we were at Ibiza or something.' (Crowe and Bradford, 2006: 341)

Bauman suggests that the virtual world's real attraction (like that of the example above) to young people is that it frees them from 'the contradictions and cross-purposes that haunt offline life' (Bauman, 2010: 15). He suggests that the sheer multiplicity of virtual relationships renders them devoid of any kind of real commitment. They are, he suggests, necessarily of short duration and are characterized by weak social bonds. Similarly, it's easy to see in the above quote from Crowe and Bradford the point that Stallabrass makes above about how games have a seductive quality that can occlude the challenges of the day-to-day material world. However, these cyber places and spaces *are*, apparently, social settings that are occupied by young people in their leisure times. In contrast to Turkle's position, Crowe and Bradford argue that young people approach these spaces with all the cultural paraphernalia of the material world (their ideas of what it means to be a man or a woman, for example), which is, largely, reproduced in cyberspace. As they argue, internet technologies and games

... and the geographical spaces and places within, have become 'cool places' in which to hang out. The virtual towns, rivers and open spaces of Runescape are not so different from those found in the material world, and the uses to which young people put them as cultural artifacts are similar to their activities in many streets and shopping malls. Again, it is sometimes possible to read these as acts of resistance, not in any heroic way but as young people marking out their sense of agency. However, we should not assume that virtuality liberates young people from the 'power of place'. On the contrary, virtual environments are social and spatial productions that entail the complex assembly of technologies, competence and imagination through which new place-based norms and disciplines evolve. (Crowe and Bradford, 2006: 343)

The meaning and significance of the interactions and relationships in which young people engage online are dependent on the social categories and frameworks that are developed there. These, Crowe and Bradford suggest, are largely shaped by the same *social* that prevails in the material world. In effect, the boundaries between material and virtual worlds (the everyday world and the gaming world) *are* porous and the 'social stuff' of one world often leaks through the boundary into the other. Drawing on the work of Goffman, Allison Cavanagh points out that cyberspace presentations of self (Facebook pages or Runescape avatars construed as cyber identities) are *strategies*. They are the means of achieving certain kinds of outcomes such as high status or power, but are also subject to the prevailing normative order (2007: 128). As such, they are irrevocably part of the social world and, to the extent that online activities contribute to identity construction, they are very important aspects of some young people's lives.

Crowe and Bradford's research on young people's use of online gaming environments made clear that in some respects, some young people saw these settings as places that had similar (and different) characteristics to places in the everyday material world. It was striking that for some of the young people who were interviewed as part of the research, there was a real sense of *belonging* in relation to places in their game worlds and there are some similarities in how young people talk about belonging in virtual and material leisure spaces.

The significance of belonging for young people (as for others) suggests the sociological importance of a conception of home. Home and belonging must be understood as being both placed and imagined. The contemporary sense of home (as a private and familiar space of particular belonging, and located in a dwelling place of some kind: a house or an apartment, for example) emerged as part of the process of modernization. Industrialization resulted in the movement of production from domestic space into the factories and workshops, resulting in the new separation of home and work, at least for the mass population.

A sense of being 'at home' (as being part of place or belonging in some way) has been central to sociology and sociological thinking from its inception. As Chapter 1 suggested, sociology's origins lie in what Polanyi (1944) referred to as the 'great transformation' of the nineteenth century in which market societies emerged through the corrosion of solidarity and community that had characterized the pre-market economies. Indeed, the major figures of early sociology were concerned with explaining these changes, although they theorized their implications in very different ways. Underlying all of their analyses, however, is an interest in belonging and belongingness. It was easy to see in *Gemeinschaft* type community where the source of belonging and solidarity lay but this was less obvious in the new capitalist and industrial market economies. The general position taken by the early sociologists, whether in Durkheim's concept of *anomie*, Marx's notion of *alienation* or Weber's *bureaucracy*, was that modernization led to a kind of 'homelessness' of the spirit.

Over to you...

Critically reflect, research and read

Consider the idea of 'home'. What does home mean to you? What words symbolize home for you? Do you think about home as place, or is it much more than that? Try to identify specific places that symbolize home and work out what it is about them that does this. While you are considering these aspects of home look at them in terms of the public and the private: to what extent is home a private space for you? You might also consider how ideas of home are mediated by social difference: by class or race, gender or disability, for example.

Much classic literature has dealt with the themes of place, home and belonging often in the context of social class and gender. In *Sense and Sensibility*, for example, Jane Austen looks at the powerful dynamics and bonds that are established between place and home, and how these are shaped by patterns of class and gender relations. A hundred years later, D.H. Lawrence wrote *Sons and Lovers*, which some critics have seen as the first novel written against a backdrop of working-class domestic life. Set in the Nottinghamshire coal mining community of Bestwood, the novel deals with a range of themes including class, poverty, gender, respectability and the significance of place and home.

Try comparing the ideas of home in both novels. Are there similarities and what are the main differences in how the authors deal with the ideas of home and place? What might a critical position on home be? Does either Austen or Lawrence suggest that perhaps the idea of home is not quite so straightforward as we might think?

Some early youth workers set up clubs as an 'alternative' home for young people whom they considered to be lacking a good home life. This has been an ongoing theme and Sue Robertson's article 'Working space. A warm safe place, an argument for youth clubs' (Robertson, 2001) about youth clubs and belongingness reflects this. If working-class homes now have private 'bedroom' space facilitated by digital technologies, perhaps youth clubs are redundant?

This sense of belonging invoked by home (and, perhaps, especially in its manifestation in place) encompasses a range of feelings: of attachment, security, and personal investment, 'a fixed point in space, a firm position from which we "proceed" (whether everyday or over longer periods of time) and to which we return in due course. This firm position is what we call "home"' (Heller, 1984: 239). Indeed, the home (typically as house or apartment) has become one of the principal sites on which a range of identity practices and identity work is performed. Increasingly complex and sophisticated home decoration and garden design are obvious examples, but home is also the space in which the objects that make up people's lives, possessions, collections of stuff of all kinds, records, books, ornaments and all the things for which they hold affection take on an almost sacred quality in creating a sense of domestic 'comfort'. In a series of portraits of some thirty households in one very ordinary street in London, the anthropologist Daniel Miller makes the point that home and the *things* that are cherished within it constitute people as *expressive* beings: objects make subjects (that is, the things that people value make them who they are) rather than vice versa (Miller, 2008). Miller's work suggests that the objects that people assemble around them, from books and CDs to cards and clothes, pictures and furniture, embed them in the place in which they live. People's objects give them a history and a present and link them to family, friends and others. Consider the photo album, for example, and its capacity for invoking memory, relationship and emotion. It is worth thinking about young people in this context and the extent to which the things and objects that they cherish make them who they are.

Suzie Scott (2009: 49–50) proposes three principal factors that give home its significance. *First*, it provides a sense of physical space – place – in which people live and which provides a base from which they can order their everyday lives. As such, home offers routine and predictability. *Second*, home signifies a place that generates a sense of familiarity that, again, provides routine and security. *Finally*, home designates the private domain, a space in which people retreat from the outside world and where they can 'be themselves'. Goffman's work was referred to earlier in terms of 'front-stage' and 'back-stage' domains. Home might be considered to be back stage in those terms, although it may be that in some ways, even at home, performance and self-presentation remain important. However, home is also the setting in which *domestic* violence and abuse are commonplace and experienced by so many women, children and young people. Front stage and back stage take on different resonances in this context. This way of thinking about home might also affect what the term *homelessness* means. There are real implications here for migrant and refugee young people. The romantic vision of home as protected and safe space has, for too many, been an illusion (Holdsworth and Morgan, 2005: 80).

Throughout Chapter 6 the significance of belonging, especially in the sense of a *place of belonging,* has been discussed. Home, for example, may signal precisely that sense of belonging for some people, although for others it evokes very different emotions based on other kinds of experience. Before this part of the discussion is concluded, and especially in the context of transnational migration, the potential significance of *nation* and how ideas of nation and place may converge is briefly considered. In a world where displacement of population through war and ethnic conflict and the movement and migration of people, especially young people, across transnational labour markets has become so common, the idea of home might be extended to the nation state.

Benedict Anderson has pointed out that nation is always an *imagined* entity in at least four ways: because no one can ever know their fellow members, commonality is therefore an act of imagination; it is imagined as *limited* because even the largest nation is finite and other nations exist beyond its boundaries; it is *sovereign* because it is based on Enlightenment principles that challenge the divinely ordained dynasties of pre-modern times; and it is imagined as *community* because it is understood (perhaps ideologically) in terms of deep horizontal relationships, regardless of patterns of inequality or exploitation that may exist within it (Anderson, 1991: 6–7). Nation is often linked with space and place, and many national groups identify particular spaces as coterminous with the nation. Scotland and the Scots provide a context in which nation and place are seemingly settled (although there is disagreement about who might count as Scottish and who controls Scottish futures in the context of broader arguments about devolution); on the other hand, consider Palestine and the Palestinians, a situation in which identity and place although powerfully connected and celebrated are simultaneously deeply fractured and contested and the focus of violence and political unrest.

Over to you...

Research and critically reflect

If you work with any groups of migrant young people, explore their understandings of home nation, place and community. Do they think about nation in terms of space and place in any particular way, or is nation a more abstract identification for them, defining what it means to be a member of a national group or minority (this might include place, of course)? Thinking about Benedict Anderson's idea that nation is an imagined community, can you find evidence of that in the way in which these young people talk about their national identity? To what extent does place (landscape or a village, a street or a whole city, for example) have significance here? You might make a comparison between migrant and non-migrant groups. Presumably, Englishness (or Scottishness, Irishness or Welshness, for example) is as much imagined as any other national identity? In terms of the spatialization of national cultures, however understood, these are saturated by representations of particular places (different kinds of landscapes or monuments, for example). Try to get young people to identify some of these: which places really capture a sense of their nationality? Let us take the example of Westfield again. For some migrant families there, the idea of their 'homeland' was sometimes very important. It appeared as a constant or fixed point in their lives, especially when times in Westfield were uncertain or troubled. Sometimes it was spoken of with a particular kind of longing (perhaps, the 'longing in belonging') and place took on a very vivid and materialized representation of where they came from. At other times, young people from migrant families seemed not to want to be reminded that they were somehow 'different' and would assert a British/English/Westfield identity rather than something that located them as 'other'.

Returning briefly to the idea of home in this context, sociology has always been concerned with modernity's potential for disrupting the sense of being (or not being) 'at home'. The American sociologist Peter Berger suggested some 40 years ago that the experience of modernity (for Berger, a Weberian sociologist, this was characterized especially by the rationalizing affects of technology, pluralization and secularization) had led to an increasing sense of *homelessness*, what he saw as a 'metaphysical loss', a deep and powerful yearning that has 'engendered its own nostalgias – nostalgias, that is, for a condition of being "at home" in society, with oneself and, ultimately, in the universe' (Berger, Berger and Kellner, 1973: 77). This was written anticipating the experience and consequence of what has come to be understood as *globalization* and it is easy to identify the contemporary presence of Berger's nostalgias.

Summary and Conclusions

Chapter 6 has explored the significance of space and place in the constitution of contemporary youth. The main point is that youth must be understood as located in both space and place (as well as time). In the chapter, *space* has been discussed in terms of its social, material, discursive and virtual dimensions. *Place*, it was suggested, is an aspect of space that is invested with specific cultural meaning by those for whom it assumes significance. Particular places (a building, a street or a city centre, for example) provide settings in which individual and collective biographies are imagined, lived and experienced, developed or constrained. Thus, space and place are both important in terms of the construction of youthful identities. Practitioners and policymakers in work with young people need a clear understanding of how place impacts on young people's life experiences. Chapter 6 has also suggested how patterns of opportunity and inequality are invariably spatialized and that growing up in particular geographic regions shapes the nature and experience of youth transitions. Space and place are factors that articulate and interact with other aspects of social difference and inequality by creating geographic patterns of opportunity and disadvantage.

Arguments about the so-called *network society* have drawn attention to the importance of digital or virtual space. For many young people online space and place has, apparently, created new prospects for spaces of engagement with others and for the creation of a sense of belonging. Online gaming, for example, appears to multiply the chances of relationships and interactions with others and some youth workers have begun to use these settings as spaces of professional intervention with young people. Chapter 6 has implicitly asked whether the multiplicity of virtual space creates new potential for the enactment of community. Sociologies of virtuality have assumed both utopian and more pessimistic positions.

On the one hand, virtual space seems to offer infinite opportunities for the development of novel social relations and for the performance of community; on the other, there is a view that virtual settings displace the capacity for *authentic* face-to-face relationships. Whichever position one adopts, it is clear that for young people, virtuality has opened up opportunities for modes of relationship and for networks that would probably not exist outside of virtual spaces, although for some young people the virtual and material are articulated. Relationships established in virtual spaces often spill over into the material world. Gaming spaces and social networking are examples of this.

The ideas explored in this chapter provide an occasion for considering big sociological questions about belonging and being 'at home' that have been raised in earlier chapters. These questions have enormous implications for how youth practitioners think about working with young people and the nature of the services that are provided for them, perhaps especially in settings where young people's sense of belonging is not strong. Part of the analysis of modernity considered here is that it has led increasingly to a sense of homelessness, and what was described in the chapter as a *nostalgia* for something lost. Perhaps virtual gaming and social networking can be understood as attempts to engender such belongingness and intimacy in an increasingly technologized, virtualized and perhaps fragmented world.

Further Reading

- Teather, E.K. (1999) *Embodied Geographies. Spaces, bodies and rites of passage*, London: Routledge.

  The chapter on 'Schoolies Week' shows the importance of embodiment and transgression in a key rite of passage in the transition from youth to adulthood.

- Foley, P. and Leverett, S. (eds) (2011) *Children and Young People's Spaces. Developing practice*, Basingstoke: Palgrave Macmillan.

  Chapters on the importance of space and place in thinking through childhood and youth transitions are key reading for youth practitioners.

- Holt, L. (ed.) (2011) *Geographies of Children, Youth and Families*, London: Routledge.

  This international collection shows why it is so important to consider the intersection of social difference and space in understanding the experiences of children and young people in a range of institutional and other settings.

7

Living in a World of Change and Constancy

Globalization, Citizenship and Youth

Introduction

Chapter 7 covers a wide-ranging and contested area, namely that of globalization and citizenship, and the significance of these for youth and young people. A number of key questions are asked. What is the relationship between globalization and citizenship? Do the two 'cross-cut' one another? Is citizenship restricted to the nation state? Is it possible to be a global citizen? Does *economic* globalization preclude (or enhance) *social* citizenship?

All these questions have been hotly disputed in politics and currently in sociology. The literature here is extensive and the area is explored by focusing on the perspectives and approaches, and particular questions that are most relevant to young people and the concept of youth. However, it is no exaggeration to suggest that *all* debates on these topics are relevant to children and young people, as they will inherit the world that emerges from current processes and developments. Citizenship is now an aspect of the curriculum in UK schools, so the exploration is concluded with a very brief consideration of the role of education in this area.

In this chapter, *citizenship* and *globalization* are the main ideas discussed. However, because the concepts themselves are contested, and this is the very substance of the debates, the chapter does *not* begin with a one or two-line definition of each. Instead, characterizations of both concepts and the relationship between them will emerge throughout the chapter. Nevertheless it is worth offering a preliminary outline of both concepts.

Over to you...

Critical reflection

Write down what you understand the term *citizenship* to mean. Don't think too long about it – just write down the first few things that come into your head.

As you proceed through this chapter, check back on these initial thoughts and see how they relate to the various discussions and debates.

As a concept, citizenship emerged in classical times in ancient Greece and applied to members of the city-state of Athens. There, certain social groups were not permitted to be citizens: women and slaves, for example. In its current, *liberal* form, citizenship signifies something quite different, referring to the *legitimate and equal membership of a society*. In the classical world, citizenship was 'obligation-based' rather than 'rights-based'. This reminds us of the 'rights and responsibilities' arguments of Third Way politics. The duality or social contract underlying citizenship discourse, that citizenship has two sides to it, rights *and* responsibilities, has been very important.

Citizenship is a concept that has been deployed historically by a range of groups, including anti-slavery campaigners, the women's movement, civil rights movements, and gay activists. The detailed definition of the concept will be contingent upon the perspective of the particular defining group. The task here is to advance an understanding of these different characterizations of citizenship, particularly in its relationship with globalization. Prior to that, the chapter briefly considers the question of change.

As earlier chapters have suggested, sociology has been preoccupied with the changes implied in the shift from *traditional* to *modern* societies, and the term *late modernity* has been used to signal contemporary times. When sociologists talk about change they refer to aspects of historical discontinuity and, in this, the concept of youth has special significance in Western societies. The universalization of youth as a social category occurred partly in relation to its value as a metaphor for making sense of social change. Questions about youth have been asked since the mid-nineteenth century, in order to evaluate the nature and condition of contemporary or future society. The post-war obsession in Western societies with youth in both working-class and middle-class forms (subculture and counterculture respectively) has reflected deep anxieties about social change in those societies and, as Davis argues, images of troubled and troublesome youth have 'come to stand in a kind of projective relationship to the formulation and diagnoses of the nature and implications of social change itself' (Davis, 1990: 217). Arguably, the extent of *actual* intergenerational conflict and social dysfunction in these societies has been overstated: despite some aspects of culture, beliefs and values clearly shifting, other elements remain constant and continuous. Nevertheless, the sense of change is strong in late modern societies. Sociologists have tended to describe change in terms of relatively unambiguous breaks between, say, tradition and modernity, or pre-industrial, industrial and post-industrial societies. The actual experience of change is much more uneven than these breaks suggest, and is entangled with aspects of continuity through which the social world is maintained and reproduced.

It is possible to think of social change as a polarity between changes that might be seen as *seismic* or *incremental*. The 1889 French and 1917 Russian Revolutions, or events in North Africa in 2011, were *seismic:* violent, rapid and politically motivated, resulting in totally reconfigured social orders. On the other hand, aspects of the shifts from feudalism to capitalism have been largely *incremental*, slower and more piecemeal, often responding to technological innovations which have entailed adjustments to social practices and relations.

Sociologists offer different accounts of social change that have attempted to analyse the process of modernization. Tonkiss (1998) outlines a useful typology (see Table 7.1).

Sociologists' exclusive focus on a modernity characterized in terms of change and complexity has contrasted with their view of traditional or pre-modern societies as distinctly *other,* conservative and implicitly lacking or backward. This has been especially so in relation to non-Western societies. The dominance of a particular account of modernity has also often failed to acknowledge the coexistence of *traditional* and *modern* aspects in one society (Tonkiss, 1998: 46). In contemporary China and India, for example, traditional and modern forms of social organization coexist, sometimes in conflict. Globalization means that both modern and traditional economies are brought into relationship.

Globalization operates at a number of different levels and a preliminary definition is offered from Ritzer who suggests that globalization is:

> ... a transplanetary *process* or set of *processes* increasing *liquidity* and the growing multidirectional *flows* of people, objects, places and information as well as the structures they encounter and create that are *barriers* to, or *expedite*, those flows. (Ritzer and Atalay, 2010: 1)

Broadly speaking, the processes of globalization signify increased connectedness between societies in different parts of the world and the

Table 7.1 Processes of social change

Change as evolutionary	This is modelled on a natural science account of change that suggests processes of increasing differentiation, specialization and adaptation across time through which new social forms emerge. Society, in this account, is understood as a social totality, a complex entity or system in itself. Growth and integration are key ideas here. This model can miss the unequal or local distribution of change, leading to social inequality
Functionalist change	Functionalism takes the metaphor of society as a living organism (a biological metaphor) that adapts to changing conditions; society is self-stabilizing to create 'steady state' conditions in its interdependent sub-systems and structures: economy, polity, social institutions and culture
Change and conflict	This account is a response to functionalist models, stressing dynamic social conflict and crisis, and the importance of revolutionary movements and agents instigating change. It points to the internal and systemic contradictions in a society to which resistance and change (instigated by social classes, for example) are inevitable responses. The Russian and French Revolutions are examples
Non-linear change	The three accounts above rely on a linear logic of *progress*. In contrast, non-linear approaches to change have used alternative explanations that entail cyclical or 'rise and fall' narratives (e.g. economic boom and bust, post-war recessions, the Depression of the 1930s). Foucault's account of the emergence of discourse (knowledge that organizes aspects of social life: such as sexuality, punishment, health and hygiene) suggests contingent, unpredictable and localized aspects of change, challenging models of systemic change that characterize the three accounts above

Source: Adapted from Tonkiss (1998)

apparent diminishing or liquidizing of boundaries, particularly those of nation states so that finance, people, ideas, goods, information and culture flow between them. The structures to which Ritzer and Atalay refer could be those imposed by nation states (for example immigration controls) or transnational organizations (for example the United Nations) that either restrict or enable those flows.

> ### Over to you...
>
> #### Critical reflection
>
> Much of the literature on globalization refers to the idea of flow; of people, culture, information and so on, that seem to characterize its processes. Can you think of examples from your own experience that seem to support the idea of 'flow' on a global scale? You might want to think about popular culture here and how many young people worldwide become embedded in an increasingly globalized youth culture.
>
> A further example is the flow of sports people and ideas across the global sporting arena. Consider, for example, the footballers currently playing for British or Italian teams and how the management of football has also become globalized. This suggests that management expertise similarly flows through international football. Tactics that have, in the past, perhaps been associated with top English or Italian teams, for example, are now commonplace.

Globalization

Globalization and citizenship could be set in opposition to each other particularly because it might be argued that citizenship *needs* the nation state. It might be suggested that the very concept of citizenship is conditional upon the existence, and strength, of the nation state whose power has been altered, even undermined and eroded by globalization. The *extent* to which globalization has eroded the power of the nation state is strongly contested (Guillén, 2001: 247–51). In arguing the complexity and uneven effects of globalization, some authors (for example Sassen, 2006) suggest that neoliberal economic globalization actually *enhances* the power of some parts of the state, including the executive and regulatory bodies, and weakens others, especially the legislature in which democracy in the liberal nation state is embodied and realized. However, other authors argue that the flows (including those of multinational corporate capital: the banks and business generally) are able to resist the capacity and authority of the nation state to control or regulate them. Indeed, supranational bodies such as the International Monetary Fund (IMF) and the World Trade Organization (WTO) regulate global capital and deal mainly with executive government that then becomes thoroughly *internationalized*. The power of the executive (that is, of the government) has also been enhanced in the post-9/11 era, although the accretion of power in this case is separate from that which is the consequence of increasingly globalized economic organization. Overall, this argument suggests shifting power relations *between* nation states as well as *within* them (Sassen, 2006). These arguments have real implications for how public services, including those for young people, are funded in any given nation state. For some politicians, globalization seems to have become an excuse for not meeting the expectations of electorates or for presenting some policy strategies as the inevitable consequence of globalization (Hirst and Thompson, 1999).

It appears, at least superficially, that nation states have less obvious power than at times in the past. National boundaries have become extremely porous. At the very least, there is considerable awareness and understanding of events taking place beyond national boundaries (globalized media have ensured this: look at the influence and reach of CNN, Fox News, or Al Jazeera). However, it does seem that there is more to this than greater public awareness of global events. At the level of the corporation, multinationalism and transnationalism are becoming almost commonplace. The ubiquitous McDonald's fast food outlets that have appeared in almost every major world city exemplify this. Financial transactions are conducted at a global level and growth in international trade has created an increasing interdependency across nations, almost continuously increasing since 1950. While international trade and flows of capital are not a new phenomenon (consider the Roman Empire, the fifteenth and sixteenth century Spanish or Portuguese explorations of the world, or England's imperial and colonial expansion from the late sixteenth and early seventeenth centuries; perhaps all examples of globalization?), it is the level and nature of these flows that has prompted many commentators to describe the current situation in terms of globalization. Although there is lively debate among sociologists and others about the nature of globalization and even whether globalization exists at all, there seems to be general and popular acceptance that globalization *is* real and that the world is becoming increasingly interrelated.

Those who challenge this position suggest that globalization is neither unprecedented nor as embedded as many seem to suggest. They argue that because trade and foreign investment are concentrated in Western Europe, North America and the Pacific Rim, what is *actually* going on is best characterized as a process of internationalization rather than globalization, as many countries are simply not involved. Guillén (2001) calls this the 'feebleness argument'. It is about capital and finance and omits the significance of what has come to be regarded as *cultural* globalization involving popular music, sport and ideas.

In broad summary, some of the questions that would need to be addressed in exploring the idea of globalization can be identified. For the purpose of this discussion you can think of globalization as the intersection of a number of key factors or forces: those shown in Table 7.2 are generally identified as important.

Table 7.2 Globalization

Factors	Characteristics and positions
Time–space compressions	Distance becomes less significant as the world metaphorically speeds up: travel across distance becomes easier and quicker; mass travel enables many people to experience different cultures first hand; electronic media bring other times and places 'into the living room'
Cultural and technological flows beyond borders	National borders become more permeable and people, ideas, technologies, information, cultural and symbolic resources (film, literature, music, and other forms of cultural expression) flow across 'borderless states'
Interconnection and interdependency	Nation states become increasingly embedded in systems of global finance and trade relations; complex relations of dependency and interdependency; social networking across boundaries and borders: Facebook, Inter-Pals, Bebo, etc. creating a sense of 'common humanity'
Networks of powerful transnational actors and organizations	These are of different kinds: transnational corporations (TNCs) such as Unilever, Sony, BP and the major supermarkets such as Tesco and Walmart have enormous market power and establish networks of trade relations through global supply chains; new bodies upholding international law (e.g. the International Criminal Court in the Hague or the European Court of Human Rights) to which nation states are increasingly accountable; international governmental organizations such as the IMF or WTO; the growth of globalized social movements and diasporas
Common world problems	A range of environmental, ecological and health factors in the form of acknowledged patterns of 'risk' shape the experiences of people in different countries: HIV/AIDS; global warming

Despite the proliferation of this activity across (most of) the globe, these globalized processes do not supplant the activities of nation states. Although the processes associated with the contents of Table 7.2 are abstract and, literally, *global* in character, they are mediated in terms of the *local*. In a country of 60 million such as the UK, the local might signify something quite different from its meaning in a country of 400,000 people, such as Malta. The mediation of the global by the local means that young people's *lived experiences* of globalization always entail a kind of *relay* between global and local factors.

Let us try to give a substantive example of this. On a recent trip to Uganda (part of the world increasingly accessible through cheap air travel), we met a group of young people in a small village in the western part of the country, next to the Congolese border. This was a part of Uganda referred to by Ugandan colleagues as 'up-country', meaning that, to all intents and purposes, it was remote, largely undeveloped in commercial or industrial terms and, in many respects, organized on traditional lines with families and very localized communities being important social institutions. These were linked in to the Ugandan model of local governance. Work in the area was organized around agriculture and the production of cassava, banana and plantain. However, all sorts of cultural artefacts originating from 'the West' had penetrated this apparently 'traditional culture'. One of the young men was wearing a Crystal Palace football shirt and although his English was limited (and my knowledge of Luganda non-existent) he was able to demonstrate a real knowledge and enthusiasm for the team, its players and its recent achievements. The shirt served as a point of contact between us and generated warmth and a degree of mutuality around a shared interest in football. Other young people there were listening to American-style hip-hop music and wore baseball caps and trainers that would not have been out of place in south London or New York.

What might be occurring here is a kind of *hybrid* of different cultures that form a link between this tiny village in Africa with London and the US. The young people's experience of the music they listen to or their enthusiasm for an English football team, and in particular the symbolic aspects of these that carry their globalized meanings, was inevitably mediated through their local setting: their location in traditional familial and community structures and their social and cultural relations. The symbolic significance of the Nike or Adidas tee shirt, the trainer logos, the Crystal Palace shirt and the music, and their meaning for local youth culture was constructed and reconstructed in the local setting. Nevertheless, these cultural artefacts formed a connection, however attenuated, between very different cultural traditions and worlds.

It is important to acknowledge the potentially 'two-way' (more appropriately *multidirectional*) traffic of globalization, at least in terms of popular culture. The Uganda example above suggests that American and UK cultural artefacts travel outwards from those cultural hubs. There are sociologists who argue that globalization should best be understood as part of the long history of what has been seen as the cultural threat of Americanization through 'Coca-Colonization': Naomi Klein's *No Logo* (2000) is a well-known example. However, Klein critically acknowledges how a new 'mono-multiculturalism' has shifted the cultural imperialism associated with American global marketing.

> Today the buzzword in global marketing isn't selling America to the world, but bringing a kind of market masala to everyone in the world. (Klein, 2000: 117)

There are, however, instances of cultural forms that travel in other directions than West–East. The Japanese *manga* and *anime* comic genres could be seen as an important Eastern influence on the West. This cultural traffic, in turn, might also be understood as a reprise of the nineteenth-century cult of *Japonism* (although there are much earlier seventeenth-century examples of the influence of Japanese art in Europe) in which highly coloured, dramatic and *exotic* wood block images of Japanese life and scenes from the Kabuki theatre became highly valued in Europe. Japonism was also influential in late nineteenth and early twentieth-century music, particularly through operas by Puccini (*Madame Butterfly*) and Gilbert and Sullivan (*The Mikado*). Manga's influence on recent and contemporary Western youth culture can be seen in the popularity of J-Pop music and the so-called 'Gothic-Lolita' aesthetic. Japanese street fashion has been popular in the UK for a long time: ASICS, Uniqlo and Superdry brands are well-known examples. There is a significant literature on these forms, including Gravett (2004) who offers a history of manga, Kinsella (2000) who identifies the gendered and racialized aspects of manga and anime, and Napier (2008) who offers an account of Japan and Japanese cultures as the focus of Western imagination and fantasy. Perhaps the point to make there is that these cultural products (in the nineteenth century and contemporarily) have acquired the cachet to become seen as cultural capital through the processes of global movement and flow.

The interesting sociological questions here in relation to both the early cults of Japonism and their later reincarnations through manga and anime concern the underlying interest in the *exotic* and, perhaps in *the exotic other,* that seem to drive these phenomena and the diverse ways in which these form or shape youth cultures and subcultures. Edward Said's well-known book *Orientalism* (1991) identified a widespread and persistent European racism focused on the Arab/Islamic world. Said argued that orientalism became a pervasive ideology shaped by imperialist assumptions of Western rationalism and cultural superiority. The Orient was seen as somehow immune from the processes of modernization that have created contemporary Western institutions and was seen as exotic, mysterious and somehow backward. The point about Said's work is that it identifies the processes and practices that create and sustain particular representations of the 'other' (and implicitly, 'us').

Perhaps there are aspects of these imaginative and representational practices underlying the current fascination with manga and anime where the cultural other becomes understood through these practices. However, these are complex questions precisely because how these cultural commodities travel is not always clear or, indeed, linear. American cartoon forms and styles inspired the original manga cartoons in the 1950s so the overall direction of cultural travel could be seen as two-way. Inevitably, these original forms become altered and hybridized in the process (Pieterse, 2010: 347).

This means, as Gidley points out (2007: 147), that simplistic arguments that suggest the globalization of culture (whether American, British or Japanese) can be understood as just another form of cultural imperialism, a specific nation or culture seeking to dominate and exploit other cultures economically or in other ways, should be rejected. Yet, the sheer market power and influence of global players such as Walmart, Coca-Cola or Tesco must be acknowledged. Cultural traffic is increasingly multidirectional and, as Gidley indicates, cultural products and artefacts are not consumed passively. Rather, as with the young people in the example from Uganda, they are adapted and combined with local cultural forms and practices to produce new and, potentially, enlivened entities.

The concept of globalization invites us to imagine a world that goes way beyond the proximate aspects of our lives that might be understood as 'near' or 'local'. In a famous essay, *The Stranger,* the early twentieth-century sociologist Georg Simmel looked at the relationship between the stranger (exemplified for Simmel by the European Jew but there are contemporary equivalents such as the international student, the refugee or the asylum seeker) and the group. Simmel suggested that the stranger's mobility and presence in one's local communities generated a kind of 'synthesis of nearness and remoteness' (Simmel, 1971: 145). In that sense, like Simmel, imagining a world beyond that understood as near cannot be avoided: the presence of the stranger ensures that everyone is made perpetually aware of the global in the local. One only has to travel through a city centre by metro or bus to see the extent to which the metro carriage becomes the synthesis of 'near and far' to which Simmel refers. For Simmel, as for contemporaries, the presence of the stranger signalled the capacity of societies to change by absorbing newness, thus becoming revitalized. This is forgotten when discussions of globalization focus solely on the stranger as threat.

Whatever else globalization signals, the idea of mobility is extremely important. Mobility implies the *physical* capacity to move around. For example, it gets easier and easier to travel rapidly to new places for holidays, commuters travel ever-greater distances to work; Americans have been accused of routinely sending prisoners from the Middle East to various countries where US surrogates extract information from them through torture (and there are accusations of the British being complicit in this); and refugees and asylum seekers from sub-Saharan Africa arrive in Europe in increasing numbers.

As well as physical mobility, there are also aspects of *virtual* mobility that have developed as a consequence of new networking capacities using information and communication technologies. Castells (2009) argues that the global is constituted in the articulation of network technologies, the spaces defined by networks and the people who control them, often powerful and protected elites.

For Castells, globalization is constituted principally in the global flow of finance, and power has come to be lodged in the networks of information through which political (small 'p') control is secured. He suggests that power itself has changed little; its sources and forms remain 'violence and discourse, coercion and persuasion, political domination and cultural framing' (ibid: 50). However, the environment in which power is exercised *has* altered and is now characterized by the articulation of global and local elements in the context of the network.

Castells' arguments, however, are broader than simply thinking about globalization in the abstract. He is also concerned with contested political legitimacy (trust in politicians is at an all time low, voter turnout at elections is almost universally diminishing and some political constituencies have come to rely on celebrity politicians – Schwarzenegger and Reagan come to mind immediately). The point here, for Castells, is that there exists a worldwide crisis of political legitimacy. He adds to this the tendency towards the fragmentation of traditional political constituencies (for example the association between social class and political parties or trade unions), increasing social mobility and processes of individualization and he suggests that a growing fissure exists between citizens and politics.

However, Castells also wants to suggest how the networks that constitute globalization can, in principle, also contribute to revitalizing political life. He shows, for example, that in the 2008 election in the US youth mobilization increased for the third election running and that this was partially a consequence of re-imagining and reprogramming communication networks (the 'Yes We Can' campaign, that was virally distributed, for example) to ensure that young Americans were registered to vote and did so in large numbers for Obama. Castells argues that digitally based communication networks have the capacity to re-establish political legitimacy by forming connections between the 'powerless segments of the population to power-making procedures' (Castells, 2009: 366). Youth is one of those relatively powerless segments.

A slightly different take on globalization is offered by the anthropologist Arjun Appadurai who has developed the idea of contemporary (global) society being constituted by a series of what he refers to as 'scapes' (an article on Appadurai's analysis can be found here: http://www.intcul.tohoku.ac.jp/~holden/MediatedSociety/Readings/2003_04/Appadurai.html).

Appadurai suggests, in common with Castells, that global capitalism has deeply fragmenting tendencies and that social life can now be understood as a series of cultural flows that shape a highly mobile and shifting world. These he defines in five ways: ethnoscapes, mediascapes, technoscapes, finanscapes and ideoscapes (see Table 7.3).

Table 7.3 The globalized world: 'scapes'

Ethnoscapes	The landscape of people who form the shifting global world: e.g. tourists, refugees, guest workers, exiles and travellers
Mediascapes	The media images of the world (with which we are perpetually bombarded: films, adverts, 'world music' and digital records of all kinds) through which we understand and 'imagine' the world around us
Technoscapes	Technology's capacity to move across borders according to politics, finance and the availability of labour to become structured in global configurations (military hardware, computer games and medicines, for example)
Finanscapes	The global flow of money and finance through currency markets, stock exchanges and various mechanisms of speculation (e.g. hedge funds)
Ideoscapes	The global flows of messages, ideas and ideology, the latter shaping conflicts between state ideologies and the counter-ideologies of social movements challenging for power

Over to you...

Critical reflection

Let us try to place this in a more concrete setting. If we return to the example of Uganda referred to earlier, we can begin to see some evidence of the ways in which these flows of culture and 'cultural stuff' become evident. We can identify at least three aspects of this.

First, one might think about the ways in which the Ugandan ethnoscape was constructed. In the village, there were people from different parts of the country and the world: locals, for example, were immediately evident. Stories of refugees and militia members from the nearby Democratic Republic of Congo had been recounted earlier that day. My own presence as a white man, a traveller, from the North of the globe also contributed to the construction of a hybridized and differentiated space. Second, aspects of a mediascape might be identified: the Crystal Palace shirt, the discussion of US hip-hop music and its influence on contemporary music-making in Uganda and the logos on trainers and tee shirts are all examples of these flows of media and this is certainly not one-way traffic. Contemporary African music is consumed almost voraciously in the North as part of the broad interest in so-called 'world music'. Third, elements of the technoscape to which Appadurai refers are evident as well. The MP3 or CD player that one of the young men was using is an example of technology (cheap and available) flowing through borders and shaping the collective culture of which it becomes a part. The CD itself is another example. And we should remember that these developments have occurred alongside the continuing presence of tradition in the form of indigenous musical forms. Look at MP3 Mondomix, for example, for lots of examples of 'cross-over' forms.

You might like to try to extend the analysis here and work out what might count as examples of finanscapes and ideoscapes. The point about all of this is that these cultural flows embed the global firmly within the local.

Appadurai suggests that these *scapes* represent a series of shifting horizons or cultural streams where apparently disjointed elements become the resources and settings in which contemporary humans imagine and make their lives in global settings. For Appadurai, it is these scapes (as imagined worlds) that create interconnections and potential solidarities. They demonstrate that borders and boundaries are no longer impenetrable. However, this raises questions of whether some borders are impenetrable to *some* groups or populations. Which groups have access and which are prevented? For *whom* are borders open and for *whom* are they closed?

Whatever else can be said about globalization, the constancy of mobility and movement is always present. As Bauman (1998) suggests, people are perpetually on the move even as they sit in front of computer screens effortlessly moving from one space to another as virtual tourists, visitors and travellers. Perhaps, as some analysts have suggested, this is conducive to the development of *global citizenship*?

Globalization and citizenship

Despite the debates, the definition of globalization suggested by Ritzer and Atalay with which this chapter began is broad enough to use as a kind of working definition that includes several key elements:

- transplanetary process or set of processes
- increasing liquidity
- multidirectional flows of people, objects, places and information
- barriers to, or which expedite, those flows.

What then of the relationship between globalization and citizenship? These two concepts are related because they raise questions of human rights and obligations held through membership of a body politic in a changing and mobile world. The classical liberal theory of T.H. Marshall, which has been very high profile in debates about citizenship in the UK and similar liberal democracies, identifies three routes to national citizenship: *work, reproduction* and *war* (Marshall, 1963).

The world of *work* as a route probably needs no explaining: stating it crudely, full-time (and, increasingly, part-time for many people) paid employment provides a contact and engagement with the external world that affords the possibility of a person becoming acknowledged as a citizen. *Reproduction,* referring literally to biological as well as to social reproduction, acknowledges the significance of experiences of family formation. Marshall's work was set in the post-war era, and so gendered social relations shaped the reproduction route to citizenship. Marshall's third route – *war* – conveys the idea of 'the soldier citizen'. If one is prepared to fight and die for one's nation, then this constitutes an obvious and direct pathway to citizenship. All three of Marshall's citizenship routes are predicated upon the existence of the nation state in which citizenship can be achieved. Workers, families and soldiers are understood unequivocally in *national* terms.

Marshall explored the historical emergence of citizenship in the context of emerging modernity from the eighteenth century onwards and subsequent industrialization and urbanization that were associated with the consolidation of modern nation states. He identified three forms of citizenship:

1. **Civil:** rights necessary for individual freedom – liberty of the person, freedom of speech, freedom of religious worship and the right to own property.
2. **Political:** the right to participate in political processes as a member of political institutions (parliament, for example) or as an elector of those.
3. **Social:** the right to participate in the life of a society according to the standards of that society. This implies the development of education and social welfare institutions and mechanisms that can support this.

Marshall's account confers citizenship on the basis of rights rather than on other criteria. It is easy, and probably appropriate in some respects, to view Marshall's 1950s concept of citizenship as dated. It certainly fails to provide (or challenge) an account of gender relations and other forms of inequality, or social participation (in labour market terms, for example) and his model was devised in a context where international and global circumstances had yet to really impact on ideas of citizenship (see Dean, 2007; Lister, 2003). However, it is also important to recognize its influence and acceptance as probably *the* principal form in which liberal citizenship has been construed in the second half of the twentieth century. Many people who had never heard of T.H. Marshall would have, perhaps even unconsciously, used these ideas in their beliefs about what constituted a 'good citizen' (even if they didn't describe this in citizenship terms). Marshall's work gives rise to at least two ways of thinking about citizenship within the nation state, namely citizenship as *status* (entitlements and responsibilities in the context of nation state) and citizenship as *practice* within the nation state (conduct that exemplifies the 'good citizen'). Both of these are important in relation to young people.

Over to you...

Critical research and reflection

How do the young people who you know understand their entitlements and responsibilities as citizens? Do they use the term 'citizen' and what meaning does it have for them? To what extent do they feel either empowered or disempowered by recent political changes? What impact might the progressive withdrawal of benefits or the imposition of increased higher education fees have on the capacity of young people in England and Wales to be good citizens?

How would you define the 'good citizen'? How do young people define good citizenship? How might your work and that of other educationalists and professionals contribute to this?

There is an argument here that higher education, for example, is not only about preparing students for their place in the labour market, but that it also has a vital role in cultivating the kinds of capacities and outlooks that can contribute to realizing the 'good citizen'. What contributions to this aim might other practices make (youth work, therapy or schooling, for example)?

The apparent erosion of the power of nation states suggests a weakening of the link between citizenship and the nation state as a consequence of increased diversity, the so-called 'cosmopolitan challenge' (Delanty and Rumford, 2005: 191). However, as suggested, the idea of citizenship has been predicated on the existence of the nation state. So, the argument goes, you can't be a French citizen without there being a French state within which that sense of citizenship is embedded and realized. It is worth recalling Benedict Anderson's argument from Chapter 6 about the nation state being an *imagined* entity: 'it is an imagined political community – and imagined as both inherently limited and sovereign' (1991: 6). By this, Anderson means that members of such a community have to hold in their minds an image of their belongingness. Because people can never have face-to-face relations with all others in the nation (as in a localized community), imagination becomes crucial in evoking 'nation', its boundaries and its significance. The media are extremely important in creating shared representations of nationhood around and through which it becomes possible to imagine membership of a national community.

Some writers have raised the question of *global citizenship*, and the extent to which, given the processes of globalization, it might be possible to imagine being a global citizen. Castells understands this as applying to a power elite that he argues is in control of 'the space of flows'. Richard Falk, suggests that time

> ... partially displaces space as the essence of what the experience of global citizenship means; citizenship thereby becomes an essentially religious and normative undertaking, based on faith in the unseen, salvation in a world to come – not in heaven, but on earth – guided by convictions, beliefs and values. (Falk, 1993: 49)

Over to you...

Critically reflect on reading

You should critically reflect for a few minutes on what Falk is saying here. What are the main points that he makes? What kinds of 'religious and normative undertaking' might count towards this idea of the global citizen? What sorts of 'convictions, beliefs and values' does Falk refer to here? Can you identify any young people who may be involved in practices that might hold the promise (for them, at least) of the kind of global communion that seems to underlie Falk's position?

Falk goes on to identify four factors that underlie global citizenship.

1. Global citizenship embodies aspiration and a politics of desire: *the importance of the ultimate unity of human experience and an affective investment in this.*

2. It implies economic integration and a 'world outlook': *a world framework (for example the G20 or the UN) embodying a sense of unity.*

3. It implies consensus on environmental matters: *the primacy of appropriate energy use, resource management, protection of the environment and the acknowledgement of potential human extinction.*

4. It incorporates transnational mobilization and militancy: *the (paradoxical) anti-globalization social movements that have embodied global politics in resistance to (invariably) neoliberal politics and economics.*

According to Falk, the achievement of a citizenship of the kind envisaged would entail a number of institutional reforms:

- increased political centralization in the form of world government
- management of transnational affairs, particularly big business and entrepreneurship
- management of globalized technologies for sustainability
- the growth of regional political consciousness: new federalisms
- the growth of transnational activism: new political communities and patterns of association and the move from a preoccupation with *spatial* to *temporal* matters (that is, the future society).

As Falk readily concurs, this is highly utopian thinking but he wants to push the idea of 'politics as the art of the impossible'.

Bryan Turner (in Braham and Janes, 2002) makes some similar points. He proposes new ways of grounding citizenship on global foundations, based upon ecological concerns, aboriginal (indigenous) rights and cultural rights such as language, freedom of religion and so on. The rise of Islam or new forms of Christianity may be consistent with the latter category. 'Aboriginal rights', for Turner, encompass Australia, New Zealand and North America. The issue at stake here is *identity* for huge numbers of people whose very existence has hitherto been concealed or ignored, let alone acknowledged in citizenship terms. Environmental concerns seem to spread across the whole globe and their movements and activism are clearly global in nature (to get a sense of how this is developing, look at http://uk.oneworld. net/guides/environmentalactivism). It is clear that young people have been extremely active in promoting these movements and their objectives, despite appearing to be disillusioned (like many adults) with national and party political membership.

Over to you...

Critical reflection

Can you identify recent or current manifestations of claims to citizenship rights on the basis of distinct cultural identities?

There have been many examples of such claims over the last 20 years. The bloody conflict that took place in the Balkans in the 1990s was very much about the reassertion of old cultural identities that had become subsumed under the nationhood of Yugoslavia. Similar tensions emerged in Iraq between Sunni and Shia Muslims and, more recently, ethnic conflict arose in Kyrgyzstan between Uzbeks and the Kyrgyz population. The resurgence of Welsh, Irish and Scottish languages is a less dramatic example. The increasing significance and influence of Islam is a very clear assertion of cultural identity and rights that seems to be extending across the globe. Reflecting on these examples, is it possible to see Benedict Anderson's idea of the nation as 'imagined community'? How much power does this evocation of 'nationhood' have in mobilizing people in their struggles for recognition and justice, and in what specific ways can you see such ideas being disseminated? Do you think that young people might have a particular role in these struggles?

Forms of global citizenship based upon concern for the environment perhaps become increasingly tenable, as communication is made easier through the use of social networking technologies such as Twitter. Many young people are able to access these digital technologies and the capacities that inhere in them (perhaps for riot and revolution), that are often inaccessible to older generations. These capacities may displace the authority of an adult elite, creating cultural distance between generations, resulting in declining trust in some settings. However, some analysts seem to have overstated the power of these communication forms. In the 2009 social unrest in Iran, for example, some media commentators suggested that social networking had the potential to overthrow the governing regime. That did not occur and it is difficult to see many immediately positive outcomes from those protests. However, it is clear that digital technologies played a role in the so-called Arab Spring in 2011, and in sending images out of Syria in 2011 and 2012. The anti-globalization movements that have emerged over recent years are other examples. There is a substantial literature on the emergence of social movements (some of which have been predicated on ideas of citizenship) in the context of globalization and in which many young people have been involved (see, for example, Offe, 1985; Tarrow, 1998; or Halcli, 2000, for good overviews). The student movement that rapidly grew in 2010 in the UK (and just as rapidly subsided) amidst a context of prospective cuts and rises in tuition fees in higher education shared some of the features of social movements. The so-called 'new social movements' (for example the anti-capitalist movement, women's movement, or human rights movement; it is sometimes difficult to know whether to refer to single or plural) have a number of common characteristics as well as their fundamentally youth-based involvement.

- They are collective attempts to resist or promote some form of social, cultural or political change: 'insurgent politics'.

- They are responses to the perceived inadequate capacity of existing political structures to properly represent the interests of those involved: it is often young people who initiate and participate.

- They broaden the range of what can be considered political: they depart from 'older' class-based politics.

- They are organized in loose and decentralized network forms: informal, fragmented and non-hierarchical.

- They often embody 'post-materialist' values that focus on lifestyle, environment, wellbeing and quality of life.

The literature suggests that a characteristic process underlies the life course of these movements as illustrated in Figure 7.1 (adapted from Macionis and Plummer, 2008). This model is based on 'traditional' social movements and may not always encompass the dynamic processes that accompany movements that have emerged in Castells' networked societies.

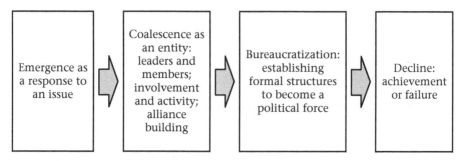

Figure 7.1 The 'natural history' of social movements
Source: Adapted from Macionis and Plummer (2008)

There are real questions about the extent to which new social movements 'coalesce': are they decentralized and do they have an existence only or mainly in virtual rather than material space, what Castells refers to as the 'new public space'? As he points out, social movements are engaged in a 'battle of images and frames, ... for minds and souls ... in multimedia communication networks' (Castells, 2009: 301–2). Castells is optimistic that social movements and 'insurgent politics' can use public space (often virtual space) in multiple ways to aim for change and autonomy by engaging in the horizontal relations that network communications promote (that is, to link with other groups and interests) and the established and mainstream media (to promote their messages and ideas). However, this will depend, he suggests, on the preservation of a free and fair system of networked communication (that is, one that is not dominated by elite interests or subject to political control or interference) and therefore freedom and 'social change, become entwined with the institutional and organizational operation of communication networks. Communication politics becomes dependent on the politics of communication' (ibid: 302).

Despite Castells' apparent optimism, the extent to which forms of environmental, aboriginal and cultural globalization are *actually* occurring (or have occurred) through the activities of new social movements is sometimes difficult to gauge. However, Falk's and Turner's arguments are, perhaps, more utopian and focused on claims for the future rather than accurate accounts or descriptions of what is occurring in the present. For Falk, modes of global citizenship should be seen as:

> ... hopeful forms arising from feelings of solidarity, concerns about equity and nature, strong impulses to combine local rootedness with planetary awareness, and the underlying belief that the security and sanctity of the human community rests, in the end, on embodying an ethos of non-violence in political practices at all levels of social organization, from the family to the world. (Falk, 1993: 50)

To conclude Chapter 7, citizenship and globalization are considered specifically in relation to young people and youth.

Globalization, Citizenship and Youth

There is very obviously a sense in which the discussion of globalization considered so far relates directly to young people. They are the future of the planet; these matters are of even more significance to them than to those who are no longer young. On the other hand, the concept of citizenship seems to be distant and even irrelevant for many contemporary young people. Young people in transition between childhood and adulthood may not be able to lay claim to any form of citizenship, however the term is defined, especially as the experiences of transition become more challenging in a declining labour market.

As suggested earlier in Chapter 7, the *global* must be understood in terms of the *local*, especially in relation to young people. Chapter 3 referred to the work of Beck and Giddens and in particular to the significance of processes of individualization in globalized late modernity. It was suggested that young people's agency is increasingly experienced by them in individual terms, as the 'project of the self' or the 'choice biography'. In 'risk societies' (where futures are continuously unpredictable, as Castells and others suggest) the capacities of flexibility and mobility are crucial if individual success and aspiration are to be realized. Recent German research shows how young people in the eastern part (post-socialist GDR) of Germany experience the consequences of global shifts and changes (in the labour market, for example) in the context of their local towns and neighbour-hoods. The work of Hörschelmann and Schäfer (2005) shows the extent to which young people's access to *social capital* (networks of interpersonal relationships) and *cultural capital* positions them in their engagement with global factors that shape labour market, life and consumer opportunities.

In Hörschelmann and Schäfer's research the capacity of middle-class, well-educated young people to deal with the uncertainties that faced them was very clear. They had the capital that would support their future aspirations, or they had the capacity to develop these. They were able to envisage life as a challenge in which they would need to be open to external influences (culture, media and people, for example), to be mobile and adapt. They had acquired 'transnational capital' that would equip individuals for life in changing and international circumstances including openness to different cultures, new lifestyles and language skills. Some of the less-well educated working-class young people experienced uncertainty and change through globalizing forces as threatening and they became marginalized in their own towns or cities, aware that their skills and knowledge would not necessarily enable them to reach their aspirations. As Hörschelmann and Schäfer point out, that is partially a consequence of:

> ... their structural position in relation to socio-cultural and economic resources, they also receive little support from parents or youth workers to develop the skills and the confidence to deal with the threats and opportunities of 'risk society'. This is all the more worrying since staying put will unlikely be an option for them in a location where training opportunities and work are of short supply, thus posing significant risks for their personal biographies. (2005: 239)

The literature on youth, globalization and citizenship has expanded significantly in the last decade. Several writers have suggested that youth culture itself could be understood as a loose non-territorial and globalized community (Bennett, 2005: 68; Scholte, 2000: 115). Cult films, popular music, slang and fashion are clear examples. The global reach of *MTV* and derivatives provides a particular manifestation of this. The youthful aspects of anti-globalization movements, as with the 1960s peace movement and anti-war movements before them could, perhaps ironically, also be characterized as global.

However, the extent to which these *are* global is perhaps inevitably questionable. Many young people in emerging economies do not, and may never, participate in any of these 'youth solidarities', and patterns of *local* identity and inequality discussed in Chapter 6 may be far more important to them. Perhaps this raises one of the main questions about globalization. That is, whether it can better be understood in some circumstances at least as more restricted but still *internationalized*. Nevertheless, as with the environmental and cultural developments referred to above, it is possible to imagine young people as constituting an important aspect of future global or international citizenship development. However, supra-territorial associations may have given some young people the possibility of a voice in a way that territorially based movements or organizations so often have not.

Over to you...

Critical reflection

Thinking about the arguments posed by Castells or Falk, for example, and reflecting on the work of Hörschelmann and Schäfer above, what forms of citizenship might be relevant to young people in the early twenty-first century? Given the erosion of (or changes to) the power of the nation state (and you may want to challenge that assertion), is it appropriate to teach aspects of traditional liberal citizenship in schools, based perhaps on the ideas that came from Marshall's work in the mid-twentieth century?

Thinking about young people that you know, is there a real possibility for environmental concerns to become the basis of new forms of global citizenship that might involve these young people? Thinking about the earlier distinction between citizenship as a status on the one hand (the argument about rights and entitlements as well as responsibilities) and as forms of practice on the other, what does being 'a good citizen' mean in the early twenty-first century? Are opportunities for practising good citizenship shaped by social difference in any way? Is it sometimes easier for either young men or young women to be seen as good citizens? How is this influenced by being black, white, Muslim, Christian or atheist?

Clearly, in political terms, citizenship is considered to be important (Bamber, 2010). In the UK, compulsory citizenship education has been included in the national curriculum in the context of fears about a 'democratic deficit', young people disengaging from political participation and failing to acknowledge the responsibilities of citizenship. Kymlicka offers a useful definition of this:

> Citizenship education is not just a matter of learning the basic facts about the institutions and procedures of political life; it also involves acquiring a range of dispositions, virtues and loyalties that are immediately bound up with the practice of democratic citizenship. (Kymlicka, 1999: 79)

In this view, citizenship embodies rights, responsibilities *and* the capacities necessary to engage in the practices of citizenship. Citizenship education is a form of socialization into a particular normative structure. For some authors, the democratic deficit (mainly understood in terms of voter behaviour) is the symptom of a wider crisis of liberal democracy across Europe and beyond and takes us back to Castells' questions about political legitimacy (Sassen, 2006).

Less than 60% of the electorate voted in the 2001 UK general election and the governing party was elected on 25% of the total vote. Compared with other groups, young people are less likely to vote or join a political party and the under-25s are four times less likely to be registered to vote than any other group (Geddes and Rust, 2000). Bentley and Oakley found that young people withdraw from formal politics because they don't see it making 'a tangible difference to the circumstances they face; that conventional politics often does not seem to achieve the things they want [and] that they are not listened to seriously' (1999: 190). Identifying adults as the problem here, the British Youth Council argued that 'rather than young people being apathetic it is in fact the politicians and parties who are indifferent, uninterested and complacent' (in Kimberlee, 2002: 89). More recently, research by Wayne et al. (2010) explored young people's views of television news and politics. This identified young people's experience of disengagement with politics in the UK, partially as a consequence of news broadcasting doing little to connect politics with young people's lived experiences. The young people in this research were not uninterested in politics and news, but were alienated by the generally negative ways in which television news programmes represented them.

In spite of evidence of a broad lack of interest in 'ballot-box politics' (but great interest in some other politics), it is the young who are the target of active citizenship discourses and citizenship education in the UK and elsewhere. Yet this still relies on a notion of citizenship grounded in the nation state rather than in global politics and has antipathy both to youth-inspired global campaigning and types of citizenship such as those derived from alternative identities such as faith and religion. It fears both and often links the latter with terrorism. Education is a powerful socializing agent in forming young people's characters and identities and in shaping their transitions to adulthood. Following Foucault, education is understood as an institution in which the skills, knowledge and dispositions (as *power-knowledge* in aspects of curriculum) necessary for *responsible* citizenship in the liberal state are cultivated (Foucault, 1980). Taking this into account, it might be inferred that the driving force behind citizenship education is the desire to form 'ideal citizens' of the future, a practice invested in by all societies but which has had particular force in the UK and similar societies through the first part of the twenty-first century as a consequence of an apparent democratic deficit. Ruth Lister (2005) points out that, although citizenship has been understood as an *inclusionary* mechanism it has latterly come to signify the importance of *exclusion*. Young people have characteristically been regarded as incomplete or 'deficit' citizens and, thus, politically and socially disengaged, hence the need to re-engage them through different forms of citizenship education. Youth, as a social relation as well as a stage in the life course, is that time in which claims to citizenship are themselves in states of transition. Lister suggests five broad models of citizenship.

1. **Citizenship as universal status:** this signifies membership of community or nation. A 'thin' version of this includes everyone and refers to relatively simple personhood. The 'thicker' version of citizenship entails belonging and having a sense of being part of something.
2. **Citizenship as respectable economic independence:** this version of citizenship relies on the individual's participation in the labour market and implies a degree of economic independence.
3. **Citizenship as constructive social participation:** this signals a positive relation to and stance towards community and the collective. It could include becoming involved in volunteering or some form of service and it privileges the notion of responsibility.
4. **Citizenship as a social contract:** this version of citizenship embodies discourses of rights and responsibilities. As such, it is a broadly liberal version of citizenship.
5. **Citizenship as the right to voice:** this refers to the right to have a say in what goes on and to participate in decision-making in the collective sphere.

There are considerable overlaps between these models.

Over to you...

Critical reflection

Now is a particularly apposite time to place the idea of citizenship (and global citizenship) on education agendas. If, as some of the literature indicates, the idea of national citizenship is being eroded and potentially being replaced by something transnational and even global, what are the implications for citizenship education? How could Lister's models of citizenship contribute to that?

What role might youth practitioners play in a broad approach to citizenship and citizenship education?

What does seem true is that for many young people the nation state and *the local* (in Castells' terms the 'space of places') are likely to form the space in which citizenship is experienced, although aspects of the global may penetrate this. Indeed, the specificity of place seems to be retained in the persistence of the local, and where people live 'continues to matter since people feel some sense of "being at home" in an increasingly turbulent world' (Savage, Bagnall and Longhurst, 2005: 12). For some, the fixed point of the local becomes the site of 'elective belonging' – chosen space in which to live and put down roots – and it opens up the potential for new kinds of solidarities and connections into the global world. Interestingly, this suggestion seeks *not* to counterpose local and global but rather to explore the interconnections of a range of complex constituted spaces in which citizenship identities and solidarities might be constructed and developed.

Summary and Conclusions

Sociologists are perhaps sometimes guilty of concentrating too much on change at the expense of clear analysis of constancy: how social relations endure over time. Chapter 7 has explored the paradox of a shifting yet also constant world in the context of the two concepts of globalization and citizenship.

The concept of globalization draws attention to the intersection of a range of forces: time–space compression, flows of different kinds, interdependencies and connections, expanding power networks and a convergence of global problems and interests. Although there is much argument about the extent to which there are precedents to globalization (for example the Roman Empire or English colonization of the world in the sixteenth century), it appears that *digitization* has created unprecedented capacities for the consolidation of power (for example in corporations, financial institutions and non-governmental organizations) across time and space, sometimes leading to negative economic consequences for nation states and communities (for example when capital is shifted from one location to another).

Globalization has important implications for the nature and experience of youth, in some ways *universalizing* youth through shared interests and solidarities, and in other ways *fragmenting* and differentiating youth by creating patterns of inequality in access to various economic and cultural assets. The idea of *flow* is a central motif in the literature on globalization, designating shifts of people, culture, finance and knowledge that have come to characterize the late modern world. Flows of cultural and symbolic resources (films, literature, fashion, music and ideas) running in different directions have contributed to the potential synchronization of global youth. Population flows, as the consequence of migration and asylum seeking, are especially familiar to those living in Western cities and often result in a varied and contested multiculturalism.

Importantly, and paradoxically, globalization draws attention to the continuing significance of the *local*. Indeed, the global is inevitably experienced *through* the local (global and local form hybrids of different sorts: examples were given from African and Japanese cultural entities) and for young people especially it is within the local that they are most likely to make claims to citizenship as a form of membership and belonging. Citizenship seems to be predicated on the notion of the nation state and Chapter 7 discussed the seminal work of Marshall in this respect. Marshall's work leads to two constitutive aspects of citizenship: citizenship as forms of *entitlement* (for example social or civil) and as forms of *practice* ('good citizenship'). It is relatively easy to see how these might be enacted in the context of the nation state but matters become more complex in a globalized world. If, as some have argued, the nation state is undermined by globalization, what sorts of claims might be made for *global citizenship*? What can be shared, what opportunities exist for agency and what sources of solidarity exist in a globalized world?

For many young people (and others), the local continues to be an important setting in which transitions occur and identities are constructed. Practitioners and policymakers will have to confront the challenges faced at local level in the shifting contexts of youth and social policy in different jurisdictions: nation states and parts of nation states. However, it is in researching and theorizing the interconnections between the local and the global that sociology can offer a better understanding of the changing yet constant nature of youth.

Further Reading

- Nayak, A. (2003) *Race, Place and Globalization: Youth cultures in a changing world*, Oxford: Berg.

  This book explores youth cultures emerging as a consequence of migration and settlement in the north east of England. The understanding of culture and cultural forms in terms of local/global relations is central to the arguments here.

- Roberts, K. (2009) *Youth in Transition. Eastern Europe and the West*, Basingstoke: Palgrave Macmillan.

  Roberts offers important comparisons between youth transitions in Europe, both East and West, including labour markets, leisure, families and politics.

- Shaw, S.M.I. (2010) *Parents, Children, Young People and the State*, Buckingham: Open University Press.

  The end chapter on 'a risk and at risk' offers a critical approach to current negative discourses of youth in the context of underlying fears about the alleged breakdown of family life in the context of international and global welfare policy.

8
Does sociology matter?

In concluding this exploration of sociology and in claiming that sociology *does* matter, several themes are rehearsed to suggest the implications for those engaged in work with young people and communities. In particular, Chapter 8 considers the production of sociological knowledge, including that by *practitioner-sociologists*, professionals (such as youth practitioners) to whose work sociological understanding can contribute an important critical dimension.

Sociology is valuable and has much to say which can broaden and deepen our understanding of youth in a social context, and which can contribute to the sensitivity and awareness necessary for working with young people as individuals and in groups. However, it is also important to make any claims for sociology in a modest way and to acknowledge that it is but one source of knowledge about the world. Sociological knowledge may, in some circumstances, make a significant contribution to improving aspects of human life. However, its capacity is necessarily limited to the range of its interests and its contribution is one among others. Sociologists should resist any tendency towards a sociological imperialism (Strong, 1979), to suggest that sociology is a superior way of knowing, and must remember the importance of other disciplines and knowledge frameworks that can help us to understand the world. That includes accounts which do not necessarily make any (scientific) claims to truth, such as novels, films, theatre, but which can nevertheless inform our understanding of questions in which sociologists are interested. Throughout this book, references have been made to these sources, and those who use sociology to enhance and develop their work should draw from them in developing their sociological imagination and understanding.

Despite disagreement among sociologists, a fundamental connection runs through the differing definitions and statements about sociology. This thread is the basic agreement that one of its main purposes is the production of knowledge which offers an analytic and empirically informed understanding of the structures, processes, relations, divisions, practices and meanings that organize and are constituted through social life. The effort made through sociology to understand that society and human relationships is a more complex area than is immediately apparent to 'common sense' and has been true since Comte first coined the term sociology in the early nineteenth century.

Throughout, the book has suggested the important role of *imagination* in sociological work. Contemporary sociologists aim to explore and explain the *social* aspects of social phenomena and in doing so they exercise their 'sociological imagination'. This is also the title of a seminal book by C. Wright Mills (2000), a sociological classic written in the US during the 1950s. Although its language inevitably reflects the style and conventions of the time, this book remains important and has a particular resonance for those who work with the young. Wright Mills' main argument is that in modern societies *biographies* (all those things construed and explained as being 'personal' or 'individual' or solely connected with individuals' own lives) are bound up with wider historical, cultural and social processes. Wright Mills' work stresses individual biographies and their relation to *shared* histories and cultures. Pierre Bourdieu makes a similar point in arguing that 'Contrary to the common preconception that associates sociology with the collective, it has to be pointed out that the collective is deposited in each individual in the form of durable dispositions such as mental structures' (1995: 18). Bourdieu indicates that the social 'gets inside' of individual consciousness, thus shaping individuals' understanding of their worlds and how they conduct themselves in those worlds. Bernstein's work similarly offers meticulous analysis of the role of language in constructing and elaborating the social (Bernstein, 2000). It is for these reasons that sociologists are interested in, for example, individual young people's accounts of their transition experiences, their family lives or their relationships with parents, peers or professionals. Their accounts tell something about the broader social processes that shape their lives and those of others.

Wright Mills makes a further connection between individual experiences and the broader social context in which they are located. He refers to *personal troubles* – unemployment, divorce or homelessness, for example – that are experienced as matters that threaten the immediate life-setting of individuals and their families; their *milieu*, in Wright Mills' terms. He connects troubles to the idea of *issues*; matters that transcend individuals' immediate worlds and that are bound up in historical, social and cultural processes. This has been an important approach in the history of youth work since the 1970s – but without the debt to C. Wright Mills being acknowledged and, indeed, without many practitioners understanding that there is sociological authority behind their approach. Youth practitioners have, characteristically, tried to understand young people as located in their social and cultural settings rather than taking a simple individualized view of them.

By exercising the sociological imagination, as Wright Mills suggests, one can illustrate the powerful, and often unacknowledged, connections between personal and social life. By doing this, one can start explaining the underlying patterns and relationships that shape human conduct and relations. In effect, good sociology moves between arguments about the general and the particular. Events in the world are invariably located within networks of *interdependency* in which individuals are variously placed and it is those networks and their consequences that form the stuff of sociology. So this might be the basis of arguing the importance of a collective, or group-based, campaigning or educational approach to work with young people, rather than an individualized treatment-based approach. For example, youth unemployment rises as a consequence of certain kinds of economic relations and processes rather than through individual fault or deficit; divorce rates increase in societies characterized by particular views of intimacy, love and personal fulfilment, rather than through individual failure.

Following Wright Mills' work, therefore, sociologists, and youth practitioners, whose interventions in the lives of young people are informed by sociology, distinguish between sociological accounts and those that rely on, say, 'natural', 'biological' or 'individual' explanations. They ask critical questions about how *relations* of class or gender might influence life expectancy or life chances. Other sociologists may be interested in how the human body – an apparently 'natural' object – is shaped in distinctively social ways. How might the body be 'socially constructed' through different grooming or disciplinary practices, or feeding regimes? Think about the complex ways in which different groups of young people use their bodies to signify identity, resistance or pleasure. This takes the debate beyond pathological representations and discourses of adolescence, and distinguishes between work which involves a focus on the personal adjustments or 'transitions' of adolescents, and that which understands that youth has other meanings associated with and shaped by social context.

Other sociologists have focused on the ways in which 'race' (for some people an apparently biologically 'fixed' category) has been used to make sense of personal and social identity in modern societies: how have 'racial identities' become constructed in particular ways? This has specific importance in relation to how practitioners respond to the experiences of different young people, address the circumstances that they face, and work within a context of policy and law that sometimes involves prioritizing social questions related to segregation, conflict and cultural misunderstandings in which race plays an important part.

In other settings, sociologists have asked about the role of violence in the formation of 'masculinity', and how violence 'works' as an element of men's social and cultural capital, drawing arguments away from natural or biological explanations. In these examples, and again following Wright

Mills, it is the specifically *social* dimensions of these phenomena, rather than any individual, 'natural', biological or psychological aspects that are of interest and importance. In everyday or common sense accounts of the world, people routinely explain events as a consequence of individual choice and action, but by identifying and analysing the social dimensions of phenomena, sociology offers other kinds of explanations. These often suggest that events in the world may not be solely the outcomes of individual conduct but the result of complex social processes over time. Such explanations enable those who work with young people to understand that in circumstances of inequality, work that aims to improve young people's situations must move beyond blaming victims or perpetrators, must travel beyond simple responses to the individual and intervene in ways that draw upon a sociological understanding.

Some examples of how sociology can enrich the way *practitioners* think about their work and offer resources for making creative and insightful responses to young people are illustrated here.

Example 1

Religion, identity and belief

As part of an educational programme on the significance of political Islam for young people, detached youth workers (street workers) in one UK city undertook some work with young men who were described as being at risk of getting involved with so-called religious fundamentalism and becoming 'radicalized'. Politicians asked how and why these young men were involved with religious groups, what were their attractions and what processes might be entailed in their association with and continuing membership of religious groups. Sociology has much to say about the importance of religion and religious faith in Western societies: religion could be understood as oppositional or resistant to dominant social values ('materialism' or 'progress', for example), it might be seen as offering space in which a meaningful and valued identity can be constructed in a society where everyday experience devalues some young people and their culture, or it might represent a strengthening of social solidarity, and it involves a knowledge frame that is self-contained and seems to offer certainties in a world which is experienced as deeply uncertain. Without understanding faith practices in terms of social relations, process and difference, it is difficult to see how interventions might be effective in helping young people to make good decisions about their lives.

Example 2

The rise of eating disorders

In a school, professional workers were becoming aware of an increasing number of young women with eating disorders. What is responsible for this increase and to what extent is it an individual problem or a social phenomenon? Why are some young women particularly vulnerable? Awareness of the difficulty among young women can alert workers to its appearance among young men. Why is the number of young men with eating disorders apparently increasing? While the individual consequences of anorexia and bulimia are potentially life threatening, sociologists have suggested that these conditions should also be understood as an expression of wider anxieties and insecurities that emerge about gender identities in modern, prosperous and globalized societies. Arguably, individual identities in late modern societies are not 'given'; they have to be 'made' from the choices and options that contemporary 'freedom' offers young women and young men. Some young people find it difficult to know how to conduct themselves in the face of a multiplicity of choices about how to look and be. Eating disorders might be understood as a longing for control and security and, perhaps, its achievement in a world where these capacities are elusive. By understanding this social explanation, practitioners enable young people to gain important insights into wider social processes.

Example 3

Spending time online

Teachers and youth workers based in a rural school tried to understand the importance of new information and communications technologies on the lives of young people in the school. Some parents and teachers were concerned about the effect on young people's development while others saw online gaming and social networking as opening up 'virtual communities' where young people might develop new and rewarding relationships. All sorts of questions emerged. How could sociology approach and imagine the phenomenon of online worlds and communities? Are they communities at all, and in what ways? To what extent do they offer the identity, association, solidarity and belonging associated with the face-to-face communities familiar in, say, neighbourhoods more generally? In talking to the young people, it was very clear that they felt part of online communities and that the friendships they described seemed just as real in one sense as those they formed in the material (or 'real') world. The online relationships that young people established sometimes spilled over into the material world and provided a foundation for new face-to-face relationships, some of which developed across national borders. The teachers and youth workers started to consider whether the internet might provide a new space in which some youth work and other educational initiatives could be located. In doing this they started to appreciate how the concepts of community,

> belonging, agency and participation are relevant to a digitized and global world. Socio-
> logical knowledge makes an important contribution to understanding a range of ways of
> understanding community and its relevance for human flourishing which must adapt to
> new situations encountered by youth.

Throughout this book, sociology has been presented as a body of knowledge concerned primarily with explanations of how and why certain kinds
of events occur. The chapters have focused especially on aspects of social
relations, social processes and social difference as constituting the social
world. Sociological theories could be understood as *stories* about how
humans interact, conduct and organize themselves in the social world. Most
sociologists would probably agree that sociological theory seeks to explain
how, why and in what circumstances social relations are established, social
processes operate and social difference 'works'. Runciman (1983) helpfully
suggests that sociology is concerned with four distinct kinds of work:

- **reporting** on events and processes
- **explaining** why things happened in the way that they did
- **describing** the experiences of the people who were involved in these
  events and the meanings that they gave to them
- **evaluating** the significance of the events for the wider society, asking
  whether they are good or desirable.

What is evident from this is that Runciman presents sociology as an
active set of practices, embodied in the work of four verbs: reporting,
explaining, describing and evaluating. For youth practitioners especially,
sociology incorporates both knowing *and* doing: it is concerned with knowledge *and* with practice. Runciman offers a particular framework for telling
a story about people in their social world and, of course, not all sociologists
will agree about the accuracy of reports, the descriptions and explanations
given for experiences and events, or the way in which significance or value
is accorded to their outcomes. Sociological stories are, in one sense, like
other stories, open to dispute because they are told from particular perspectives that embody different traditions. When it comes to it, judgements
have to be made on the veracity and truthfulness of sociological accounts.
Sociological knowledge, like any other knowledge, is produced in the
context of the particular practices of a community (a community of sociologists) and thus acquires meaning in a collective or social setting.

Runciman's idea of **reporting** the social world and the events and processes that shape it is an important starting point which makes a great deal of sense in the practice context. Reporting demands a particular kind of perspective: rigorous, reflexive and critical, constantly asking, 'What is going on here?' This is not easy. The objects of sociology (family, community or work organizations, for example) are already well known to sociologists, as they are to others. They are familiar through common sense encounters in day-to-day life and are the objects of 'tacit' or 'personal' knowledge that people build up from their experiences over time (Polanyi, 1962), and that professional workers build on the basis of their work experiences (Schön, 1983). The common sense knowledge derived from ongoing experience is a potentially rich, but non-systematic, body of knowledge that enables people to sustain normal everyday social and working life. However, when matters are reported only in common sense terms, reports invariably contain routine understandings, prejudice, distortions, half-accounts and misunderstanding as well as the characteristic perspectives that are generated from particular social or cultural positions. The boundary between common sense and sociological thinking can never be watertight as everyone is absorbed in day-to-day practices and routines, deploying the practical knowledge necessary to 'get along'. People do not query motives and meanings as a matter of course unless problems or questions about conduct arise. However, throughout this book it has been suggested that sociology encourages *precisely* such critical and reflexive understanding of the social world. It seeks to challenge the self-evident nature of what is already known and to disrupt its 'taken-for-grantedness' thereby gaining a different or extended understanding of events and processes. This is particularly important for those practitioners who have the power to intervene in the lives of others and who carry a weight of responsibility for the ways in which they exercise their powers.

Explaining the world suggests that sociology can somehow account for why and how things happen the way they do. In this book, the importance of historical *processes* has been identified. For example, as earlier chapters have suggested, the concept and meaning of youth emerged as a consequence of the major historical changes that occurred in the nineteenth and early twentieth centuries and has developed in a way that reflects further changes and processes. This was discussed in terms of an emerging *modernity,* entailing the growth of nation states, expansion of capitalism and industrialization, urbanization, new systems of education and training, developing regimes of surveillance and new knowledge frameworks that claimed to explain the phenomenon of youth and adolescence. Psychology as a newly codified body of knowledge was especially significant here. Without this overall historical account, it would be impossible to explain how contemporary meanings of youth have come about.

To be able to explain means that one has to *understand*. Sociologists seek to understand the social world in a disciplined way. The discipline of the so-called scientific method is a deeply contested area in sociology because there are different approaches to science and scientific understanding. It does mean that sociological work is bound by rules of evidence and that methodology is important in assessing the 'validity' of the knowledge produced by sociological work. However, it does not mean that the sociologist should adopt a crude 'scientistic' perspective, with simplistic explanations of cause and effect, or use empirical evidence as though it were self-evident. Human beings are much more complex than the inanimate objects and processes which were the subject of study of the early scientists from whose work the rules of scientific method were formulated. In particular, human beings give subjective meanings to their worlds and, as we have suggested, they are in a constant process of creating and inventing these worlds and their identities in it. Rejecting a scientistic approach and attempting to explore subjective meanings involves interpretive practices that involve the use of 'self' by the sociologist. However, this does not mean that the sociologist should 'get too close' to the people or subject being studied. What it does necessitate, following Bauman and May (2001), is that the sociologist adopts 'responsible speech', ensuring that the practice of sociological work itself (defining a sociological problem, undertaking data collection, analysis and interpretation) is transparent and that claims are supported by evidence and argument that can be subjected to the scrutiny of others (a professional community of sociologists and or practitioners). Objectivity in sociology consists in the approach and methods taken, rather than in its findings or results. Methods must be *appropriate* to the subject matter. For youth practitioner-researchers using sociology, this is especially important (Bradford and Cullen, 2012).

In **describing** the world, sociologists cannot take a 'God's eye view' on the matters they study: there is no neutral perspective or position from which any social process or social entity can be studied and judged. The processes in which sociologists are interested are social productions, constructed through the detailed practices of actors in specific social settings and shaped by broader social and historical processes in which they are set. It is those practices and their contexts in which sociologists are interested but of which they are also part. Insofar as young people are identified as a distinct social group, then youth is a focus of sociological attention. While the concept of youth can be explored in its range of meanings, the realities of young people's lives are dynamic and changing with time and place and one's view is always and forever partial. Sometimes, deep insights can be provided by sociological investigation into a section of a particular population but the boundaries to that understanding must be recognized.

When sociologists come to analyse and describe what is going on in the social world, they sometimes refer to the importance of *reflexivity*. To be reflexive means to consider one's own position, one's approach to knowledge as shaped by a range of social factors. Gender, age, race or class might all be important here in forming the 'durable dispositions' to which Bourdieu refers above and which shape thinking and imagination, including that of sociology. Reflexivity entails working out how the personal position of the sociologist or youth practitioner influences the knowledge generated through the research and reflection that they undertake and in the claims to knowledge and truth made. One's routine assumptions, interests and preoccupations can hide underlying social processes and relations, and sociology can be powerful in *problematizing* what is taken for granted. The social world is extraordinarily complex and it is that complexity for which good sociology tries to account. It is crucial that one's own position and perspective are acknowledged in the activities to which Runciman refers. If youth practitioners are unable to be *reflexive* (that is, acknowledge their position and understanding) their accounts, analysis and understanding of the world and young people's place in it will be extremely limited.

Runciman's final sociological activity, **evaluating**, draws attention to sociology's ethical stance in which it seeks to ask questions about value and, implicitly, the question of what sociology is for. David Silverman (1985) suggests three potential positions that sociologists might take up, all of which have potentially serious ethical and political implications.

- The sociologist as *scholar:* in this characterization of sociology, the objective is knowledge for its own sake (that is, to generate truth). Truth emerges as a consequence of the conscience of the sociologist-scholar and a commitment to responsible speech and scientific method. This is a liberal version of scholarship, sometimes critiqued from the point of view that it might uphold existing power relations, as the sociologist may unwittingly be co-opted into serving the interests of powerful groups, particularly pertinent in view of the relative powerlessness of young people in social institutions.

- The sociologist as *state counsellor:* this depiction of sociological work has the sociologist serving the state bureaucracy, providing evidence to identify and map out social problems and drive policy. This inevitably raises ethical tensions for sociologists in engaging with evidence in the service of state or organizational power-knowledge. The so-called 'evidence-based' approach to policy and practice might entail sociologists becoming involved in this position as they organize evidence in the pursuit of policy goals, in this case, with reference to young people.

- The sociologist as *partisan:* Howard Becker (1967) elaborated this position in asking the question 'whose side are we on?' The sociologist as partisan reflects political engagement and a commitment to siding with the underdog, arguing perhaps for the interests of disenfranchised youth, migrant populations or those in poverty. It is easy to see how in this case, because of commitment, the priority of one set of values being adopted over another clearly opens the possibility of truth being subordinated to ideology.

There may be a tendency in any of these positions, perhaps especially the latter two, to assume the 'grand conception' of sociology's role (Hammersley, 1999) in which sociology is construed as a radical and emancipatory project established to evaluate and change the world. This view has its roots in the nineteenth century as discussed in Chapter 1 and contrasts with a more modest view that the role of sociology is to understand social relations and processes and thus to inform social practices. The ongoing question of what sociology is for seems to lie in tensions between the positions that Silverman identifies above.

Much of the debate about whether the knowledge sociology produces is 'objective' and true or 'subjective' and biased has been based upon a mechanical and a somewhat methodologically obsessed notion of 'science' – an idealized model of methodological restrictions which does not actually reflect the development of natural science at all (Latour and Woolgar, 1986). Science – 'real science' – is not just about rigidly controlled experiments, careful observations and rigorous, logical reporting. It is also about glorious mental leaps-in-the-dark, creative thought, hunches and intuition. Wright Mills quotes Percy Bridgman, a Nobel Prize-winning physicist, as saying there is no scientific method as such, 'but the vital feature of the scientist's procedure has been merely to do his utmost with his mind, *no holds barred*' (2000: 69).

There are several strands of argument in the debate about the scientific status of sociology. These are important matters for practitioner-sociologists who are interested in using sociological knowledge to inform policy and practice. Max Weber advanced the classic argument for the scientificity of sociology, suggesting that the sociologist could and should be 'value neutral'. This neutrality would, Weber argued, ensure that sociological knowledge would be objective and scientific. He makes the distinction between 'factual judgement' and 'value judgement', the latter for Weber at least, having no place in science. This is a position referred to by Silverman above as 'sociologist as scholar'. In practice it means that sociologists should not 'take sides' in their studies of social phenomena.

An alternative argument is that no single objective social reality exists; only alternate subjective or *positioned* experiences of the social world.

Therefore, it is not possible for a sociologist to present such experiences as representing any kind of independent 'objective' viewpoint. Some sociologists have argued that it is important to throw out spurious notions of objectivity and actively takes sides on social issues, as Becker suggests: 'The question is not whether we should take sides, since we inevitably will, but rather whose side are we on?' (Becker, 1967: 239). This is the position to which Silverman refers above as the 'partisan' approach, and suggests that partisan sociology (particularly in social research) may have a gloss of radical chic, but in departing from sociological rigour its claim to be distinguished from 'polemic or investigative journalism must rest on its ability to comprehend the perspectives of top dogs, bottom dogs and, indeed, lap dogs' (Silverman, 1985: 178).

Some feminists and critical theorists (see, for example, Lather, 1991; Ribbens and Edwards, 1998) have taken the position that *gendered* social structures and relations in patriarchal and capitalist systems powerfully shape individual subjectivity and identity, and that the role of the social scientist is to render the relationship between meaning and structure explicit. In much of this work, the attempt is made to reconfigure the relationship between objectivity and subjectivity by allowing the 'voice' of the marginalized or the powerless to have a place in social research. Such researchers have been accused of presenting their work as a 'partnership' in which the experience of marginalized groups (including women, LGBT young people, members of minority ethnic groups) takes epistemological precedence over scientific method, essentially a claim that knowledge can be reduced to experience. This has been vigorously challenged and deliberation about truth and objectivity is ongoing (Moore and Muller, 1999; Hammersley, 1999; Young, 2008). What is really at issue here is the basis upon which truth claims are made. Emancipation of whatever kind, Silverman argues, cannot be the purpose of social science as that is to confuse 'fact and value'. The utility of research is a question of value, but the establishment of truth, for Silverman and others, is a matter of rigorous social scientific work. Silverman asks the question, if social science statements are merely one kind of account among others (common sense or journalism, for example), why should we pay attention to them? What is it that makes them *better* accounts than those of others?

Youth practitioners and practitioner-sociologists committed to positions of *social justice* in their work have to consider how their values shape their sociological work. It is important to see that values lead to particular questions (rather than other questions) being interesting and important to sociologists. Values influence and shape the questions sociologists and practitioner-sociologists ask: why *this* question, why not *that* question, how is the problem to be framed and asked? Distinguishing important from non-important questions is vital. This is often referred to as the consideration of *value relevance* and it means that sociological questions are connected to the cultural values of a society, have meaning for members of a society and are relevant to the particular problems of a society at any given time. The British Sociological Association's website, and its pages on ethical practice, is very helpful in this regard (http://www.britsoc.co.uk/media/27107/StatementofEthicalPractice.pdf). The BSA points to the potential *political* position in which sociological research is set, and urges sociologists to be cautious of how their work might be used by others. Powerful agents (managers, politicians or policymakers) may, partially, make policy and practice decisions on the basis of sociological work, so this is especially important for practitioner-sociologists. Insofar as young people act in a way that appears distinctive from other groups, insofar as there are institutions designed with a particular focus on youth, and insofar as policy and practice decisions have a particular focus on young people, then there is a specialist as well as a general relevance to the youth practitioner.

For example, there was considerable value relevance in researching the position of youth in the various regime changes in North Africa and the Middle East in 2011 or in looking at the street disturbances and riots in which young people were involved in London and Vancouver in the same year. These events indicate much about the importance of power, inequality, generations and the social position of youth. In the example of the riots, different positions might be taken in relation to particular sociological questions. Were the riots a consequence of individual criminality, the activities of organized gangs, a growing 'feral underclass', the absence of good male role models, poverty and inequality or merely opportunism in a context where the normal rules of the social contract were suspended? Good sociology, in deploying Wright Mills' sociological imagination would try to make connections between the particular circumstances in specific neighbourhoods (perhaps looking at events that could work as 'flashpoints', the particular identities of those involved, relations between different groups, key actors, media representations of isolated events that become part of a social narrative or moral panic) and possible broad social and historical processes that provide a context to the events themselves (shifting configurations of authority and deference, sharpening patterns of inequality related to global shifts, declining social solidarity and shared values, changing notions of 'morality', complex race, class and gender relations).

Clearly, positions vary. Despite the methodological arguments advanced by protagonists in debates about the nature of sociological knowledge, there is a level at which, for practical purposes, a compromise has to be reached (or at least an understanding established between the different positions). Sociological theorizing and research are inevitably and rightly shaped by views of the events under examination and these lead to very different sociological questions. Indeed, from sociology's earliest days, the problems taken on by sociologists were the problems of the day. As Chapter 1 showed, Marx, Weber and Durkheim were all preoccupied with aspects of capitalism and modernity and the impact of these on social order, social conflict and social relations. Their accounts of society implied particular ideas of what counted as the *good society* and what *human flourishing* might be in such societies. Sociology in the first decades of the twenty-first century may not have lost its interest in the good society, but its focus may appear to have altered as a consequence of social change occurring over the last century. Sociology is more interested in acknowledging the experiences and problems of *particular* social groups and their members perhaps because it has become increasingly difficult to identify shared beliefs and values (which is not to say that they do not exist) in societies that have become highly differentiated through, for example, global shifts and flows. Sociologists and practitioner-sociologists are interested in looking, for example, at the distinctive experiences of young women, young people from specific ethnic groups or young working-class men's transitions in order to explore what these might say about *broader* social processes. Sociology offers a way of critically understanding the social world and informing practitioner-sociologists' actions in it and, thus, contributing to its improvement. However, it can only do this if it argues and explains matters convincingly, if it demonstrates coherence in those arguments and if it invokes support from a knowledge community in giving it legitimacy.

Further Reading

- Bradford, S. and Cullen, F. (eds) (2012) *Research and Research Methods for Youth Practitioners*, London: Routledge.

  This book considers the significance of social research and argues that it is central to effective policy and practice.

- Wright Mills, C. (2000) *The Sociological Imagination, 40th Anniversary Edition*, Oxford: Oxford University Press.

  This is a sociological classic. Wright Mills shows how the social shapes the lives of all and of everything as he encourages the exercise of an imagination that forms connections between individual lives and social and historical processes in which they are set.

References

Aapola, S., Gonick, M. and Harris, A. (2005) *Young Femininity. Girlhood, Power and Social Change*, Basingstoke: Palgrave Macmillan.

Alden, P. (1904) 'The Problem of East London', in R. Mudie-Smith (ed.) *The Religious Life of London*, London: Hodder and Stoughton, 19–43.

Alexander, C. (1996) *The Art of Being Black: The creation of Black British youth identities*, Oxford: Oxford University Press.

Alexander, C. (2000) *The Asian Gang: Ethnicity, Identity, Masculinity*, London: Berg Publishers.

Alexander, C. (2008) *Rethinking Gangs. Gangs, Youth Violence and Public Policy*, London: Runnymede Trust.

Ali, S. (2003) *Mixed-Race, Post-Race, Gender, New Ethnicities and Cultural Practices*, London, Berg Publishers.

Anderson, B. (1991) (revised edition) *Imagined Communities. Reflections on the Origin and Spread of Nationalism*, London: Verso.

Archer, M. (2000) *Being Human. The Problem of Agency*, Cambridge: Cambridge University Press.

Archer, M. (2007) *Making our Way Through the World. Human Reflexivity and Social Mobility*, Cambridge: Cambridge University Press.

Bhabha, H. K. (1994) *The Location of Culture*, London: Routledge.

Ball, S.J. Maguire, M. and Macrae, S. (2000) *Choice, Pathways and Transitions Post-16. New Youth, New Economies in the Global City*, London: Routledge Falmer.

Bamber, P. (2010) 'Educating for Global citizenship', in H. Gadsby and A. Bullivant (eds) *Global Learning and Sustainable Development*, Abingdon: Routledge, 56–75.

Barron, M. and Bradford, S. (2007) 'Corporeal controls: Violence, bodies and young gay men's identities', *Youth and Society*, 39(2): 232–61.

Barry, N. (1987) *The New Right*, London: Routledge.

Bauman, Z. (1993) *Postmodern Ethics,* Oxford: Blackwell.

Bauman, Z. (1998) *Postmodernity and its Discontents*, Cambridge: Polity Press.

Bauman, Z. (2001) *The Individualized* Society, Cambridge: Polity Press.

Bauman, Z. (2004) *Identity: Conversations with Benedetto Vecchi (Themes for the 21st Century)*, Cambridge: Polity Press.

Bauman, Z. (2007) *Liquid Times, Living in an Age of Uncertainty,* Cambridge: Polity Press.

Bauman, Z. (2010) *44 Letters from the Liquid Modern World*, Cambridge: Polity Press.

Bauman, Z. and May, T. (2001) *Thinking Sociologically*, Oxford: Blackwell Publishers.

Beck, U. (1992) *Risk Society: Towards a New Modernity*, London: Sage Publications.

Beck, U. and Beck-Gernsheim, E. (1995) *The Normal Chaos of Love*, Cambridge: Polity Press.

Beck, U. and Beck-Gernsheim, E. (2002) *Individualization. Institutionalized Individualism and its Social and Political Consequences*, London: Sage Publications.

Beck-Gernsheim, E. (2002) *Reinventing the Family. In Search of New Lifestyles*, Cambridge: Polity Press.

Becker, H. (1963) *Outsiders. Studies in the Sociology of Deviance*, New York: The Free Press.

Becker, H. (1967) 'Whose side are we on?' *Social Problems*, 14, 239–48.

Bell, D. (1996) *The Cultural Contradictions of Capitalism*, twentieth anniversary edition, New York: Basic Books.

Bell, D. (1976) *The Coming of Post-Industrial Society*, New York: Basic Books.

Ben-Amos, I.K. (1994) *Adolescence and Youth in Early Modern England*, New Haven and London: Yale University Press.

Bennett, A. (2001) *Cultures of Popular Music*, Maidenhead: Open University Press.

Bennett, A. (2005) *Culture and Everyday Life*, London: Sage Publications.

Bentley, T. and Oakley, K. (1999) *The Real Deal: What young People Think About Government, Politics and Social Exclusion*, London: Demos.

Berger, P.L., Berger, B. and Kellner, H. (1973) *The Homeless Mind. Modernization and Consciousness*, New York: Random House.

Berlin, I. (1969) *Four Essays on Liberty*, Oxford: Oxford University Press.

Bernstein, B. (1971) *Class, Codes and Control, Volume 1, Theoretical Studies towards a Sociology of Language*, London: Routledge and Kegan Paul.

Bernstein, B. (2000) *Pedagogy, Symbolic Control and Identity. Theory, Research and Critique*, Lanham, MD: Rowman and Littlefield.

Bessant, J. (2008) 'Hard Wired for Risk: Neurological Science, the Adolescent Brain and Developmental Theory', *Journal of Youth Studies*, 11(3): 347–60.

Blackman, S. (1995) *Youth: Positions and Oppositions*, Aldershot: Avebury Press.

Blumer, H. (1969) *Symbolic Interaction*, Englewood Cliffs, NJ: Prentice Hall.

Bolton, S.C. (2005) *Emotion Management in the Workplace*, Basingstoke: Palgrave Macmillan.

Bourdieu, P. (1984) *Distinction, A Social Critique of the Judgement of Taste*, Cambridge, MA: Harvard University Press.

Bourdieu, P. (1986) 'The Forms of Capital', in J. Richardson (ed.) *Handbook of Theory of Research for the Sociology of Education*, New York: Greenwood Press, 241–58.

Bourdieu, P. (1995) *Sociology in Question*, London: Sage Publications.

Bowling, B. and Phillips, C. (2007) 'Disproportionate and Discriminatory: Reviewing the Evidence on Police Stop and Search', *The Modern Law Review*, 70(6): 936–61.

Bradford, S. (2004) 'The Management of Growing Up: youth work in community settings', in J. Roche, S. Tucker, R. Thomson and R. Flynn (eds) *Youth in Society*, Sage Publications, 245–54.

Bradford, S. (2007) 'Practices, policies and professionals: emerging discourses of expertise in English youth work', 1939–1951, *Youth and Policy*, 97/98, Autumn/Winter, 13–28.

Bradford, S. and Clark, M. (2011) 'Stigma Narratives: LGBT transitions and identities in Malta', *International Journal of Youth and Adolescence*, 16(2): 179–201.

Bradford, S. and Cullen, F. (eds) (2012) *Research and Research Methods for Youth Practitioners*, London: Routledge.

Bradford, S. and Hey, V. (2007) 'Successful Subjectivities? The Successification of Class, Ethnic and Gender Positions', *Journal of Education Policy*, 22(6): 595–614.

Bradford S. and Hey, V. (2010) 'Successful Subjectivities? The Successification of Class, Ethnic and Gender Positions', in M. Simons, M. Olssen and M. Peters (eds) *Re-Reading Education Policies. A Handbook Studying the Policy Agenda of the 21st Century*, Sense Publishers, 605–24.

Braham, P. and Janes, L. (eds) (2002) *Social Differences and Divisions*, Oxford: Blackwell Publishing in association with the Open University.

Brake, M. (1985) *Comparative Youth Culture. The Sociology of Youth Cultures and Youth Subcultures in America, Britain and Canada*, London: Routledge and Kegan Paul.

Brent, J. (2009) *Searching for Community. Representation, power and action on an urban estate*, Bristol: Policy Press.

Brooks, R. (ed.) (2009) *Transitions from Education to Work. New Perspectives from Europe and Beyond*, Basingstoke: Palgrave Macmillan.

Burke, E. (1790) *Reflections on the Revolution in France and on the Proceedings in Certain Societies in London Relative to that Event*, London: J. Dodsley.

Butler, A. (1993) 'The end of post-war consensus: reflections on the scholarly uses of political rhetoric', *The Political Quarterly*, 64(4): 435–46.

Castells, M. (2000a) (2nd edn) *The Rise of the Network Society*, Oxford: Blackwell Publishers.

Castells, M. (2000b) 'Materials for an exploratory theory of the network society', *British Journal of Sociology*, 51, 5–24.

Castells, M. (2009) *Communication Power*, Oxford: Oxford University Press.

Cavanagh, A. (2007) *Sociology in the Age of the Internet*, Maidenhead: Open University Press.

Clarke, J. (1976) 'The skinheads and the magical recovery of community', in S. Hall and T. Jefferson (eds) *Resistance through Rituals. Youth Subcultures in Post-war Britain*, London: Hutchinson, 99–102.

Clarke, J. and Newman, J. (1997) *The Managerial State*, London: Sage Publications.

Coffey, A. (2004) *Reconceptualizing Social Policy. Sociological Perspectives on Contemporary Social Policy*, Buckingham: Open University Press.

Cohen, A. (1955) *Delinquent Boys: The Culture of the Gang*, Chicago: Free Press.

Cohen, P. (1972) *Subcultural Conflict and Working Class Community*, Working Papers in Cultural Studies (2), Birmingham: Centre for Contemporary Cultural Studies.

Cohen, S. (1972) *Folk Devils and Moral Panics. The Creation of the Mods and Rockers*, London: McGibbon and Kee.

Coleman, J.S. (1989) 'Social Capital and the Creation of Human Capital', *American Journal of Sociology*, 94, Supplement, 95–120.

Collins-Mayo, S. (2010) 'Introduction', in S. Collins-Mayo and P. Dandelion (eds) *Religion and Youth*, Farnham: Ashgate, 1–6.

Comte, A. (2010) *The Positive Philosophy of Auguste Comte, Volume* II, New York: Cosimo Inc.

Connell, R.W. (1987) *Gender and Power: Society, the Person, Gender and Politics*, Cambridge: Polity Press.

Critcher, C. (ed.) (2006) *Moral Panics and the Media*, Maidenhead: Open University Press.

Cross, G. (2008) *Men to Boys. The Making of Modern Immaturity*, New York: Columbia University Press.

Crowe, N. and Bradford, S. (2006) 'Hanging out in Runescape': identity, work and play in the virtual playground', *Children's Geographies*, 4(3): 331–46.

Cullen, F. (2010) '"I was kinda paralytic": pleasure, peril and teenage girls' drinking stories', in C. Jackson, C. Paechter, and E. Renold (eds) *Girls and Education 3–16: Continuing Concerns, New Agendas*, Milton Keynes: Open University Press, 183–96.

Davies, A. (2008) *The Gangs of Manchester. The Story of the Scuttlers, Britain's First Youth Cult*, Preston: Milo Books.

Davis, J. (1990) *Youth and the Condition of Britain. Images of Adolescent Conflict*, London and Atlantic Highlands, NJ: The Athlone Press.

Day, G. (2006) *Community and Everyday Life*, London: Routledge.

Dean, M. (2007) *Governing Societies*, Maidenhead: Open University Press.

Delanty, G. and Rumford, C. (2005) *Rethinking Europe. Social Theory and the Implications of Europeanization*, London: Routledge.

Delsol, R. and Shiner, M. (2006) 'Regulating stop and search: a challenge for police and community relations in England and Wales', *Critical Criminology*, 14(3): 241–63.

Department for Children, Schools and Families (2009) *Statistical First Release: Participation in Education, Training and Employment by 16–18 year olds in England*, London: DCSF.

Department for Education and Employment (1999) *Learning to Succeed: A new framework for post-16 learning*, London: The Stationery Office.

Department of Social Security (1998) *New Ambitions for Our Country: A new contract for welfare*, Cm 3805, London: The Stationery Office.

Department of Education and Science (1967) *Immigrants and the Youth Service, A Report of a Committee of the Youth Service Development Council*, London: HMSO.

Department of Education and Science (1969) *Youth and Community Work in the 70s*, Proposals by the Youth Service Development Council, London: HMSO.

Dorling, D., Rigby, J., Wheeler, B., Ballas, D., Thomas, B., Fahmy E., Gordon, D. and Lupton, R. (2007) *Poverty, Wealth and Place in Britain, 1968 to 2005*, Bristol: Policy Press.

Douglas, M. (1996) (2nd edn) *Natural Symbols. Explorations in Cosmology*, London: Routledge.

Douglas, M. (2002) *Purity and Danger. An Analysis of Concept of Pollution and Taboo*, London: Routledge.

Durkheim, E. (1970) *Suicide*, London: Routledge and Kegan Paul.

Durkheim, E. (1976) *The Elementary Forms of the Religious Life*, London: Routledge and Kegan Paul.

Durkheim, E. (1982) *The Rules of Sociological Method and Selected Texts on Sociology and its Method* (ed. S. Lukes), New York: The Free Press.

Durkheim, E. (1984) *The Division of Labour in Society*, Basingstoke: Macmillan – now Palgrave Macmillan.

Edmunds, J. and Turner, Bryan S. (2002) *Generations, Culture and Society*, Buckingham: Open University Press.

Eisenstadt, S. (1956) *From Generation to Generation: Age Groups and Social Structure*, Glencoe: Free Press.

Englander, D. (1998) *Poverty and Law Reform in Nineteenth Century Britain, 1834–1914. From Chadwick to Booth*, London: Addison, Wesley, Longman Ltd.

Esping-Andersen, G. (1990) *The Three Worlds of Welfare Capitalism*, Cambridge: Polity Press.

Falk, R. (1993) 'The making of global citizenship', in J. Brecher, J.B. Childs and J. Cutler (eds) *Global Visions. Beyond the New World Order*, Montreal: Black Rose Books, 39–50.

Farrington, D. (1996) *Understanding and Preventing Youth Crime*, Social Policy Research Findings, 93, York: Joseph Rowntree Foundation.

Field, J. (2003) *Social Capital*, London: Routledge.

Foster, V., Kimmel, M. and Skelton, C. (2001) 'What about the boys?' An overview of the debates, in W. Martino and B. Meyenn (eds) *What About The Boys? Issues of Masculinity in Schools*, Buckingham and Philadelphia: Open University Press, 1–23.

Foucault, M. (1970) *The Order of Things. An Archaeology of the Human Sciences*, London: Tavistock Publications.

Foucault, M. (1977) *Discipline and Punish, The Birth of the Prison*, London: Allen Lane.

Foucault, M. (1979) *The History of Sexuality, Volume 1, An Introduction*, London: Allen Lane.

Foucault, M. (1980) *Power/Knowledge: Selected Interviews and Other Writings, 1972–1977* (ed. C. Gordon), Brighton: Harvester.

Foucault, M. (1988) *Politics, Philosophy, Culture: Interviews and Other Writings, 1977–1984*, New York: Routledge.

Fowler, D. (2008) *Youth Culture in Modern Britain, c. 1920–1970*, Basingstoke: Palgrave Macmillan.

Frankenburg, R. (1966) *Communities in Britain: Social Life in Town and Country*, Harmondsworth: Penguin.

Fraser, N. (2000) 'Rethinking Recognition', *New Left Review*, 3, 107–20.

Fraser, N. (2009) *Scales of Justice, Reimagining Political Space in a Globalizing World*, New York: Columbia University Press.

Frost, L. (2001) *Young Women and the Body. A Feminist Sociology*, Basingstoke: Palgrave Macmillan.

Frost, L. (2003) 'Doing bodies differently? Gender, youth, appearance and damage', *Journal of Youth Studies*, 6(1): 53–70.

Frost, L. (2005) 'Theorising the young woman in the body', *Body and Society*, 11(1): 63–85.

Garnett, J. and Matthew, C. (1993) *Revival and Religion Since 1700, Essays for John Walsh*, London: Hambledon Press.

Geddes, M. and Rust, M. (2000) 'Catching them young?' *Youth and Policy*, 69, Autumn, 42–61.

Gelder, K. (ed.) (2005) *The Subcultures Reader* (2nd edn), London: Routledge.

Gerth, H.H. and Wright Mills, C. (1967) *From Max Weber: Essays in Sociology*, London: Routledge and Kegan Paul.

Giddens, A. (1991) *Modernity and Self-Identity. Self and Society in the Late Modern Age*, Cambridge: Polity Press.

Giddens, A. (1998) *The Third Way. The Renewal of Social Democracy*, Cambridge: Polity Press.

Giddens, A. (2000) *Runaway World. How Globalisation is Reshaping our Lives*, London: Profile Books.

Gidley, B. (2007) 'Youth culture and ethnicity: Emerging youth inter-culture in South London', in P. Hodkinson and W. Deicke (2007) (eds) *Youth Cultures. Scenes, Subcultures and Tribes*, London: Routledge, 145–57.

Gillis, J. (1974) *Youth and History: Tradition and Change in European Age Relations, 1770–Present*, New York: Academic Press.

Goffman, E. (1959) *The Presentation of Self in Everyday Life*, New York: Anchor Books

Goldsmith, C. (2008) 'Cameras, cops and contracts: what anti-social behaviour management feels like to young people', in P. Squires (ed.) *ASBO Nation. The Criminalisation of Nuisance*, Bristol: Policy Press, 223–37.

Goode, E. and Ben-Yehuda, N. (2009) *Moral Panics. The Social Construction of Deviance*, Oxford: Wiley Blackwell.

Gravett (2004) *Manga, Sixty Years of Japanese Comics*, London: Lawrence King Publishing.

Griffin, C. (1993) *Representations of Youth. The Study of Youth and Adolescence in Britain and America*, Cambridge: Polity Press.

Griffin, C. (2004) 'Representations of the Young', in J. Roche, S. Tucker, R. Thomson and R. Flynn (eds) (2nd edn) *Youth in Society*, London: Sage Publications, 10–18.

Griffiths, P. (1996) *Youth and Authority. Formative Experiences in England 1560–1640*, Oxford: Clarendon Press.

Guillén, M.F. (2001) 'Is Globalization Civilizing, Destructive or Feeble? A Critique of Five Key Debates in the Social Science Literature', *Annual Review of Sociology*, 27, 235–60.

Halcli, A. (2000)'Social Movements', in G. Browning, A. Halcli and F. Webster (eds) *Understanding Contemporary Society. Theories of the Present*, London: Sage Publications, 463–75.

Hall, S. (1990) 'Cultural Identity and Diaspora', in Rutherford, J. (ed.) *Identity: Community, Culture and Difference*, London: Lawrence and Wishart, 222–37.

Hall, S. and Gieben, B. (eds) (1992) *Formations of Modernity*, Cambridge: Polity Press, in association with Blackwell Publishers Ltd. and the Open University.

Hall, S. and Jefferson, T. (eds) (1976) *Resistance through Rituals. Youth Subcultures in Post-war Britain*, London: Hutchinson.

Hammersley, M. (1999) 'Sociology, What's It For? A Critique of Gouldner' Sociological Research Online 4(3) (http://www.socresonline.org.uk/4/3/hammersley.html).

Harne, L. and Radford, J. (2008) *Tackling Domestic Violence: Theories, Policies and Practice*, Maidenhead: Open University Press.

Harrison, S and Dourish, P. (1996) 'Re-Place-Ing Space: The Roles of Place and Space in Collaborative Systems', in *Proceedings of CCSW '96*, Cambridge, MA: ACM Press, 67–76.

Haywood, C. and Mac an Ghaill, M. (2003) *Men and Masculinities: Theory, Research and Social Practice*, Buckingham: Open University Press.

Hebdige, D. (1979) *Subculture. The Meaning of Style*, London: Methuen.

Heelas, P., Lash, S. and Morris, P. (eds) (1996) *Detraditionalization*, Oxford: Blackwell Publishers.

Heller, A. (1984) *Everyday Life*, London: Routlege and Kegan Paul.

Henderson, S., Holland, S., McGrellis, S., Sharpe, S. and Thomson, R. (eds) (2007) *Inventing Adulthoods. A Biographical Approach to Youth Transitions*, London: Sage Publications.

Hendry, J. (2008) *An Introduction to Social Anthropology: Sharing our Worlds*, Basingstoke: Palgrave Macmillan.

Henriques, J., Holloway, W., Urwin, C., Venn, C. and Walkerdine, V. (eds) (1984) *Changing the Subject: Psychology, Social Regulation and Subjectivity*, London: Routledge.

Hetherington, K. (2005) 'Blank Figures in the Countryside', in K. Gelder (ed.) *The Subcultures Reader*, London: Routledge, 246–55.

Hey, V. (1997) *The Company She Keeps. An Ethnography of Girls' Friendship*, Buckingham: Open University Press.

Hey, V. and Bradford, S. (2006) 'Re-engineering Motherhood? Surestart in the Community', *Contemporary Issues in Early Childhood*, 7(1): 53–67.

Hirst, P. and Thompson, G. (1999) *Globalization in Question*, Cambridge: Polity Press.

HMSO (1969) *Youth and Community Work in the 70s* (The Fairbairn-Milson Report), London: HMSO.

HMSO (1975) *Adult Education: The Challenge of Change* (The Alexander Report), Edinburgh: HMSO.

Hochschild, A. (1983) *The Managed Heart: Commercialization of Human Feeling*, Berkeley, CA: University of California Press.

Hodkinson, P. and Deicke, W. (eds) (2007) *Youth Cultures. Scenes, Subcultures and Tribes*, London: Routledge.

Holdsworth, C. and Morgan, D. (2005) *Transitions in Context. Leaving Home, Independence and Adulthood*, Maidenhead: Open University Press.

Holt, L. (2010) 'Embodying and Destabilising (Dis)ability and Childhood', in Hörschelmann, K. and Colls, R. (eds) *Contested Bodies of Childhood and Youth*, Basingstoke: Palgrave Macmillan, 203–14.

Hörschelmann, K. and Schäfer, N. (2005) 'Performing the global through the local – Young people's practices of identity formation in former East Germany', *Children's Geographies* 3(2): 219–42.

Huskins, J. (1996) *Quality Youth Work With Young People. Developing social skills and diversion from risk*, Bristol: John Huskins.

Huskins, J. (1998) *From Disaffection to Social Exclusion, A Social Skills Approach to Developing Active Citizenship and Lifelong Learning*, Bristol: John Huskins._

IEA Health and Welfare Unit (1996) *Charles Murray and the Underclass: The Developing Debate*, Choice in Welfare, No. 33. London: IEA Health and Welfare Unit in association with the *Sunday Times*.

Jackson, C. (2006) *Lads and Ladettes in School. Gender and a Fear of Failure*, Maidenhead: Open University Press.

Jenks, C. (2005) *Subculture. The Fragmentation of the Social*, London: Sage Publications.

Johnston, C.E. (2011) The Other Side of the Bridge: A Study of Social Capital in further Education Provision for Young People with Disabilities, unpublished PhD thesis, Uxbridge: Brunel University.

Jones, G. (2002) *The Youth Divide: Diverging Paths to Adulthood*, Buckingham: Open University Press.

Jones, G. (2009) *Youth*, Cambridge: Polity Press.

Kemp, P. (2005) 'Young people and unemployment: From welfare to workfare?' in M. Barry (ed.) *Youth Policy and Social Inclusion. Critical Debates with Young People*, London: Routledge, 139–56.

Kenway, J., Bullen, E., Fahey, J and Robb, S. (2006) *Haunting the Knowledge Economy*, London: Routledge.

Kimberlee, R. (2002) 'Why don't British young people vote at general elections?' *Journal of Youth Studies*, 5(1): 85–98.

Kinsella, S. (2000) *Adult Manga: Culture and Power in Japanese Society*, London: Routledge.

Klein, N. (2000) *No Logo: No space, No Choice, No Jobs*, New York: Flamingo.

Knowles, C. and Alexander, C. (eds) (2005) *Making Race Matter: Bodies, Space and Identity*, Basingstoke: Palgrave Macmillan.

Kuhn, A. (2002) (2nd edn) *Family Secrets: Acts of Memory and Imagination*, London: Verso.

Kymlicka, W. (1999) 'Education for citizenship', in J.M. Halstead and T.H. McLaughlin (eds) Education and Morality, London: Routledge, 79–102.

Langhamer, C. (2000) *Women's Leisure in England, 1920–1960*, Manchester: Manchester University Press.

Lather, P. (1991) *Getting Smart. Feminist Research and Pedagogy With/in the Postmodern*, London: Routledge.

Latour, B. and Woolgar, S. (1986) *Laboratory Life: The Construction of Scientific Facts*, Princeton, NJ: Princeton University Press.

Lee, N. (2001) *Childhood and Society. Growing Up in an Age of Uncertainty*, Buckingham: Open University Press.

Lee, N. (2005) *Childhood and Human Value. Development, Separation and Separability*, Buckingham: Open University Press.

Le Roux, B., Rouanet, H., Savage, M. and Warde, A. (2008) 'Class and cultural division in the UK', *Sociology*, 42(6): 1049–71.

Levitas, R. (1996) 'The concept of social exclusion and the new Durkheimian hegemony', *Critical Social Policy*, 16(46): 5–20.

Levitas, R. (2004) (2nd edn) *The Inclusive Society? Social Exclusion and New Labour*, Basingstoke: Palgrave Macmillan.

Lincoln, S. (2004) 'Teenage Girls' "Bedroom culture": Codes Versus Zones', in A. Bennett and K. Khan-Harris (eds) *After Subculture: Critical Studies in Contemporary Youth Culture*, London: Palgrave, 94–106.

Lister, R. (2003) (2nd edn) *Citizenship: Feminist Perspectives*, Basingstoke: Palgrave.

Lister, R. (2005) 'Young people and citizenship', in M. Barry (ed.) *Youth Policy and Social Inclusion. Critical debates with young people*, London: Routledge, 33–55.

Livingstone, S. (2009) *Children and the Internet*, Cambridge: Polity Press.

Livingstone, S. and Bober, M. (2005) *UK Children Go Online. Final report of key findings*, London: Economic and Social Research Council.

Longhurst, B. (2007) (2nd edn) *Popular Music and Society*, Cambridge: Polity Press.

MacDonald, R. (ed.) (1997) *Youth, the 'Underclass' and Social Exclusion*, London: Routledge.

Macionis, J.J. and Plummer, K. (2008) (4th edn) *Sociology. A Global Introduction*, Harlow: Pearson.

Mannheim, K. (1943) *Diagnosis of our Time, Wartime Essays of a Sociologist*, London: Kegan Paul, Trench, Trubner and Co. Ltd.

Mannheim, K. (1952) *Essays on the Sociology of Knowledge*, New York: Oxford University Press.

Marshall, T.H. (1963) *Sociology at the Crossroads*, London: Heinemann.

Martin, B. (1983) *A Sociology of Contemporary Cultural Change*, Oxford: Basil Blackwell.

Marx, K. (1906) *Capital,* Vol. 1, London: Lawrence and Wishart.

Marx, K. (1973) *Grundrisse*, Harmondsworth: Penguin Books.

Marx, K. and Engels, F. (1968) *Selected Works*, London: Lawrence and Wishart.

Marx, K. and Engels, F. (1970) *The German Ideology*, London: Lawrence and Wishart.

Matza, D. (1964) *Delinquency and Drift*, New York: John Wiley and Sons.

McCleod, J. (2002) 'Working out Intimacy: Young People and Intimacy in an Age of Reflexivity', *Discourse: Studies in the Cultural Politics of Education*, 23(2): 211–26.

McRobbie, A. (1994) *Postmodernism and Popular Culture*, London: Routledge.

McRobbie, A. (1998) *British Fashion Design. Rag Trade or Image Industry?* London: Routledge.

McRobbie, A. (2000) (2nd edn) *Feminism and Youth Culture*, New York: Routledge.

McRobbie, A. and Garber, J. (1976) 'Girls and Subcultures', in S. Hall and T. Jefferson (eds) *Resistance Through Rituals, Youth subcultures in post-war Britain*, London: Hutchison, 209–22.

McRobbie, A. and Garber, J. (2005) 'Girls and Subcultures', in K. Gelder (ed.) (2nd edn) *The Subcultures Reader,* London: Routledge, 105–12.

Mead, G. (1934) *Mind, Self and Society*, Chicago: University of Chicago Press.

Miller, D. (2008) *The Comfort of Things*, Cambridge: Polity Press.

Miller, W. (1958) 'Lower Class Culture as a Generating Milieu of Gang Delinquency', *Journal of Social* Issues, 14(3): 5–20.

Ministry of Education (1960) *The Youth Service in England and Wales,* Report of the Committee Appointed by the Minister of Education in November 1958 (The Albemarle Report), London: HMSO.

Mizen, P. (2004) *The Changing State of Youth*, Basingstoke: Palgrave Macmillan.

Morgan, D. (2009) *Acquaintances: The Space Between Intimates and Strangers*, Maidenhead: Open University Press.

Morgan, D.H.J. (2011) *Rethinking Family Practices*, Basingstoke: Palgrave Macmillan.

Moore, R. and Muller, J. (1999) 'The discourse of "voice" and the problem of knowledge and identity in the sociology of education', *British Journal of Sociology of Education*, 20, 189–206.

Napier, S. (2008) *From Impressionism to Anime: Japan as Fantasy and Fan Culture in the Mind of the West*, Basingstoke: Palgrave Macmillan.

O'Donnell, M. and Sharpe, S. (2000) *Uncertain Masculinities: Youth, ethnicity and class in contemporary Britain*, London: Routledge.

Offe, C. (1985) *Disorganized Capitalism: Contemporary Transformations of Work and Politics*, Cambridge: Polity Press.

Offe, C. (2006) 'Some Contradictions of the Modern Welfare State', in C. Pierson and F.G. Castles (eds) (2nd edn) *The Welfare State Reader*, Cambridge: Polity Press, 66–76.

Osgerby, B. (1998) *Youth in Britain Since 1945*, Oxford: Wiley Blackwell.

Osgerby, B. (2004) *Youth Media*, London: Routledge.

Pahl, R. (2000) *On Friendship*, Cambridge: Polity Press.

Parker, H., Williams. L. and Aldridge, J. (2002) 'The Normalisation of "Sensible" Recreational Drug Use, Further Evidence from the North West England Longitudinal Study', *Sociology*, 36(4): 941–64.

Parkin, F. (1982) 'Social closure and class formation', in A. Giddens and D. Held (eds) *Classes, Power and Conflict. Classical and Contemporary Debates*, London: Macmillan – now Palgrave Macmillan, 175–84.

Parsons, T. (1942) 'Age and sex in the social structure of the United States', *American Sociological Review*, 7, 604–16.

Pieterse, J.MN. (2010) 'Hybridity, So What? The Anti-Hybridity Backlash and the Riddles of Recognition', in G. Ritzer and Z. Atalay (eds) *Readings in Globalization. Key Concepts and Major* Debates, Oxford: Wiley Blackwell, 347–51.

Polanyi, K. (1944) *The Great Transformation: The Political and Economic Origins of Our Time*, Boston, MA: Beacon Press.

Polanyi, M. (1962) *Personal Knowledge. Towards a Post-Critical Philosophy*, London: Routledge and Kegan Paul.

Prensky, M. (2001) 'Digital Natives, Digital Immigrants', *On the Horizon*, 9(5): 1–6.

Price, P. (2004) *Dry Place: Landscapes of Belonging and Exclusion*, Minneapolis: University of Minnesota Press.

Putnam, R.D. (1995) *Bowling Alone. The Collapse and Revival of American Community*, New York: Simon and Schuster.

Reay, D. (2008) 'Psychosocial Aspects of White Middle-class Identities: Desiring and Defending against the Class and Ethnic "Other" in Urban Multi-ethnic Schooling', *Sociology*, 42(6): 1072–88.

Reay, D., Crozier, G. and James, D. (2011) *White Middle Class Identities and Urban Schooling*, Basingstoke: Palgrave Macmillan.

Reynolds, T. (2006)'Bonding Social Capital within the Caribbean Family and Community', *Journal of Community, Work and Family*, 9(3): 273–90.

Reynolds, T. (2007) 'Friendship Networks, Social Capital and Ethnic Identity: Researching the Perspectives of Caribbean Young People in Britain', *Journal of Youth Studies*, 10(4): 383–98.

Ribbens, J. and Edwards, R. (eds) (1998) *Feminist Dilemmas in Qualitative Research: Public Knowledge and Private Lives*, London: Sage.

Ritzer, G. and Atalay, Z. (eds) (2010) *Readings in Globalization. Key Concepts and Major Debates*, Oxford: Wiley Blackwell.

Robb, M. (ed.) (2007) *Youth in Context: Frameworks, Settings and Encounters*, London: Sage Publications in conjunction with Open University.

Roberts, K. (2009) *Youth in Transition. Eastern Europe and the West*, Basingstoke: Palgrave Macmillan.

Robertson, S. (2001) 'Working space. A warm safe place, an argument for youth clubs', *Youth and Policy*, 70, 71–7.

Rogaly, B. and Taylor, B. (2009) *Moving Histories of Class and Community: Identity, Place and Belonging in Contemporary England*, Basingstoke: Palgrave Macmillan.

Rojek, C. (2010) *The Labour of Leisure. The Culture of Free Time*, London: Sage Pulications.

Rose, N. (1999) (2nd edn) *Governing the Soul. The Shaping of the Private Self*, London: Free Association Books.

Rowbotham, S. (1973) *Women, Resistance and Revolution: A History of Women and Revolution in the Modern World*, New York: Random House.

Runciman, W.G. (1983) *A Treatise on Social Theory. Volume 1: The Methodology of Social Theory*, Cambridge: Cambridge University Press.

Said, E. (1991) *Orientalism*, London: Penguin Books.

Sassen, S. (2006) *Territory, Authority, Rights. From Medieval to Global Assemblages*, Princeton, NJ: Princeton University Press.

Savage, M., Bagnall, G. and Longhurst, B. (2005) *Globalization and Belonging*, London: Sage Publications.

Scholte, J.A. (2000) 'Cautionary Reflections on Seattle', *Journal of International Studies*, 29(1): 115–21.

Schön, D.A. (1983) *The Reflective Practitioner. How Professionals Think in Action*, New York: Basic Books.

Scott, S. (2009) *Making Sense of Everyday Life*, Cambridge: Polity Press.

Secretary of State for Education and Science (1982) *Experience and Participation, Report of the Review Group on the Youth Service in England and Wales*, Cmnd 8686, London: HMSO.

Sennett, R. (1996) *The Uses of Disorder. Personal Identity and City Life*, London: Faber and Faber.

Sennett, R. (1998) *The Corrosion of Character. The Personal Consequences of Work in the New Capitalism*, New York: WW Norton.

Sewell, T. (1996) *Black Masculinities and Schooling: How Black Boys Survive Modern Schooling*, Stoke-on-Trent: Trentham Books.

Sewell, T. (2009) *Generating Genius: Black Boys in Search of Love, Ritual and Schooling*, Stoke-on-Trent: Trentham Books.

Shildrick, T.A. and MacDonald, R. (2006) 'In defence of subculture: Young people, leisure and social divisions' *Journal of Youth Studies*, 9(2): 125–40.

Shildrick, T.A. and MacDonald, R. (2007) 'Biographies of exclusion: Poor work and poor transitions', *International Journal of Lifelong Education*, 26(5): 589–604.

Shilling, C. (2005) 'Embodiment, emotions and social order', in J. Alexander and P. Smith (eds) *The Cambridge Companion to Durkheim*, Cambridge: Cambridge University Press, 211–38.

Silverman, D. (1985) *Qualitative Methodology and Sociology*, Aldershot: Gower Press.

Simmel, G. (1971) *On Individuality and Social Forms, Selected Writings*, Chicago: University of Chicago Press.

Skeggs, B. (2002) *Formations of Class and Gender*, London: Sage Publications.

Smart, C. (2007) *Personal Life. New Directions in Sociological Thinking*, Cambridge: Polity Press.

Song, M. (2005) 'Global and local articulations of Asian identity', in C. Knowles and C. Alexander (eds) *Making Race Matter: Bodies, Space and Identity*, Basingstoke: Palgrave Macmillan, 60–75.

Spencer, L. and Pahl, R. (2006) *Rethinking Friendship. Hidden Solidarities Today*, Princeton: Princeton University Press.

Squires, P. (ed.) (2008) *ASBO Nation. The Criminalisation of Nuisance*, Bristol: Policy Press.

Stacey, M. (1960) *Tradition and Change: A Study of Banbury*, Oxford: Oxford University Press.

Stallabrass, J. (1993) 'Just Gaming: Allegory and Economy in Computer Games', *New Left Review*, 198: 83–106.

Standing, G. (2009) *Work after Globalization. Building Occupational Citizenship*, Cheltenham: Edward Elgar.

Stanley, K. (2005) 'Young asylum seekers and refugees in the UK', in M. Barry (ed.) *Youth Policy and Social Inclusion. Critical Debates with Young People*, London: Routledge, 187–203.

Strong, P.M. (1979) 'Sociological imperialism and the profession of medicine. A Critical Examination of the thesis of medical imperialism', *Social Science and Medicine*, 13, 199–215.

Tarrow, S. (1998) (2nd edn) *Power in Movement: Social Movements and Contentious Politics*, Cambridge: Cambridge University Press.

Thomas, B. and Dorling, D. (2007) *Identity in Britain: A Cradle to Grave Atlas*, Bristol: Policy Press.

Thomson, R. (2009) *Unfolding Lives. Youth, Gender and Change*, Bristol: Policy Press.

Tinkler, P. (1995) *Constructing Girlhood: Popular Magazines for Girls Growing up in England, 1920–1950*, London: Taylor and Francis.

Tizard, B. and Phoenix, A. (1993) *Black, White or Mixed Race? Race and Racism in the Lives of young People of Mixed Parentage*, London: Routledge.

Todd, S. (2005) *Young Women, Work, and Family in England, 1918–1950*, Oxford: Oxford University Press.

Tonkiss, F. (1998) 'Continuity/Change', in C. Jenks (ed.) *Core Sociological Dichotomies*, London: Sage Publications, 34–48.

Tönnies, F. (1955; 1887) *Community and Association*, London: Routledge and Kegan Paul.

Turkle, S. (1997) *Life on the Screen: Identity in the Age of the Internet*, New York: Touchstone.

Turner, B.S. (1992) *Regulating Bodies. Essays in Medical Sociology*, London: Routledge.

Turner, E. (2012) *Communitas. The Anthropology of Collective Joy*, New York: Palgrave Macmillan.

Turner, V. (1975) *Dramas, Fields, and Metaphors. Symbolic Action in Human Society*, Ithaca, NY: Cornell University Press.

Utting, D. (ed.) (2009) *Contemporary Social Evils*, Bristol: Policy Press in association with Joseph Rowntree Foundation.

Van Gennep, A. (1961) *The Rites of Passage*, Chicago: University of Chicago Press.

Valentine, G. (2003) 'Boundary Crossings: Transitions from Childhood to Adulthood', *Children's Geographies*, 1(1): 37–52.

Vickerstaffe, S. (2003) 'Apprenticeship in the "golden age": Were youth transitions really smooth and unproblematic back then? *Work Employment and Society*, 17(2): 269–308.

Walby, S. (2004) 'The European Union and gender equality: Emergent varieties of gender regime', *Social Politics*, 11(1): 4–29.

Watt, P. and Stenson, K. (1998) 'The Street: "It's a bit dodgy around there", safety, danger, ethnicity and young people's use of public space', in T. Skelton and G. Valentine (eds) *Cool Places, Geographies of Youth Cultures*, London: Routledge, 249–65.

Wallace, R.A. and Hartley, S.F. (1988) 'Religious elements in friendship: Durkheimian theory in an empirical context', in J.C. Alexander (ed.) *Durkheimian Sociology: Cultural Studies*, Cambridge: Cambridge University Press, 93–106.

Wayne, M., Petley, J., Murray, C. and Henderson, L. (2010) *Television News, Politics and Young People: Generation Disconnected?* Basingstoke: Palgrave Macmillan.

Weedon, C. (2004) *Identity and Culture: Narratives of Identity and Belonging*, Maidenhead: Open University Press.

Wilkinson, R. and Pickett, K. (2009) *The Spirit Level. Why Equality is Better for Everyone*, London: Allen Lane.

Willis, P. (1977) *Learning to Labour. How Working Class Kids Get Working Class Jobs*, Farnborough: Saxon House.

Willis, P. (1978) *Profane Culture*, London: Routledge and Kegan Paul.

Wilmott, P. and Young, M. (1960) *Family and Class in a London Suburb*, London: Routledge and Kegan Paul.

Wilson, B. and Atkinson, M. (2005) 'Rave and Straightedge, the Virtual and the Real Exploring Online and Offline Experiences in Canadian Youth Subcultures', *Youth and Society*, 36(3): 276–311.

Woodman, D. (2009) 'The mysterious case of the pervasive choice biography: Ulrich Beck, structure/agency and the middling state of theory in the sociology of youth', *Journal of Youth Studies*, 12(3): 243–56.

Wright Mills, C. (2000) *The Sociological Imagination*, Oxford: Oxford University Press.

Wrong, D. (1961) 'The oversocialized conception of man in modern sociology', *American Sociological Review*, 26(2): 183–92.

Wyn, J. and White, R. (1997) *Rethinking Youth*, London: Sage Publications.

Young, J. (1971) *The Drugtakers. The Social Meaning of Drug Use*, London: Paladin.

Young, M.F.D. (2008) *Bringing Knowledge Back In. From Social Constructivism to Social Realism in the Sociology of Education*, London: Routledge.

Index

Note: 'f' denotes a figure and 't' denotes a table.